Theoretical

Perspectives in

Architectural

History and

Criticism

Mark Rakatansky, editor

Massimo Cacciari

Translated by Stephen Sartarelli

Introduction by Patrizia Lombardo

Architecture and Nihilism: On the Philosophy of Modern Architecture

Yale University Press

New Haven and London

Published with assistance from the Mary Cady Tew Memorial Fund.

Designed by Sylvia Steiner.
Set in Sabon type by Tseng Information Systems, Inc., Durham, North Carolina. Printed in the United States of America by Vail-Ballou Press, Binghamton, New York.

Library of Congress Cataloging-in-Publication Data
Cacciari, Massimo.
[Essays. English. Selections]
Architecture and nihilism : on the philosophy of modern architecture / Massimo Cacciari ; translated by Stephen Sartarelli ; introduction by Patrizia Lombardo.
p. cm. — (Theoretical perspectives in architectural history and criticism)
Essays substantially revised and translated for this publication.
Includes bibliographical references.
ISBN 0-300-05215-4 (cloth)
        0-300-06304-0 (pbk.)
1. Architecture, Modern—20th century—Philosophy. 2. Negativity (Philosophy) I. Title. II. Series.
NA680.C24   1993
720.1—dc20   92-33713CIP

A catalogue record for this book is available from the British Library.

The paper in this book meets the guidelines for permanence and durability of the Committee on Production Guidelines for Book Longevity of the Council on Library Resources.

10 9 8 7 6 5 4 3 2

Contents

Part III   **Loos and His Angel**

Contents

Preface

This book brings together my most significant essays on certain aspects of modern architecture viewed in the light of aesthetic-philosophical problematics. In the first part I have included my short volume *Metropolis* (Rome, 1973) and a chapter from another book, *Walter Rathenau e il suo ambiente* (Bari, 1979). The second part contains the essay "Loos-Wien" (published in M. Cacciari and F. Amendolagine, *Oikos*, Rome, 1975), another piece, perhaps my most important work on the great Viennese *Baumeister, Loos e il suo angelo* (Milan, 1981), as well as several brief essays from my book *Dallo Steinhof: Prospettive viennesi dell'inizio del secolo* (Milan, 1980). I would also like to refer American readers to the translation of my essay "Eupalinos or Architecture," published in *Oppositions* 21 (1980), which may provide a general frame of reference on the history of modern architecture as a whole for the basic themes developed here. The epilogue, "On the Architecture of Nihilism," written expressly for this edition, is an essay of an aesthetic-philosophical nature that might seem not a little disagreeable to specialists of architectural history; but these same readers will find the same ideas, in a context perhaps more congenial to them, in chapter 10, "Loos and His Angel."

I have considerably revised all these essays for their publication as a single whole, and I am deeply grateful to my friend and translator, Stephen Sartarelli, whom I have caused to suffer more than a little with my "etymologies," and to Mark Rakatansky, who was able to overcome some misgivings on my part as to the timeliness of publishing these "old" works of mine today. I have not altered the essential substance of the theses I put forward in them, nor have I enlarged or updated the critical apparatus. Such an undertaking would, no doubt, have led me to write still *other* books. On the other hand, the manner in which the *ratio* of modern architecture is examined in these essays, and the uncommon aesthetic and philosophical references cited therein, have since enjoyed a certain diffusion and influence, demonstrating their fecundity even in the more specific area of the history of architecture and urbanism. In the last few years I have written much less on these subjects but have continued to take an active interest, especially in my university courses, in the relation, or rather in the unbroken metaphorical thread, between architecture and philosophy throughout our intellectual tradition. When writing these essays, I did not yet have a clear idea of just how "Vitruvian" they were. I have always considered architecture to be *scientia pluribus disciplinis et varii eruditionibus ornata,* and the architect he who rises *ad summum templum architecturae,* a true *author,* a *demiourgos,* that is, a creator with the ability to work *cum auctoritate,* since his labor consists *ex opere et eius ratiocinatione.* It is precisely this *ratiocinatio,* this reflexive-meditative ability ever present in the master "builders" of our century, that I have sought to illustrate here in all its tensions and conflicts. Of course, readers will notice differences in tone and perspective between the most recent pieces and the earlier ones collected in this volume, but it is my hope that they will also grasp an internal consistency or at least a certain unchanging obstinacy in my attempt to understand the essential and constituent problems of this difficult *tekné* beyond all fashionable trends and all mere documentary interest—and beyond all deadly academicism.

Massimo Cacciari
Venice, June 1992

Preface

Introduction:
The Philosophy
of the City

Ne suis-je pas un faux accord
Dans la divine symphonie,
Grâce à la vorace Ironie
Qui me secoue et qui me mord?

(Am I not a discordant note
In the divine symphony,
Thanks to voracious Irony
That shakes me up and bites into me?)

—Charles Baudelaire
"L'Héautontimorouménos"
Les Fleurs du Mal

Architecture and Nihilism is the first book by Massimo Cacciari
to be published in English. Until now, one article, "Eupalinos
or Architecture," has been translated in *Oppositions* in 1980.
It is an Heideggerian reflection on the concepts of building and
dwelling as well as a comment on Manfredo Tafuri and Francesco Dal Co's *Modern Architecture*. Cacciari is one of the most
important and productive philosophers in Italy today, and his
works are available in German, French, and Spanish. *Architecture and Nihilism* brings together three essays written between

the early seventies and the early eighties: "The Dialectics of the Negative and the Metropolis" (1973), "Loos and His Contemporaries" (1975), and "Loos and His Angel" (1981). While the Europeans mainly translated recent production, this English-language edition, approved by Massimo Cacciari, focuses on the first and, so to speak, middle Cacciari; it does not represent his work of the past ten years, namely that which has been most engaged in a mystical and religious meditation inspired by Heidegger.

The essays in *Architecture and Nihilism* offer a good overall view of Cacciari's philosophical trajectory, from the Marxian-oriented investigation on the German urban sociologists of the beginning of the century to the metaphysical inquiry into some *aporias* in the work of the Viennese architect Adolf Loos. The reader will follow Cacciari's critique of ideology, which is central in the first essay; then his interpretation of Adolf Loos in the light of this same critique, specifically focused on the Metropolis seen both as the extreme utopia of rationalization and the failure of that same utopia; and finally, the multivalent interrogation of Loos himself, no longer perceived from an external point of view but from what I would call an internal one. As Cacciari suggests in his epilogue, the reader may find discrepancies among the essays, but there is also a continuity, rooted in Cacciari's concept of the metropolis. I call his theory—in the etymological sense of procession—the philosophy of the city.

The continuity among Cacciari's many works, as well as in the essays translated here by Stephen Sartarelli, is also centered in his constant involvement with Walter Benjamin. Benjamin himself encompasses Marxist and mystical components: any serious interest in this writer so crucial for our current cultural debates on a global scale presupposes that Marxism and mysticism are not mutually exclusive. Undoubtedly, these two persuasions are present in Benjamin at any one time, whereas for Cacciari they seem to constitute a first and then a second step in his intellectual search. "Loos and His Angel" gives a clear insight into the direction Cacciari took after 1980, away from his first intellectual concerns as they appear in "The Dialectics of the Negative and the Metropolis" and in "Loos and His Contemporaries." But he is not yet fully immersed in the metaphysical and theo-

Introduction

logical language of, for example, *Dell'Inizio* (1990). As Mark Rakatansky remarked in one of our conversations, in "Loos and His Angel," the Benjaminian balance is still there.

The choice of texts for this English translation is faithful to many crucial aspects of Cacciari himself, to his philosophical development, and suggests that there are at least two ways of interpreting Cacciari's transformations through time. One interpretation would stress his disinvolvement with Marxism after 1980—after *Dallo Steinhof*, his important study on the Vienna of Wagner, Wittgenstein, and Loos. The other interpretation— to which I am personally more inclined, as will be evident from my reading—perceives the persistence of the concept of *crisis* as a key theme in all of Cacciari's works from the early seventies. *Krisis: Saggio sulla crisi del pensiero negativo da Nietzsche a Wittgenstein* (1976), one of his most important works, sums up his early investigations and paves the way for *Dallo Steinhof* and his subsequent endeavors.

This English translation of Cacciari also speaks directly to cultural and political issues in this country that are often central to literary and architectural debates. Whoever is interested in theory should read Cacciari. His work is an essential contribution to cultural studies, including architectural theory, which took in the mid-seventies and eighties a very precise form, that of a historical and theoretical debate on architecture transcending national frontiers and academic disciplinary divisions.

In this introduction I shall not discuss Cacciari's opinions on the main figures treated in *Architecture and Nihilism*: Simmel, Weber, Benjamin, and Loos. I am not interested in making explicit whether I agree or disagree with Cacciari's interpretation of those figures, nor do I attempt to show how Cacciari's reading differs from other readings. But I try to reconstruct Cacciari's perspective on these figures, and I aim at contextualizing Cacciari's concerns within a network of references that are often unfamiliar to the American reader and that, to my knowledge, have not been gathered in Italy nor anywhere else. My interpretation of Cacciari is founded on what can be called the interplay between the global and the local, because even when I dig into the most particular experiences, I try to show how they are part of a broad movement reaching beyond national borders and

Introduction

situate them within other cultural experiences or intellectual endeavors in Europe or in the States. I would say that in my attempt to reconstruct the context of *the philosophy of the city* I proceed both internally and externally. The internal contextualization implies a close reading of Cacciari's text and language, as well as of what may be called the intertextual stream, that is, the identification of other texts that Cacciari is explicitly or implicitly responding to—or in dialogue with, to use Bakhtin's term for the working of the text.

The external contextualization takes into account Cacciari's political, institutional, and intellectual milieus since the late sixties. In my opinion, it is necessary to comprehend these events in order to understand his work. For this reason I focus on the political life of the late sixties, on Cacciari's relation with the Italian Communist Party, on the role of the journal *Contropiano,* and on the role of the Istituto di storia dell'architettura (later renamed the Dipartimento di analisi critica e storica), directed by Manfredo Tafuri within the School of Architecture in Venice. The work of Tafuri, known in this country since the seventies, and that of Alberto Asor Rosa, whose major texts have not been translated in English, are essential background for reading Cacciari, especially the parts I and II of the present volume. For part III, the philosopher Emannele Severino is an important reference for Cacciari's current research but less relevant for architectural theory.

As parts I and II of *Architecture and Nihilism* were published in the early seventies, I make an effort to reconstitute the atmosphere of a historical period that at once seems very recent and very distant. Although this reconstitution implies what Roland Barthes would call the sense of recognition and at the same time lack of recognition that we have when we look at the pictures of our youth, it occurred almost naturally to me because the history of that time is connected to personal memories of my college years. These memories are staged on a precise scene, that of Cacciari's political and intellectual activity: the city of Venice. The philosophy of the city is then, for me, for my interpretation of Cacciari—inevitably, impeccably, ineluctably—the philosophy, or a philosophy, of Venice.

Venice's Spleen

Venice, June 1973: The city was overrun by the national Festival dell'Unità, the yearly festivities of the PCI, the Italian Communist party. Venice itself was transformed: in every *campo* (square) there were red flags, bookstalls, public speeches, food, wine, music, songs, *compagni* (comrades) from everywhere, Italy and abroad, of every age, every social class. One could hear a lot of discussion, a mixture of voices and accents from various regions of Italy, with different local political experiences and also different political lines, following the tendency of a given Federazione, or even Sezione (the hierarchical organizations of the Communist party, active at the levels of the nation, region, city, town, suburb). In the city there was a sense of feast, the pleasure of the crowd, of community life, of the *polis,* of political debates. Venice was ours; it was the "red city" for a few days, in spite of the Christian Democratic tradition of the Veneto, the most "white" region of Italy. Maybe the Revolution—a word used in those years, not yet bereft of its sound and meaning—is like a great Festival dell'Unità in an unreal city like Venice, a huge coming together, a vast Communist International, workers and intellectuals together, as if there were no gap. We were all there at the culminating moment of the Festival, when the general secretary of the Communist party, Enrico Berlinguer, spoke:

> It is the first time that a national festival of the Unità takes place in Venice and in the Veneto region. The choice of Venice is a good one, because in this city—unique in the world— the activity and initiative of comrades, friends, workers made the festival a mass-event. It represented a new and unusual experience for the city, for all Venetians, as well as for our Party. The Venetian people responded enthusiastically to the Party's initiative proving how fake is the conception of those who believe that only a small elite can enjoy culture, art and science, and would like to give to the people nothing but a vulgar and commercialized under-culture.
>
> It is not by chance that the will to make culture belong to all people is coming from a Party like ours. We want the working class to inherit all the progressive, beautiful, true

things that mankind created in its secular path. We want the working class to embody the new universal values that will renovate social and economic life, the relation between people and classes, as well as the science, art and culture of the whole world.[1]

We students and intellectuals of Venice's Sezione Universitaria, listening to that redemptive, humanistic language, felt as Stendhal did in a church, not believing but being deeply moved by the ritual of the Mass. We were thrilled by the crowd, the city, and the event but, obviously, could not believe in those sentimental words about progress, universal new values, new relations among classes. We knew Cacciari's lesson, as he writes in "Dialectics of the Negative and the Metropolis"[2] (part I of this English edition), a collection of materials discussed in Manfredo Tafuri's seminars at the School of Architecture on the history of German architecture and the German sociology of the city: "In a metropolitan situation, the revolutionary process itself is totally *intellectual*. The 'geometric clarity' with which, in the final analysis, class interest is posited, eliminates all possible teleological or ethico-sentimental synthesis."

To deny the metropolitan situation means to believe in the conservative nostalgia of a better, more natural human life, or in the progressive utopia of a realized good society. To eschew the Metropolis, as Cacciari says, inevitably means to propose a backward attitude: "Therefore *any* discourse (discussion) on the city itself necessarily becomes at this point reactionary." How could anyone speak in the second half of the twentieth century about culture for everybody, progress, art, and science? We were nevertheless aware that the public square where Berlinguer spoke to the masses was not our group at the Sezione Universitaria nor Tafuri's seminar at the Istituto di storia dell'architettura. But we were especially aware that behind Berlinguer's celebration of Venice and the Party there was a political project that would eliminate any Stalinist mentality: he had been secretary since 1972 and, when he was vice-secretary, at the 24th Congress of the Soviet Communist party in Moscow, he had already stated that every Communist party had the right to follow an autonomous line dictated by the specific conditions of

Introduction

every country. He was opening the way within the left to a different understanding of politics and alliances.

A few months after Venice's Festival dell'Unità, Berlinguer proposed to the country the *compromesso storico* (historical compromise)—a new relation of collaboration between the Italian left and center, and a Communist party for all of Europe. Berlinguer obviously disturbed many of the old generation in the PCI who were attached to a centralized party structure; at the same time he disgusted the revolutionary purists so typical of the extreme left in those years after 1968 who so virulently opposed any institutional structure. But, together with the clear tendency toward social-democratic positions, a new wind was blowing within the Italian Communist party, an organization that traditionally represented the working class voice, constituted a large oppositional presence within the Italian Parliament, and was always more than a simple electoral machine: an institution really connected to the mass movement of workers and students. This made it possible for Cacciari to join the Party. He was coming from an extreme left *operaista* experience (supporter of the doctrine that power should be given to the workers), and his collaboration with the review *Contropiano* marked his move in the direction of the Party. *Contropiano* was started in 1968; its title was clearly indicative of its stand against capitalist planning (from economic to urban planning), and the first issue opened with Antonio Negri's article on Keynes and capitalist state theory in 1929, followed by Mario Tronti's study of the changes in the content of working-class struggles at the international level from the 1930s to the 1960s.[3] The first issue of *Contropiano* listed three editors: Antonio Negri, from Padua, who was the leader of the group *Potere Operaio;* Alberto Asor Rosa, from Rome, who was a member of the PCI and had always been committed to an operaista direction within the party;[4] and Cacciari, from Venice. Cacciari had been active in factory agitations and other working-class fights since 1968, when new contracts were negotiated among trade unions, government, and the employers of the largest Italian factories and corporations. Fiat in Turin and Pirelli near Milan, as well as the huge area next to Venice, Mestre and Porto Marghera (with its chemical plants of Montedison and thousand of workers,[5]) made indus-

Introduction

trial northern Italy from 1968 to 1970 one of the centers of the struggle between working class and capital—as one said at that time in "straightforward" Marxist language.

Cacciari's theory of the Metropolis reflects on problems of organization, from work and revolution to services and industrial growth, to State and institutions. The militant practice in the factory necessarily confronts questions of organization. Cacciari, together with others writing in *Contropiano*, had given much thought to the question of the relation between the workers' struggles and an institution like the PCI, even when he was politically active outside the Party and sometimes strongly critical of it. The debate over the PCI and the *entrista* position (which favored joining the party in spite of disagreements with its main tenet) brought about the schism with Negri, who reinforced the operaista, interventionist, anti-state position. Negri's article on Marx in the second issue of *Contropiano* was his last as he left the direction of the journal, which continued under Asor Rosa and Cacciari through 1971. That crucial second issue of 1968 began with an eloquent editorial stressing the complex class situation and the necessity "to get rid of an excessively unilateral vision of theoretical and political work" (p. 240). This editorial insisted on the balance between theory and action, but nevertheless considered the reflexive component as indispensable "before" experience or political action: "We will continue to think that the working-class slant on capitalist society implies, if correctly formulated, a clear and totally demystified description of the object to be known and a similarly clear indication to transform that knowledge into action" (p. 241). Knowledge and action—or theory and practice—were perceived as equally important, but the emphasis on the priority of knowledge, description, and analysis of phenomena implied the criticism of an agitation for its own sake. This criticism, particularly important coming from operaisti activists, shows a certain faith in institutional forms and implies the recognition that the modern and contemporary world is made of abstraction: the process of intellectualization, understanding, and rationalization presides over all activities from economy to politics to law to everyday life, as in the metropolitan situation where institutions, the circulation

Introduction

of money, and the transformation of any material reality into figures shape experience itself.

The question of how to relate mass movements to institutions and institutions to mass movements was important to *Contropiano*'s political exploration, at a time in Italy when the line between action and terrorism was to become tragically blurred. Nevertheless Cacciari did not romanticize the Party and its role, as he had clearly pinpointed in public speeches, meetings, and writings that there are phases and crises in the relation between party and class movements. In *Ciclo capitalistico e lotte operaie: Montedison Pirelli Fiat 1968,* he saw a radical change since 1960: the workers began to form essential avant-gardes who contested the traditional role of the party at the moment it was losing control of the class movement and seemed incapable of organizing the workers' struggles.[6] Cacciari wrote extensively on the workers' movement in the sixties, and, already in a review article on the events of May 1968 in France, he spoke of the difference between the situation in Italy and that in France, where the students' movement had been attacked by the official Communist newspaper, *L'Humanité,* and by the Communist trade union, the CGT. Both were blocked in an old position, a frozen institution, incapable of making the vital link between movements and party. Cacciari focused on the strength of the Italian workers' movements as indispensable in determining the interactions among working class, Party, and trade union. He also stressed the role of the "political mediation that the party expresses at the institutional level."[7] Cacciari voiced his suspicion of immediacy, of any spontaneous agitation without organized structures, and his belief that the intervention of the party can be larger and stronger than that of any group. The overture toward the Italian Communist party was clear; at the same time, within the party, there was an openness to social forces and to people capable of renewing the Party itself.[8] After the first issues of *Contropiano* appeared, Cacciari joined the PCI, where Berlinguer's line would dust off an old way of understanding politics.

As we stood there at the Festival dell'Unità, we had no populist dreams of an idyllic society nor any illusion about a subversive

Introduction

culture, or a subversive use of culture. We were convinced that art and culture have "an inevitable bourgeois nature," as Asor Rosa writes in a 1968 article on Trockij and Majakovskij, where he attacks the literary Stalinism of the first Congress of Soviet Writers (1934) as founded on the utopia of the coincidence between the intellectual and the revolutionary. He was aiming at that myth constantly present in the avant-garde attitude:

> In our opinion, the use of art and literature as instruments to communicate the political discourse should be completely rejected. . . . Socialism has never been necessary to make good literature. Writers will not be necessary to make revolution. Class struggle, if it is real class struggle and not just populist protest, peasant agitation, sentimental admiration for the masses' virgin strength, does not need to take the road of this illusion. Class struggle has other voices to express itself, to make itself be understood. And poetry cannot keep track of it, because poetry, great poetry speaks a language where *things*—the hard things of everyday strife and fatigue—have already taken the value of a symbol, of a gigantic metaphor of the world. The often tragic price of poetry, the price of its greatness is that what it says is not practice, nor will ever get back to it.[9]

We were suspended between feeling and intellect, the inevitable emotion of the great ethico-sentimental synthesis sketched in Berlinguer's speech and the scorn for that community vision, conscious as we were that there is no reality other than the tough, tragic "geometrical clarity" of the Metropolis, with its endless social and political tensions. We had no choice other than intellect, or *Verstand:* we had *negative thought* in our veins.

In order to understand the concept of negative thought, so essential to reach the architecture of completed nihilism, it is necessary to keep in mind Cacciari's network of references. I would say that this configuration operates in a whirl movement, where synchronic and diachronic elements of various orders clash, in a disorderly order, as in a theater, where the actor's voice, the physical presence of people and objects, the setting of the scene, the visible and invisible work that makes everything possible come together. There is no linear history and,

Introduction

probably, intellectual history should be conceived like a choreography constructed by the intellectual historian who makes practical choices to sketch the puzzle that is historical analysis.

Cacciari's choreography is formed by the political experience of the working-class movements and the Communist party; by the passage from an avant-garde position to membership in a large party institution; by the four years of intense work for *Contropiano,* equally devoted to class analysis and what would be called today in the United States cultural criticism or cultural studies; by the interdisciplinary and radical setting of Venice's Istituto di storia, directed by Manfredo Tafuri since 1968 and committed to a Marxian critique of ideology and of the ideology of architecture. In this complex choreography made of various people and institutions—a party, a school, a journal— at least two names are indispensable: Alberto Asor Rosa, whom I have already cited, and Manfredo Tafuri, whose importance will be stressed below. Then, of course, there is Venice, the city and its inland, with its Porto Marghera, whose chimneys one can see from the Giudecca Canal, as in a De Chirico painting where the desolate and dark towers of a warehouse or a factory are juxtaposed with the ancient columns of a white, classical square. One can also think of that photograph of Aldo Rossi's floating theater built for the 1979–80 Venice Biennale: the theater seems almost attached to the Punta della Dogana, to the Salute Church, moving in the water between the Giudecca and the Grand Canal; its roof points to the line of ancient palaces followed by one row of wrecking cranes and then another of industrial chimneys fading away in the distance.[10]

This juxtaposition of Palladio's churches and Marghera's factories suggests why one of the most sophisticated and difficult theories of the Metropolis came from the city that seems most untouched by the contemporary world. It is as if in Venice one finds a reaction against its mellow and touristic image, an elaboration of a philosophy that fuses together political militancy, Adolf Loos' hatred of ornament, Baudelaire's vision of Paris, Georg Simmel's "nervous life," and Walter Benjamin's understanding of anguish and shock as the basis of modern experience. Maybe the contrast between the city in the Adriatic lagoon and the industrial setting is so visible, so violent in the Vene-

Introduction

tian skyline that the philosopher or the cultural critic can forge exactly from this contrast the difference between city and Metropolis, together with the ideological construction that hides, in the very heart of the modern mode of production and life, the metropolitan reality, while fabricating the illusion of a city with human relationships. Venice, small and ancient as it is, with no cars, apparently so ideal as a refuge from the hustle and bustle of today's world, allows a powerful intuition of modernity. Venice overcomes its physical dimension and becomes larger than Paris, London, or New York; it becomes an allegory, as the buildings of Paris did for Baudelaire in "Le Cygne," the famous metropolitan poem of *Les Fleurs du Mal* that is a splendid commentary on Haussmann's great works of urban renovation:

Paris change! mais rien dans ma mélancolie
N'a bougé! palais neufs, échafaudages, blocs,
Vieux faubourgs, tout pour moi devient allégorie.

(Paris changes! but nothing changed in my melancholy!
New buildings, scaffoldings, blocks,
Old suburbs, everything to me becomes allegory).[11]

Real Allegory

The term "Metropolis" is an abstraction, an allegory, as Cacciari suggests by using the capital letter. Today, we would say that the Metropolis is an impersonal agent. Negative thought, or the negative, or negativity, should be synonymous with Metropolis, if the Metropolis is correctly understood in its total impersonal reality and its power of abstraction. Cacciari's philosophy of the Metropolis should not be interpreted in simple realistic terms. Of course, behind it there is the concrete experience of Porto Marghera's fights in the late sixties and early seventies, but, in the texts in this English edition, Cacciari is not speaking of a specific city with precise chronology and statistical data, even if Paris ("capital of the nineteenth century" for Benjamin) and the German *Werkbund* and Vienna at the beginning of the twentieth century constitute clear references. Cacciari grasps, through the concept of the Metropolis, the German urban sociology of Weber, Simmel, and Benjamin, the nihilistic architecture of Adolf Loos, the real allegory of the modern (as

Introduction

in *L'Atelier du peintre: Allégorie réelle,* the title of Courbet's famous painting that questions the status of pictorial representation itself). Cacciari stresses the modern condition of a crisis that is and should be completely assumed as the inevitable foundation of life, experience, subjectivity itself. His work is not historical research but philosophical illumination. His work is strictly interpretative: interpretation of interpretations, illuminations and sparks that provoke a sort of general understanding of abstractions or give keys to further readings of important moments in the making of our modernity.

The Metropolis is the reality and the metaphor of the modern world, and also our contemporary world as Cacciari defines it in part 1: "The general form assumed by the process of the rationalization of social relations," following the "rationalization of the relations of production." The Metropolis implies traffic, factories, services, commercial life, market economy, offices, administrative institutions, the State, political organization, crowds, social tensions, the constant law of the circulation of money. The Metropolis in a nineteenth-century world constitutes the opposite of nature, the country, the village, the suburb. But the metropolitan tendency was already typical of the European medieval city, studied by Max Weber, at the moment it forsook tribal life. The Metropolis shows the impossibility of synthesis, the impossibility of the city as synthesis where conflicts would disappear or be hidden or preventively repressed (see part 2). The Metropolis defeats any community mentality: the conservative or regressive attitudes, from family life to the image of people coming home from work to "cultivate their kitchen gardens," as well as the progressive ones, from the image of technological comfort and individual freedom to the dream of mass liberation and to the vision of Venice as unique city in the world. Any progressive attitude becomes backward because, in spite of its futuristic glamor, it dreams of old types of relationships among people.

Cacciari's militant experience in the factory could not but help his formulation of the political problem of the Metropolis as capitalist system and as site of social conflict. The factory experience would offer ground for reflection within a review whose aim was to present "Marxist materials." *Contropiano* was com-

Introduction

mitted to political and theoretical rigor in "an epoch of deep change," as the political situation of Western Europe's working class was transformed by "the breaking off of the Soviet system and the global return of the European working class to the revolutionary front." [12] (This was written more than twenty years ago.) In that rich, exalting, "multiple and contradictory class situation" that "manifested itself at several levels," the review stressed its working-class point of view while "facing an extremely vast gamut of interests," providing therefore a thorough critique of ideology from economics to working-class history, architecture, urban planning, literature, film, and philosophy.[13] *Contropiano* insisted on its negative role, centered on the destruction of bourgeois culture yet refusing the illusion of constructing a working-class culture; in the political language of the time, when we spoke of "bourgeoisie" and "working class," the editors of the review refused to be hampered by "any exclusive discourse" and planned to offer various hypotheses and themes of research.[14]

In those exhilarating years of political confrontation and intellectual creativity, there was no fundamental discrepancy then between Cacciari's article, "Porto Marghera's Montecatini-Edison," and his essay on "The Genesis of Negative Thought" [15] —both philosophically connected to the Nietzschean insight of "The Dialectics of the Negative and the Metropolis." There was no contradiction between Asor Rosa's readings of "The Young Lukacs, Theoretician of Bourgeois Art" or "Thomas Mann or Bourgeois Ambiguity," and "Trade Union and Party after Salary Contracts" or "Class Composition and Workers Movements." One could continue the list, showing that it was part of the same intellectual battle to publish Mario Tronti's essays on the working class, on extremism and reformism, Antonio Negri's study on John M. Keynes, and Manfredo Tafuri's reading of Weimar or of Vienna socialist urban planning from 1920 to 1933.[16]

Cacciari's philosophy of the city—or of the Metropolis—was the logical continuation of his political activity, in the double practice of militancy and intellectual research. Asor Rosa had put it in his cutting operaista tone, which would be a perfect antidote against what I would call the *campus* illusion of cultural studies in this country: the academic community as politically

Introduction

radical because leftists fight to introduce new fields of study and new content in the curriculum. In the 1966 preface to the second edition of *Scrittori e popolo*, Asor Rosa clarified his position:

> We were saying that the elimination of cultural battle meant for us the full assumption of the political discourse of class. . . . To practice cultural analysis . . . is impossible—*doesn't have any sense*—if one is not capable of fully carrying on the political work that the situation demands. We do not simply allude to the plurality of levels that a serious movement must keep present all at once: but, in a very direct and elementary way, we speak even of the physical simultaneity of the two levels [of political work and cultural analysis] in the persons themselves of the comrades-researchers.[17]

The plurality of levels or doubleness in physical terms, even beyond the level of political militancy, is an almost necessary condition of modern life, of modern subjectivity. Cacciari suggests here in his epilogue that the "inconsistencies and conflicts" between the seventies' essays and his later work on Loos (1981) are not as strong as they seem at first and represent a development in his inquiry of nihilism. I would say that they are coherent parts of an intellectual movement centered on a plurality of levels and on the continuous acknowledgment of contradiction or breaking off. Lacan would say that the subject is constantly displaced; Derrida that difference is endlessly at work. Cacciari is even more double or multiple or inhabited by differences than any of the well-known gurus of the late twentieth century: for almost twenty-five years he has been a professor in Tafuri's Department of Historical and Critical Analysis (what was before the Istituto di Storia dell'Architettura), an intellectual and a public political figure, moving back and forth between the local and the national levels.

First, as said before, an activist in the factory at the time of the *operaisti* movements, later a well-known Communist deputy in the Italian Parliament (from 1979 to 1984), then briefly within the PDS (Democratic Party of the Left), after Ochetto gave a new direction to what was the PCI until a few years ago, Cacciari is today an independent on the left (he created the group Il Ponte, the bridge), and is a key figure in the political life of Venice:

Introduction

he nearly became mayor in 1990 and is now a member of the city council. But in order to grasp the multifaceted mind of Cacciari, it would be enough to focus on the different layers of his writings. Beside the richness of his references coming from various disciplines—from literature to economics—the most evident scandal is his move from his early works to his late ones. Up to *Krisis* (1976) his research can be defined in the terms of his commitment to Marxist analysis. From *Icone della Legge* (1985) to the third edition of *L'Angelo necessario* in 1992,[18] Cacciari pursues a theological investigation, studying ancient Greek, Christian, and Jewish texts as well as the mystical component of Benjamin, Rilke, and Heidegger. But if one considers how important Benjamin has always been for Cacciari, there is no scandal then, not even a conversion, because mysticism and Marxism are the two halves of Benjamin's work. One can rather find what can be called a conversation, the constant dialogue that one work has with another, regardless of time and location. As Maurice Blanchot said, "a book is nothing but the making of a book out of other books" (*la mise en livre d'autres livres*).

Conversations

To insist on the theory of the Metropolis is for Cacciari the full, almost physical awareness of the fact that cultural analysis cannot eschew political work. To insist on the Metropolis means to grasp, via the urban theme so important in Benjamin, the most basic Marxist touchstones: the factory, capital, the cycle of money and goods, State organization as the foundation of political economy. As Benjamin understands it, there is continuity from factory work to metropolitan life. He compares the uniformity Poe saw in the attire, behavior, and facial expressions, of the metropolitan crowd to the uniformity Marx of industrial labor, where in the assembly line the workers have to move like automatons.[19] The Metropolis, Cacciari insists, is a system, "a multi-articulated urban type—*a comprehensive service* . . . a qualified organization of the labor force: a scientific reserve-supply for industrial growth; a financial structure; a market: and the all-inclusive center of political *power*." The Metropolis implies the physical space of the city as well as the network of ideological constructions of different kinds around it; it em-

Introduction

bodies both the awareness of urban proletariat and the abstract dimension of work: the reality of the factory and the sophisticated cycle of the circulation of money.

The theory of the Metropolis, combined with the militant practice in the factory at the time when Italy experienced its own industrial revolution through workers' struggles, confronts the devouring strength of advanced capital that is capable of restructuring itself through its own crisis, the conflicts antagonizing it. The Cacciarian theory perceives crisis as fundamental to capitalist development; then the point becomes, in strictly militant terms, how to use it, how to make the crisis functional to the working class and not to the capital. For the sake of cultural analysis it is worthwhile to identify tendencies and formulate, as suggested by *Contropiano*'s editorial, "a clear and totally demystified description of the object to be known." In this way Cacciari perceived negative thought and a dialectic of it, or negative thought in motion.

In his essay "On the Genesis of Negative Thought," Cacciari analyzes Schopenhauer, Kirkegaard, and Nietzsche as the thinkers of negative thought. Their critical readings of Hegel marks the beginning "of a rigorous systematization of an anti-dialectical thought." [20] Cacciari opposes dialectics and negative thought. Dialectics is historically positive, operates in a logical and temporal order, synthesizes everything, even what appears as "eccentric" or unfamiliar "to the structure, needs and purposes of that order." [21] Cacciari states that, in contrast to this positive side of dialectics, he calls "negative" that mode of thought that rejects the dialectical synthesis and tries to determine as central what is eccentric, what is crisis. The purely philosophical analysis encompasses ideological awareness, as Cacciari continues: "There is no doubt that the opposition [of what he defines, that is, negative thought] to dialectics *means* the criticism of the ideological and social structure of the bourgeois system, as well as the refusal to be integrated positively and actively in its process of rationalization." [22] At this point takes place a switch that is not a reversal but what can be called a leap, or better a trembling (to borrow a term used by Roland Barthes—when he wants to say that when we speak we are condemned to signify, he finds that language is "tremblé de sens,"

Introduction

(trembles with meaning). The trembling of negative thought makes it the most refined engine of the development of the system it wants to reject. Negative thought becomes functional in the system exactly because it is capable of interrogating all the nonfunctional—today we would say marginal—elements that cannot be synthetically absorbed into the system itself. Cacciari leaps to the extreme consequence: "Precisely because of its negativity, of its obstinate radical refusal of bourgeois system and ideology, the anti-dialectic thought can present itself as ideological *function* of this same system."[23]

Cacciari, in his philosophical investigation, was echoing Antonio Negri's inquiry on economy and law. In the first issue of *Contropiano*, Negri launches his reading of 1929 and John Maynard Keynes:

[The year] 1929 represents a moment of exceptional importance. . . . 1929 sweeps away even the nostalgia for those values that 1917 destroyed. In the black Thursday of Wall Street, in the catastrophic falling down of the Stock Exchange, are rightly falling the state myths, the political myths of a century of renewed bourgeois hegemony on the working class. . . . It is the end of *laissez-faire*. . . . The beginning of a new period in the history of the contemporary state is marked by the fact that, in this already socialized world, the recognition of the emergency of the working class—and of the ineliminable character of this antagonism—can no longer be denied. . . . The capitalist reconstruction of the state is conceived on the discovery of the radical antagonism of the working class."[24]

But in addition to this conversation with Negri's economic analysis, Cacciari was pinpointing, in what I called the trembling of negative thought, the tragedy of any radical thought, from the political radicals like Marx, obsessed by the fact that he had to use the language of capitalism, to the poetic or aesthetic radicals like Baudelaire who knew the devouring shocks of irony.

Cacciari's interpretation of the German sociologists continues that of Schopenhauer, Kirkegaard, and Nietzsche, while the Nietzschean insight is integrated in "The Dialectics of the Negative and the Metropolis." Both Simmel and Benjamin reached

Introduction

the negativity of the Metropolis, but at a different level and with different implications.

According to Cacciari, Simmel grasped the metropolitan "nervous life," that disaggregation of subjectivity typical of the modern. He pictured the violence of the process of intellectualization that determines every gesture in the metropolitan reality. But Simmel could not stand up to the most radical consequences of what he himself perceived: at the very limit of modern tragedy, he found the signs of the freedom and development of humankind. He found the individual, and not the capitalist machine that grinds away all possible human condition, all possible synthesis. Therefore Simmel operated an ideological construction, where the Metropolis ended up being human, like the community, the city, the big consumer city, as in the past. Close to Simmel is Lukacs, reader of Simmel, who, although he perceived the impressionistic character of the German sociologist, tamed the sharpness of negative thought considering the literary form of tragedy as the form of essence—whereas there is no essence in negative thought, only leaps and points of breaking off. Benjamin, moving up from the position of Simmel, perceived the radical negativity of the Metropolis. Together with Benjamin, Nietzsche appears in "The Dialectics of the Negative and the Metropolis" as the one who did not return to nostalgic positions of synthesis and fully understood the inevitability of tragedy with no hope of consolation.

Cacciari is actually interested in two positions that can be called *almost* negative and *fully* negative: the utopian and the tragic; or the synthetic and the radical; or one oriented toward historical continuity and one embracing crisis as the engine of changes that defy programmatic prediction. Nevertheless, the failure of prediction should not be interpreted as the tendency toward an irrational explosion or as the praise of irrational forces. Cacciari is suspicious of immediacy even in political fights, and, as a philosopher interested in a critique of ideology, he rejects as ideological construction any irrationalist interpretation even of the Romantic period—of Novalis and Schlegel— that precedes what he calls negative thought.[25] No rhizomes, no philosophy of *imagination au pouvoir* (imagination in power) in the Italian theory of the Metropolis.[26] The reader should then

Introduction

be aware that there are two types of rationality or rationalizations: one positive, hopeful, sunny, even if in contact with modern negativity, and the other dark, with no hope, no nostalgia, no projects, but endlessly at work as a process of rationalization, capable of integrating the failure of reason into its total rationalization. As Cacciari phrases it in his 1980 *Oppositions* article, "The uprooted spirit of the Metropolis is not 'sterile' but productive par excellence." [27]

Many rapprochements are possible, connecting the theory of the Metropolis to other important European trends of the sixties and the seventies, fashionable in the States since the eighties. One could disregard what I would call more internal discrepancies and, in a sort of flight over the most important theories of the second half of the twentieth century, see the proximity of Cacciari's philosophy with Derrida's, as if Cacciari constructed a deconstructionist thought not on language but on the allegory of the Metropolis. The Derridian input is justified both by Cacciari's emphasis on difference and by the fact that Cacciari was introduced to Derrida's work by his aesthetics' professor at the University of Padua, Dino Formaggio. One can also see, in spite of Cacciari's short critical note against Lacan in part I, some affinity with the Lacanian project. What else is Lacan's psychoanlytical theory, after all, if not the last, gigantic rationalist effort, the more so because his unconscious is at work exactly where the cogito fails? All these are theories of reason below degree zero, where the old reassuring rationality is broken and negativity colors everything with its dark hue. But there is no alternative, no hymn toward irrational forces finally liberated after the oppression. Such is the harsh law of negative thought.

The various authors mentioned by Cacciari would finally enter either in the position of the quasi-negative or in that of the fully-negative thought. But Cacciari's ability—and difficulty—lies in that he is constantly juggling with that unbalanced point where one position drastically changes into the other. The reader follows Simmel for several pages as example of negative thought, while Cacciari gives a voice to that negative thought; at the same time they hear another voice combined with Simmel's—Cacciari's voice—and they are already warned by a few sentences here and there that the German sociologist will not finally reach

Introduction

the fullness of the negative. When the reader gets to Benjamin and Nietzsche, he or she is brought back to the almost negative position by the rich debate within the Werkbund, by the reading of Goethe, by the critique of Lukacs as a reader of Simmel.

Cacciari's philosophy offers an insight to all those who believe that architecture is, more than constructing a building, a complex act condensing visible and invisible political and ideological implications, aesthetic and moral choices. Cacciari does not help those who want more detailed information about Vienna, the German Werkbund, Loos, or Benjamin, although he offers a daring interpretation of all these figures and movements, sketching what Pierre Bourdieu would call an intellectual field where various agents take up various positions.[28] In Cacciari's lectures and essays always resounds a tone that does not come from the quiet of the classroom nor the peace of the library. Sure, one can find the obscurantism and the love for abstract terms typical of philosophy (one would perhaps say, in the States, Continental philosophy), but this attitude is the most superficial flavor of Cacciari's writing. One should see in it the power of a cutting word or a condensed sentence that needs to reach a conclusion when agreement is urgent to come to a decision, to conclude a final negotiation.

Cacciari's style does not have the political illusion of the avantgarde: changing the world through language, or feeling different, radical because a few oppositional stereotypes are combined with an approved set of references and quotations. His language is broken by the practice of political activism in the real world, and shows the existence of an untenable contradiction: the fact that there is a cultivated, preposterous language for professors and that there are words burning with action, loaded with work and rage, and nevertheless controlled, intellectual in their formulation. Cacciari's words aim at a political effect, a cold reason overcoming the simplistic opposition of victory and defeat, while continuing a precarious balance, veering to identify the right targets. Cacciari's rhetoric, perhaps even more brutal in English, cannot obey the rules of radiant clarity and soft persuasion of the ancient polis. His style recaptures the spoken word in the Metropolis where there is no warmth for passions nor peace for reflection, but the anguish to master reality,

Introduction

failing which, one is overwhelmed by the traffic, the crowd, the unexpected event. In the Metropolis, unlike the polis, meetings do not take place in a reassuring public space but in a hall next to the noise of the assembly line, next to the acid smell of chemical products. The rhythm of metropolitan life and metropolitan relations is embodied in Cacciari's language, in the spasms of allusions, ellipses, endless inverted commas and italics, harsh German philosophical terms used every two lines without translation as if they were provocatorily breaking the classical musicality of Italian vowels. This language, continuously chopped in short sentences obsessively constructed on the third person singular of the verb *to be,* is disturbing, nonharmonious, violent; it carries the trace of the harshness of metropolitan life, what Baudelaire called:

l'heure où sous les cieux
Froids et clairs le Travail s'éveille, où la voirie
Pousse un sombre ouragan dans l'air silencieux

(The hour when, under the cold and clear skies,
Work is waking up, when works in the streets
Scream like a dark tornado in the silent atmosphere.)[29]

The reader should hear in Cacciari's difficult, nervous, broken, repetitive style the echo of discussions in moments of struggle, the raising of the voice when the contractual tension comes to a crucial point; the sharpness of a political assurance that corners those who think differently and are not as quick as the speaker; the pauses to let other people talk, while the speaker is nevertheless thinking about his next intervention in that effort of listening and at the same time mentally organizing his own reply; the hammering of a conviction that must become evident and effective in lobbying. In the fights in factories, where a minute is money for both workers and capitalists, there is no time for demagogic effects nor for the seduction of great humanitarian visions. Even political rage has to be controlled, intellectual: it aims to the metallic clarity of figures. Everything has the dryness of a contract, the cruel logic of a negotiation under pressure, in a confrontational peak, where no passion is allowed because it would create confusion. The Italian *autunno caldo* (warm fall) of 1969, the period of violent strikes that lead to new agreements between workers and capital, left its indelible imprint in Cacciari's style. That imprint will also mark his later books, even if they seem so far away from the preoccupations of the sixties and seventies.

Architectural Theory Against Italian Cultural Tradition

Cacciari devoted a chapter of "The Dialectics of the Negative and the Metropolis" to artistic representation, clearly leading to Loos's architecture of nihilism. Against any irrationalist illusion of redemption by art,[30] of an art that would finally save the world by proposing a different use of itself or new contents, Cacciari identifies the tragic dimension of some artistic languages that do not try to eschew the negativity of the Metropolis. Poe, Baudelaire, Kafka, and Nietzsche speak the language of contradiction, displaying all the signs of alienation, dismissing any hope in any possible alternative. This is the true nihilistic position that also frames Loos's architecture, as Cacciari writes in "Loos and His Contemporaries": "All anti-expressive, anti-synthetical, anti-natural composition is nihilistic." The repetition and calculation of Poe's short stories recalls that of Loos's architectural exteriors: they mimic the standardized production of the Metropolis and are "pure use value—as in the 'coach' of the Stein house (1910) and the house at Northartgasse (1913)." That artistic choice is searching for neither salvation nor consolation nor escape: the great, tragic forms of the artists mentioned by Cacciari can do nothing but be analogous with the negativity of the Metropolis. They describe obsessively, present the hard lines of alienation in the most literal sense of the term, *alius,* other, always different, never coincident with anything, never reconciled with a supposed origin or nature.[31]

Poe, Baudelaire, and Kafka are also writers on whom Benjamin concentrated in constructing his reading of the effects of metropolitan life on human perception and everyday life.[32] The line from Poe to Benjamin constitutes a crucial trajectory for any radical thought.[33] The texts by Cacciari collected here are contained within a reading of Benjamin; it could be said, using a term so important in "Loos and His Angel," that they are commentaries on passages from Benjamin. They are comment and

Introduction

not criticism, since their aim is not to explain Benjamin but to follow the associations inspired by his texts, or fragments and images coming from his texts.

There is an Italian modern trend in the twentieth century that caught and even enhanced the European dimension of urbanization[34] and metropolitan life: Giorgio De Chirico's metaphysical cities and squares; Mario Sironi's urban industrial landscape; Alberto Savinio's enigmatic irony; the architect Sant'Elia's buildings that seem to belong to a science-fiction film; Italo Svevo's novels where the tormented inhabitant of Trieste lives all the contradictions of the modern. The list could continue, stressing Italo Calvino's mathematical literature that is forged by the cruel logic of metropolitan life. It would be impossible to leave aside the feeling of harsh metropolitan emptiness and uprootedness that derives from Aldo Rossi's Fontana di Segrate, or from many of his sketches where all natural dimensions are perverted, where a coffeepot is as big as a building. Or one can think of the totally unnatural, stony scenarios of Massimo Scolari's paintings.

This important Italian anti-organic, metropolitan tendency fiercely opposes the construction of a little Italy(!), a "Strapaese" totally immersed in village life, peasant, petit-bourgeois reality, pathological provincialism.[35] The peasant type of Italy is imbued with a populist ethos that has a nineteenth-century origin, when Italy had a huge historical delay in its economic and political development compared to England and France. The peasant type is also the image of an agrarian Italy that corresponded to the fascist economic plan, the populist vein of fascism as well as a left-wing populism attached to the image of the national-popular. In his complex reading of Gramsci in *Scrittori e popolo,* Asor Rosa pinpointed the paternalistic position of Gramsci, who himself insisted that the new literature cannot but be historical, political, and popular:

It must tend to elaborate what is already existing, polemically or in whatever other way; what really matters is that it should be rooted in the *humus* (earth) of popular culture, as it is, with its taste and inclinations, etc., with its moral and intellectual world, even if it is backward and conventional.[36]

Introduction

The theory of the Metropolis, its non-nostalgic negativity, its favorite references from Paris as capital of the nineteenth century to Vienna as capital of the early twentieth century, express very well the multicultural frame of mind of a technological age; at the same time they reject the sentimentalism, the tears, the countryside and the rural dream of two or three centuries of Italian literature. This ideology seems to survive and to propagate the most conventional, folkloric image of Italy: Giuseppe Tornatore's film *Cinema Paradiso*, cited at the Cannes Festival in 1989 and quite well-known in the United States, is one example. This sentimental and successful film reinforces a nostalgic view of the simple, preindustrial community life in a Sicilian village, while some Italian metropolitan films are completely unknown outside Italy, such as Ricky Tognazzi's *Ultrà,* or Marco Risi's *Meri per sempre* (1989) and *Ragazzi fuori* (1991). Tognazzi presents a metropolitan and violent Italy in his story of young hooligans going from Rome to Turin; Risi depicts a desperate Palermo. For the two young directors the metropolitan dimension does not lie just in the story about urban realities but also in the formal rhythm of the film itself, mimetic of the nervous, fragmented life of the metropolitan experience.[37]

Frederic Jameson, in his 1985 article entitled "Architecture and the Critique of Ideology," pinpointed the peculiar blend of the Italian weariness with the Gramscian vision: "There are, of course many reasons why radical Italian intellectuals today should have become fatigued with the Gramscian vision, paradoxically at the very moment when it has come to seem reinvigorating for the Left in other national situations in Europe and elsewhere." Jameson, who criticized Tafuri for his "stark and absolute position," proposed a position that "may be called neo–Gramscian,"[38] recalling "the 'organic' formulations" of the classical Marxian text. Jameson is fully aware of the Italian reaction against the "thirty-year institutionalization of Gramsci's thought within the Italian Communist party" and suggests that Gramsci is assimilated, "in the Italian context, to that classical form of dialectic thought which is everywhere repudiated by a Nietzschean post–Marxism."[39] But Jameson prefers to read Tafuri within the frame of mind of what I would call a general history of Marxist thought, not within the frame of mind of

Introduction

a theory of the Metropolis, which I consider the indispensable perspective for approaching both Tafuri and Cacciari.

The theory of the Metropolis uproots any organic nature, any *humus*, any belonging, just as architectural theory, as developed at the University of Venice Department of Critical and Historical Analysis, breaks through comfortable divisions of disciplines and habits of thought. If this perspective has its historical reasons within Italian culture, it cannot be locked in a deterministic pattern and should be seen as a conceptual device that allows one to rewrite history—or the history of architecture, or the analysis of the work of a single architect, such as Adolf Loos.

The notion of the Metropolis is not static like a thematic category, but rather has the dynamic movement, the nervous life of a work-in-progress. Lewis Mumford, for example, collected examples of cities, but he did not construct a theory of the Metropolis.[40] Or, to cite another example, Raymond Williams uses the theme of the country and the city to explain different phenomena: this opposition identifies a tension present in many cultural attitudes of the West.[41] The opposition of country and city has an almost positivistic calm, serving the purpose of ideological analysis, always present in Williams's enterprise. Nevertheless, Williams's opposition does not get to that trembling contradiction undermining any statement in the whirlpool of positions continually on the verge of turning upside down.

The notion of Metropolis is neither thematic nor historiographic. It belongs to the antihistoriographic mode of Cacciari, a chapter of what I call a conversation with Tafuri, since conversations can be ideal, but also part of an institutional enterprise.

Any serious evaluation of cultural studies and its institutionalization today in this country should consider not only the famous experience of the Birmingham Centre for Cultural Studies,[42] but also the Venetian experience of Tafuri's department at the School of Architecture, and the interplay between political and cultural struggles suggested above.

I emphasize Cacciari's collaboration with *Contropiano*, where Tafuri published articles that later became well-known books, in Italy and abroad, like his *Progetto e Utopia* (1973), which constitutes a whole rewriting of his 1969 *Contropiano* article, "For a Criticism of the Ideology of Architecture."[43] Cacciari

Introduction

started to teach at Tafuri's department in the early seventies, and the interwoven activity of politics and culture is quite clear in the Venetian experience. It should now be stressed how it challenged the typical historiographic tradition of more than a century of Italian education and academic production, founded on a linear idealistic development: history, or the history of a given discipline, understood as a series of authors and movements to be orderly categorized according to a seemingly linear definition of the various disciplines.

This anti-historicist stand was also taken by Asor Rosa—who was teaching at the University of Rome, not at the Venice School of Architecture—in his *Scrittori e popolo,* which is organized around clusters of investigation: the nineteenth century, the period between the two wars, the Italian resistance to fascism, and then specific writers such as Carlo Cassola and Pier Paolo Pasolini. In his 1988 preface, he writes that *Scrittori e popolo* "wanted to be a decisively anti-evolutionist, therefore anti-historicist, and therefore anti-progressist book." He then identified the link between the nihilist attitude and the opposition to the historical mode of thinking: "The criticism of History was then parallel to the criticism of bourgeois culture, while representing its secret justification: and we cannot hide that already at that time a substantial nihilistic attraction nourished our anti-historical position." [44] Asor Rosa stresses his intention of "doing intellectual work," not of continuing "a cultural tradition" and even less that "particularly absurd form of cultural tradition, that is the national cultural tradition, with which, hopefully, we always succeeded in never identifying." [45]

Tafuri suggests a similar anti-historical position—in the sense of opposing linear history. His 1971 *Contropiano* article, "Austrian Marxism and City: *das Rote Wien,*" starts with a complaint about the textbooks of history of modern architecture: Hitchcock, Zevi, and Benevolo ignored the "historically exceptional episode of Vienna's social-democratic administration, between 1920 and 1933." [46] Tafuri notes that only in political history, or in specific works on that Viennese period, one could find documentation of that event, forgotten by the history of the discipline. In *Theories and History of Architecture,* Tafuri takes a clear stand on the question of modern architecture and

Introduction

the "eclipses of history"—such is the title of the first long chapter. Tafuri criticizes much of the historiographical tradition, what he calls, in a preface to the second edition, the "worn-out idealist historicism" and even the "watered-down official Marxism" of Lucien Goldmann and Galvano Della Volpe. Here he aims, as in *Architecture and Utopia: Design and Capitalist Development,* to question the idea of architecture itself, always proposed as if it were an untouchable reality, an eternal value and not an ideological construction, an institution, a contingent reality. He specifies that the term "ideology" means the structure "of the false consciousness that intellectuals offer to the ruling classes."[47] Later, moving towards a more Foucauldian understanding of history, he modifies this straightforward Marxist definition and reads architecture and its languages as discursive practices that forge reality. But, beyond the Marxian tone or within it, Tafuri indicates already in *Theories and History of Architecture* a different way of writing history, that rejects the paradoxically nonhistorical mode of linear history.[48]

In the above-mentioned article on Tafuri, Jameson stresses the three perspectives in which he thinks Tafuri's work should be examined: the Marxist context in which it was produced, the context of a contemporary event on a global scale, and the discursive form in which Tafuri works. The Marxist context is that trend of contemporary Marxism which repudiated "what the Althusserians called Marxist 'humanism,'" in which Jameson includes "very specifically its 'Utopian' component as symbolically represented by Marcuse and by Henri Lefebvre."[49] Jameson calls this trend post-Marxism and places within it the French *nouveaux philosophes* and "Tafuri's collaborator, Massimo Cacciari"; Jameson also perceives "some kinship with T. W. Adorno's late and desperate concept of a purely 'negative dialectics.'"[50] The vaster contemporary event, which has American equivalents, is "the critique of high modernism, the increasingly omnipresent feeling that the modern movement itself is henceforth extinguished" (pp. 38–39). Finally, the perspective of Tafuri's discursive form, that is, historiography (or better, narrative history) confronts Tafuri himself "with the problem of writing history, and in this case of writing the history of a discipline, an art, a medium" (p. 39).

Introduction

Jameson understood the dilemma that the writing of history poses to anyone who wants to do more than "small-scale semiotic analyses of discrete or individual text or buildings," referring to the well-known "crisis in narrative or story-telling history since the end of the nineteenth century" (pp. 38–39). At the same time, he aims at the description of the postmodern condition as the determining feature of the Tafurian dilemmas, all the more so because Tafuri himself did not mention postmodernism. Jameson does not miss the formal quality of Tafuri's work, and, in a cogent analysis, compares Tafuri's *Architecture and Utopia* with Adorno's *Philosophy of Modern Music* and Barthes' *Writing Degree Zero:* "What the three books I have mentioned have in common is not merely a new set of dialectical insight into literature, but the practice of a peculiar, condensed, allusive discursive form, a kind of textual *genre,* still exceedingly rare, which I will call dialectical history" (p. 40). Nevertheless, Jameson's wish to give the correct ideological formulation of Tafuri's work pushes him to rush to the labels post–Marxism and postmodernism. These terms can categorize an episode and indeed be clarifying, but they imprison an intellectual effort in definitions that paradoxically reinforce the linear, historicist approach of what Jameson himself could not help calling "the history of contemporary Marxism," even if he grasps the rare achievement of what he calls "dialectical history" (p. 38). In other words, I think that rather than emphasizing the Adornian kinship, Tafuri and Cacciari are to be placed in what I call the Benjaminian project, or the conceptual tension of the Metropolis.

The stand against linear histories implies another historical choice: rereading the past with a clear concern for the present situation—the present from which we are looking at the past—and trying to read the past in that dramatic moment in which events produce the ephemeral spark of their own brief present. But these events are intense and complicated by a network of personal intentions, failures of those same intentions, institutional struggles, historical memory and oblivion, and conscious and unconscious factors at the collective and individual levels. How could this complexity be contained in the simple sequence of events told by linear history, in the notion of author with

Introduction

a chronology of works and places, or the notion of movement with a series of names? To give the sense of the type of history that rejects the historicist flatness, one could quote Benjamin's "Thesis on the Philosophy of History," where he discusses the French historian Fustel de Coulanges, the prototype of nineteenth century positivistic history, what in France is called *histoire historisante*. Benjamin criticized this approach:

> To historians who wish to relive an era, Fustel de Coulanges recommends that they blot out everything they know about the later course of history. There is no better way of characterizing the method with which historical materialism has broken. It is a process of empathy whose origin is the indolence of the heart, *acedia*, which despairs of grasping and holding the genuine historical image as it flares up briefly.[51]

Benjamin defined historicism as being without a theoretical armature and culminating in universal history: "Its method is additive: it musters a mass of data to fill the homogeneous, empty time."[52] Tafuri rejects this homogeneous time and conceives his history and theories of architecture on what Benjamin called "a constructive principle," typical of materialistic history.

Only an ornamental understanding of intellectual work limits the role of technique to that of mere embellishment. Only "the indolence of the heart" leads to the belief that history is an accumulation of data. The way in which the object of investigation is chosen, composed, presented, even mistreated, makes a difference. Benjamin describes this other type of investigation, which sums up a direction of research, typical of the second half of our century, in which history and theory are interwoven:

> Thinking involves not only the flows of thoughts, but their arrest as well. Where thinking suddenly stops in a configuration pregnant with tensions, it gives that configuration a shock, by which it crystallizes into a monad. A historical materialist approaches a historical subject only when he encounters it as a monad.[53]

It is in this antihistoricist mode of understanding history that I propose to read Cacciari and Tafuri.[54] In the first section I presented an epoch, an endeavor, and a place that, in my opin-

Introduction

ion, are indispensable background for reading *Architecture and Nihilism,* and in the next section I shall examine the intellectual presence of an institution, the University of Venice's Department of Historical and Critical Analysis.

The Shock of History
In 1975, when Cacciari published in Italy the essay "Loos and His Contemporaries," the Department of Historical and Critical Analysis was in what I would call its golden age: it had a definite profile and a publisher, Officina in Rome, where Cacciari published both *Metropolis* and his study on Loos.[55] The department played a clear role within Venice's School of Architecture representing an interrogation on the architectural profession itself, an end to the illusion of producing thousands of architects who would have the opportunity to build. The *Contropiano* ethos left its mark in academic research, in the teamwork oriented towards the critique of architectural ideology such as *The American City: From the Civil War to the New Deal* (1973), which brought together four essays by Giorgio Ciucci, Francesco Dal Co, Mario Manieri Elia, and Tafuri, all of whom taught in the department. The preface of *The American City* shows both the type of nonhistoricist historical commitment as well as the work of the critique of ideology (which obviously challenges historicism):

> What, in effect, we have discovered with our research, is not a differing history but certainly another history [of the New World]. . . .
> Our efforts have been directed at demonstrating how the levels of integration of cultural products and ideologies is based not only on an implicit vocation but also on a well defined complex of techniques, which, in its turn, is even partly shaped by the intellectual production as a whole. The direct transformation and utilization of ideology and culture as a technique—even where the ideology is the most regressive, the culture weakest, and the technique least evident—appears to us the most important fact to emerge from our studies.[56]

Against the additive method of historicism, this book also concentrates on blocks and clusters, as in Tafuri's *History and Theo-*

Introduction

ries. For example, in the first chapter, "Modern Architecture and the Eclipse of History," Tafuri identifies a crystallized moment, a moment of shock where the problem of history and the negation of history emerges well before twentieth-century artistic avant-gardes with their typical rejection of history. The moment chosen by Tafuri is the Toscan fifteenth century. A new image of Brunelleschi emerges: far from rooting him in the architectural tradition of an unbroken classical antiquity, Tafuri shows how the architect dehistoricizes the language of the past translating historical values into the present, founding a new language on fragments of the classical world. The quotations and allusions of Brunelleschi were aiming at constructing a new reality and therefore burn away their historical value. The churches of San Lorenzo and Santo Spirito and the dome of Santa Maria del Fiore are "autonomous and absolute"[57] architectural objects that break the order of the medieval city.

But the shock is not simply provided by Brunelleschi, as if Tafuri were moving from a historicistic analysis to a formalist-linguistic approach. The shock is produced by the double movement of dehistoricization offered by Brunelleschi's symbolic system as well as by what Tafuri calls "the philological rehabilitation" of Alberti's *De re aedificatoria*. Brunelleschi and Alberti face each other as two poles of a stand toward history: the first represents a conception of the past as usable for the present and disembodied from its connection with antiquity, whereas the second represents a heroic vision of the past as evasion from the dullness of the present.

Similarly, Cacciari's "Loos and His Contemporaries" culminates with the two poles of Loos's "Roman" period and the seminal house attributed to Wittgenstein. The reading of Loos and his contemporaries is a monad, a crystallized moment where Cacciari performs his critical construction. Cacciari's essay is not a monograph, neither historical nor philosophical but what Benjamin calls "a configuration pregnant with tensions." The first tension is the notion of the Metropolis as seen in the first essay, "The Dialectics of the Negative and the Metropolis," which gives the constructive principle where tensions are incessantly at work. Cacciari couples Loos's essays of the early twentieth century with the journalism of his friend Karl Kraus:

together they constitute a thorough criticism of the German Werkbund and the Viennese Werkstätte. Cacciari focuses on that period at the beginning of the twentieth century where two avant-gardes—the Vienna Secession and the "negative" group of Kraus and Loos—seem to represent two poles: the community utopia and the full consciousness of metropolitan alienation. The community utopia, represented by two architects of the Secession, Josef Hoffmann and especially Ernst Olbrich, is based on the illusion of recuperating a use-value of work: handicraft labor appears as pure quality escaping the alienation of exchange-value. The reader will find in "Loos and His Contemporaries" arguments that continue to draw on the basic features of utopias, like the idea that the artist is a free creator and can be emancipated from the horror of money's circulation and the loss of human quality that it implies. Loos's attack against ornament has nothing to do with a stylistic attack, Cacciari insists, but rather emanates from the metropolitan awareness, the metropolitan logic, his refusal to look for a lost world of use-value.

As usual, Cacciari is interested in the point of instable balance where intellectual positions shift or are ambiguous, what he sometimes calls "unresolved dialectics," as when he discusses the architect Otto Wagner, who insists on the importance of the functional aspect of architecture and opposes the art of building to style. "Wagner's critique of the idea of the garden city" is a critique "of the city as an image of community." But the metropolitan ideal of Wagner is to liberate the Metropolis from the vampire of speculation through artistic form; in this way he can be reintegrated in the ideology of the Werkbund, the Werkstätte, and the Viennese Secession.

In his reading of the Ringstrasse, Carl Schorske offers a similar interpretation of Wagner and of what Cacciari calls his unresolved dialectics, "from the 'tattooed' house, the Majolikahaus of 1898–99, to the buildings of the Neustiffgasse; from the autumnal, floral, almost Olbrichean interiors of the first Wagner villa, to the perfectly 'apparent,' comprehensible space of the Postspaarkasse." Schorske stresses the link between Klimt and Wagner, who called the painter "the greatest artist who ever walked the earth." [58] If Klimt's search for the modern man "was essentially Orphic and internal, a quest for that *homo psycho-*

Introduction

logicus who had already emerged in the literature of the early 1890's," Wagner's search presented a different type of modern man:

> An active, efficient, rational, modish bourgeois—an urban man with little time, lots of money, and a taste for the monumental. Wagner's metropolitan man suffered from only one pathological lack: the need for direction. In his fast-moving world of time and motion, what Wagner called "painful uncertainty" was all too easy felt. The architect must help to overcome it by providing defined lines of movement. The style of Klimt and the Secession helped Wagner in this effort.[59]

Whereas Schorske follows Wagner's movements from the primacy of function to his commitment to the symbolic language of the Secession, Cacciari sees in Wagner the discrepancy between his understanding of functional architecture and his Secessionist tendency to worship art. The difference between Schorske and Cacciari lies in the form of their research. Schorske confronts the dehistoricization of modern man in historical terms: the analysis of Klimt or Wagner or Freud is concerned with a chronological accuracy and situated in the most precisely reconstructed network of cultural exchanges, friendships, and beliefs. Here one can find not the flatness of historicism, but a genre of comprehensive research where personal, institutional, and political histories are fused within a closely argued textual analysis of written as well as visual and musical materials that always shows the contradictions of intellectual programs, intentions, and realizations. I would say that the actors of the Viennese Secession are present, as present as concrete realities like the street: the Ringstrasse becomes the physical center of the confrontation between two artistic generations, and the tension culminates with the figures of Camillo Sitte and Otto Wagner, "the romantic archaist and the rational functionalist" who "divided between them the unreconciled elements of the Ringstrasse legacy."[60]

Cacciari, on the other hand, obsessively moves all the characters of his early-century Vienna on the conceptual grid of the Metropolis. This grid twists any biographical continuity and narrative structure toward the impossible, unreachable, devouring point that would be the achievement of the Metropolis—or

Introduction

the completion of nihilism. Cacciari couples Wagner with Loos in a comparison where Loos appears as the one who grasped the multiplicity of languages of the Metropolis and its necessary distortions, from which it will never be liberated because these distortions are "*inherent* in the language of the Metropolis." But Loos is not the last term of the metropolitan tension, as Wittgenstein constitutes the other extreme of the response to Wagner's unresolved dialectic.

Cacciari's thesis rejects the historiographic tradition that simplifies Loos as a rationalist or protorationalist architect.[61] Cacciari is aware of Loos's unresolved dimension, of his ideological switch after World War I that may have increased the tendency to include his work in the category of rationalism. Up to a certain point the discrepancy between the exterior and the interior of a building parallels the multiplicity of languages of the Metropolis. But, after the war, the conflict between outside and inside becomes more and more directed to the recuperation of the "artistic nature" of the interior. At this point another monad comes onto the scene, already prepared by glimpses and allusions, when Cacciari speaks about Loos's logico-philosophical attack on the Werkbund. Wittgenstein, one of Loos's contemporaries, is already present, in the words and productions of the architect—as Kraus is part of the same struggle against ornament fought by Loos. But toward the end of Cacciari's essay, the philosopher returns as an architect, as if philosophy materialized into architectural forms. How could a historicist history of architecture pay attention to this episode, so small—one house built by a philosopher, a *capriccio* that does not fit with the orderly sequence of buildings, architects, movements, and styles which fill the homogeneous time of historicism?

But within the structuring notion of the Metropolis, in a history concentrated on tensions, the Wittgenstein house, *oikos*, constitutes a culminating moment. The terrible silence of oikos —a theorem, in "its impenetrability and anti-expressivity"— is coupled to Loos's notion of Roman architecture as similar and yet opposite. In spite of his lucidity in understanding the metropolitan condition and criticizing his contemporaries at the beginning of the century, in spite of the blunt difference between the exterior and the interior of his buildings, the later Loos, in his

Introduction

xliii

reading of Roman architecture, according to Cacciari brought a dimension of sociality: "From the Romans, says Loos, we have derived the technique of thought, our power to transform it into a process of rationalization." Technique and time are values: technique is transmitted and confirms the temporal trajectory expressed by "from." Architecture has a value within public life. At the other extreme, Wittgenstein's house never looses its quality of being a theorem, "infinitely repeatable, infinitely extraneous to all value—but also infinitely *unicum*."

The City of Scrambled Alphabets

In "The Dialectics of the Negative and the Metropolis," the concept of the Metropolis culminates as a totally assumed negativity—such as that of Benjamin or writers like Poe, Baudelaire, and Kafka. In "Loos and His Contemporaries" the concept of the Metropolis reaches its highest point with the multiplicity of languages—an argument Loos fully grasped. Cacciari writes that Loos does not see art as transcending handicraft and industry; his emphasis is "on the reciprocal 'transcendence' of *all* these terms: that is on the functional multiplicity of the languages." Cacciari continues: "To separate means to set-in conflict: not to establish abstract hierarchies of value, but to measure-calculate specific differences, on the basis of specific functions as well as specific 'histories' and traditions. Where the Werkbund 'imagines' bridges, Loos posits differences."

Cacciari warns against what can be called the postmodern temptation, even if he never uses this term, neither in the seventies nor in the eighties. He suggests that it would be completely wrong to interpret Loos's multiplicity as compositional eclecticism:

> What is most important here is not the variety of languages but their common logical reference: the need for every element and every function to formulate its own language and speak it coherently and comprehensively, to test its limits and preserve them in every form—to remain faithful to them, not wanting idealistically or romantically to negate them.

Exactly because of this, "in the 'regressive' atmosphere of the postwar period," of Loos's Roman, the *Chicago Tribune* project

Introduction

can be understood as Tafuri (quoted by Cacciari) describes it: as "a polemical declaration against the Metropolis seen as the universe of change," "a paradoxical phantom of an ordering outside time," and at the same time as an incredible attempt at control, a "total possession of the compositional elements."[62] Loos is testing the limits of languages and functions. The *Chicago Tribune* project is not a divertissement, which would be an eclectic explosion, a game, a fantasy. What Tafuri calls its gigantic and pathetic will to exist "in the face of the Metropolis" represents the awareness of what happens to languages when they are not preserved, when one does not remain faithful to them. In his *Scientific Autobiography* (1981), Aldo Rossi,[63] another reader of Loos, could not help thinking of Loos in New York, at the very moment Rossi grasped the truth of the equivalence he always posited between city and architecture since his *Architecture of the City:*

> New York is a city of stone and monuments such as I never believed could exist, and on seeing it, I realized how Adolf Loos's project for the *Chicago Tribune* was his interpretation of America, and not of course, as one might have thought, a Viennese divertissement: it was the synthesis of the distortions created in America by an extensive application of a style in a new context.[64]

The multiplicity of languages is an important motif in "Loos and His Contemporaries" but it does not become a practice until "Loos and His Angel." Here Cacciari does not just announce the multiplicity of languages; his own text *is* this multiplicity. One may think of his references not as simple notes but as conversations with Benjamin, Scholem, Kraus, Loos, Rilke, Heidegger, Derrida, Levinas, Canetti, Agamben, Severino, Savinio, Tafuri, Schmitt, Andreas-Salomé, and others, or, in other terms, most of the mental adventures that made our century, the languages of our century, from political and legal thought to mysticism and religion, from the investigation of the foundations of Western metaphysics to the practices that resist the aporias of thought, from the persistence of a old logo-centric tradition to its fragmentation, its feminization. Because the Metropolis is finally all this: the immense effort to rationalize and the defeat of reason;

Introduction

the place of exchange-value, of the circulation of money, and of their opposite, the intimacy, the noncirculation of Andreas-Salomé's buttons that she collected as a child, or the patient artisanal work of Joseph Veillich, Loos's friend, on whom the architect wrote what Cacciari calls some of his "most beautiful" pages.

Surprisingly, after the insistence on Loos's criticism of the Werkstätte's nostalgic attitude, of their handicraft ideal of quality objects in the epoch of exchange-value, Cacciari discovers another Loos who "tells us with what patience and *endless care* Veillich worked at his furniture." Should one see in Cacciari's interpretation a conversion from the hardness of the theory of the Metropolis to vernacular and to tradition, as if an organicistic faith had corrected the previous position? Should one see in Cacciari's essay a move similar to the one that took place in architecture, going from what Robert Venturi has called the moral rigor of the modern movement to that eclectic, pluralistic, quotational mood of the so-called postmodern architecture? Did negative thought become postmodern, did it become a written divertissement, after so much political and theoretical commitment?

It would be misleading to perceive a contradiction between the two texts of the early seventies and "Loos and His Angel" (1981). One should be patient and reread this text—patient like Loos's Viellich, or like the reader Nietzsche longs for at the beginning of the *Genealogy of Morals,* a reader who would have "the skill to ruminate." There is a strict logical movement that leads from Wittgenstein's oikos to a further reading of the Viennese philosopher and the entire beginning of the century in Vienna: between "Loos and His Contemporaries" and "Loos and His Angel" Cacciari wrote his crucial work on Vienna, *Dallo Steinhof* (1980). Or one should proceed with Cacciari's texts as we are supposed to with Loos's buildings, going from an exterior to an interior that does not try to accommodate the exterior, but is different, and different at every moment. That Loosian gap, with no hierarchy between the exterior and the interior already participates of the multiplicity of languages. One should always keep in mind the passage from "Loos and His Contemporaries" cited above about the Loosian multiplicity of

Introduction

languages, the need that every element has to formulate its own language, "to test its limits and preserve them in every form—to remain faithful to them."

The multiplicity of languages inevitably poses the problem of tradition, and of "being loyal" to it. In the section of "Loos and His Angel" called "Being Loyal," Cacciari stresses Loos's insistence on tradition. The Michaelerplatz is an attempt to solve compositional questions "in the term of our old Viennese masters." Loos's view of tradition stood as a criticism of the creativity of the architect, "the architect as Dominator,"[65] wanting to establish the hegemony of one meaning over the others. Wittgenstein talked about the absurdity of a single language that pretends to represent the world, and Loos's craftsman does not impose the unicity of a language; he does not create but rather interrogates. He continuously questions "language as *a combination of linguistic games,* a repetition of the assertion that to speak of *one* language (of *one* game) is mere abstraction." And Cacciari continues: "Language is tradition, use, praxis, comprehension, and the contradiction existing among the various openings onto the world." All this means transformation.[66]

This logic of transformation—as Cacciari notes in his epilogue—rejects any idea of overcoming, or rearrangement of elements in hierarchical order. The thought of multiplicity, difference, and transformation appears in a 1977 essay by Cacciari on Deleuze and Foucault. Here Cacciari criticizes a fundamental naturalism in the conception of desire as formulated by the two French philosophers,[67] and ends his discussion opposing another understanding of game to their conception of desire as game. "Game" for Cacciari does not correspond to the liberation of desire, to its totalizing image. Game "shows the new space of the multiplicity of languages" as well as "the plurality of techniques and the conventional character of their names." Game requires rules that are not invented but assumed, transmitted. Only by recognizing this cruel conventional, not natural structure of game "it is possible to affirm its transformability."[68] In order to transform, it is necessary to know the rules, not to have the "indecent pretense" to create the game.

Cacciari indicates in "Loos and His Angel," that Loos's crafts-

Introduction

man represents exactly the link between game and habit, knowledge of the rules and new combinations:

> The deeper one's participation in a game, the more these "openings" issue from practice itself, from "habit." The truly present has deep roots—it needs the "games" of the "old masters," the languages of the posthumous. Hence, the tradition of which we are speaking here does not unfold from book to book, drawing to drawing, "line" to "line," but follows the long detours, the waits, the labyrinths of the games among the languages, of linguistic *practices*.

"Loos and His Angel" insists on the idea of game, which is also important in Cacciari's investigation of Wittgenstein in *Dallo Steinhof*, the text that bears testimony to Cacciari's will to pursue manifold directions of research: "The possibility of variants are immanent to the game—otherwise the rules of the game will be sublimated in new ideal forms, in new Invariants."[69]

Nothing could be farther from Cacciari's concept of game than postmodern free association and immediacy, that mode in which some architectural productions or critical productions freely quote, patching together pieces from here and there without listening to their specific languages, without being loyal to them.[70] Against any fanciful chattering stands the severity of a desperate transparence that does not communicate—such as the glass of Mies van der Rohe, or of Loos's American Bar, completely different from the glass Scheerbart talked about, enthusiastically foreseeing a new glass civilization. In his reading of Mies van der Rohe, Cacciari wrote: "The sign must remain a sign, must speak only of its renunciation of having value—and only by means of this renunciation will it be able to recognize its true functions and its own destiny: only a language illuminated by its own limits will be able to operate."[71] Clearly the renunciation of the farce of value, great synthesis, and free fantasy goes together with the consciousness that any construction—written, musical, visual, or architectural—is an assemblage of parts. It is worthwhile to cite again, as Cacciari does, Mies van der Rohe's wish that building should "signify truly and only building" and his conviction that "the building is an assemblage of parts, each of which speaks a different language, specific to

Introduction

the material used."[72] Tautology and vernaculars are at the limits of language.

The Fleeting Gaze of the Angel

In that Nietzschean meditation on the writing of history that is "The Historical Project" (the preface to *The Sphere and the Labyrinth*), Tafuri also faces the question of the multiplicity of languages and warns against the danger of *wirkliche Historie* (real history): to conceive history as recognition, that is to say on the presupposition that there is a unity of history, "based on the unity of the structures on which it *rests*, on the unity, as well, of its single elements."[73] Then Tafuri quotes Foucault and his cruel "will to knowledge" that does not allow the consolation of universal truth. But Tafuri also warns against the other danger, very strong today, that the awareness of multiplicity becomes again the reconstitution of some unity:

> The danger that menaces the genealogies of Foucault—the genealogies of madness, of the clinic, of punishment, of sexuality—as well as the disseminations of Derrida, lies in the reconsecration of the microscopically analyzed fragments as new unities autonomous and significant in themselves. What allows me to pass from a history written in the plural to a questioning of that plurality?[74]

Tafuri is the historian who knows what I would call, borrowing from the terminology of architecture, the historical material, the various historical materials, their nature, limits, characteristics, resistance, capability to endure time. Tafuri is aware of the importance of the historical project, the calculations that ensure its realization, and the artisanal work—the *giochi di pazienza* (game of patience) as the historian Carlo Ginzburg calls it—required to put together the historical puzzle. Tafuri explores the risks of every position, the questions one should ask the material and the work—patiently, endlessly, ready to catch the necessity of an adjustment, continually adding nuance to the reciprocal input of theory and practice, of documents and concepts. What really matters is the ability to listen to the voice of transformation, to dare to change—that is the only way of being truly loyal. One should not therefore be astonished that the Tafurian

Introduction

research of the eighties, such as his *Venice and the Renaissance* seems to have abandoned the cutting edge of Marxian analysis and adopted the mode of investigation typical of the Annales School.[75] Moreover, an accurate understanding of the conceptual direction that the Annales School gave to historical analysis is inconceivable without that questioning of institutions—and the institution of history—coming from Marxism.[76] In a 1985 article Tafuri posed the terms of the problem:

> If one wants to grasp the complexity of the relational network of contemporary art, it is better to give up the simplistic mode of traditional classifications, or at least recompose in another way its divisions. A history of architecture that would replace this same history into its social and political context, will give little importance to purely linguistic phenomena and will reread texts and documents in the light of *mentalités* history.[77]

The point is not to be imprisoned in an orthodoxy that sticks to dogmatic formulas that are reassuring in their fixity. This is the profound lesson of Benjamin.[78] There is no abandonment of the initial positions of *Theories and Histories* in Tafuri's recent research, which shows the influence of *mentalités* history. On the contrary, there is the loyalty of a transformation. One of the founding fathers of the Annales, Lucien Febvre, rejects linear history as strongly as Benjamin does. It would be enough to quote Febvre's paradoxical and emphatic exclamation against what Benjamin would have called *acedia* and what Febvre called "intellectual laziness" of the historicist mode: "The Past does not exist, the Past is not a given data. The Past is not a collection of cadavers nor should the historian's function be that of finding all these cadavers, giving them a number, taking pictures of each one of them, and finally identifying them. The Past does not produce the historian. It is the historian who gives birth to history." [79]

Cacciari writes in the first part of "Loos and His Angel" that, for Loos and Kraus, the "past is transformed into the vision and hearing of a living, incessant questioning—into a problem par excellence," but they never seek in it an "eternal image." If Tafuri adopts the patience of the historical work, Cacciari follows to its limits the Benjaminian investigation on history, as the entire third part of *Architecture and Nihilism* is inspired by Benjamin's famous image of "Angelus Novus":

A Klee painting named "Angelus Novus" shows an angel looking as though he is about to move away from something he is fixedly contemplating. His eyes are staring, his mouth is open, his wings are spread. This is how one pictures the angel of history. His face is turned towards the past. Where we perceive a chain of events, he sees one single catastrophe which keeps piling wreckage upon wreckage and hurls it in front of his feet. The angel would like to stay, awaken the dead, and make whole what has been smashed. But a storm is blowing from Paradise; it has got caught in his wings with such violence that the angel can no longer close them. This storm irresistibly propels him into the future to which his back is turned, while the pile of debris before him grows skyward. This storm is what we call progress.[80]

This passage, not fully quoted in "Loos and His Angel," is a constant reference; it can be said, in the words of Nietzsche, to be an aphorism that "stands at the head of that essay, and the body of the essay forms the commentary."[81] Tafuri, the historian, firmly looks into the debris of history, into its blinding whirl; Cacciari, the philosopher who has been deeply touched by Heidegger's questions, traces the movements of the figure of the Angel. He follows its image and writes a commentary on it.

The passage from the first essays to "Loos and His Angel" is marked by the movement away from the language of critique of ideology—even if this language was never compact, unique, as in Cacciari's passages on Loos's interiors and exteriors that fully belong to the mode of art criticism, or in the last pages on oikos that defy any definition of genre and, like the best passages of "The Dialectics of the Negative and the Metropolis," burst out in a sort of sharp philosophic-poetic brevity. Cacciari does not reject or condemn the language of the critique of ideology but rather perceives its function and understands that it is a language among others. Studying Wittgenstein in *Dallo Steinhof,* Cacciari focuses on the crucial difference between philosophy and mysticism. Philosophy stumbles on the "fetishism" of show-

Introduction

ing and describing the world as it is, while the mystical "shows from inside the limits of possible propositions."[82] Cacciari is fully aware of the dream "of an immanent and forever alert 'criticism of ideology,'" as he calls it in his epilogue. He knows that it belongs to nihilism, to its opposition to synthesis as well as to mere games of fantasy. He also knows that this lucidity is part of the utopia "of the project of completed nihilism," of its productive will to rationally control everything, to reach "an order of fully transparent function." To recognize this extreme utopia means to test the limits of nihilism itself, the limits of language, the murmur of the multiplicity of languages.

The language of "Loos and His Angel" is inhabited by multiple voices: it is commentary. As indicated by Cacciari, his essay has "the melancholic rhythm of a stroll" rather "than the insistent rhythm of a critique." The stroll is that mode of seeing, thinking, and writing that confronts the limits, not knowing what can be anticipated, not wanting to reach a conclusion. The stroll is a metaphor for the commentary; it can also indicate the practice of the one who looks into architectural forms, traditions, and habits, wanders into space and meanings,[83] and reads "the *difference* existing between their present function and their previous significations."

The stroll also allows the opportunity of looking at the visible, but with an eye to the invisible, with no expectations nor solutions, as in the initial lines of *Dallo Steinhof* that seem to describe a stroll to Wagner's Steinhof church:

> Two symmetrical rows of thoroughfares, at the foot of the Viennese forest, lead to Saint Leopold church. . . . Wagner's church, at the top of the buildings for the psychiatric hospital of the city of Vienna, comes out of the deep green wood with its shining copper dome. It is impossible to say what this work anticipates—it is impossible to say what reaches it.[84]

In his epilogue, Cacciari points out the utopia of nihilism, the aporia of what he calls the architecture of completed nihilism. In the Heideggerian vein, he tries to reach that uncunning point of thought where difference, flickering like a flame, can never be grasped but sheds light in perennial movement, and therefore no definition is ever possible as the final word, as the solution.

Introduction

Cacciari forces the limits of language, with notions like the completion of the architecture of completed nihilism, which nonetheless can never be completed. One would say that he wishes to be submerged by the limits of the architecture of nihilism, inaugurated by Loos's Café Nihilismus. The trajectory of the theory of the Metropolis brings negative thought to the mode of commentary, mystically—not philosophically—conceived as a plunge into the limits of language.

In *Dallo Steinhof,* Cacciari quotes Kraus, who says that we are at war with language; he stresses the continuous character of this fight: "The limit of language is not providentially assigned to us so that we can simply put order inside it."[85] And citing Wittgenstein, Cacciari suggests the necessity of the immersion, the "shipwrecking" into the limits of language. The Cacciarian determination to face the limits of language also means facing the limits of the architecture of nihilism, Cacciari's research is part of his proximity to Wittgenstein's reflection on the expressible and the inexpressible, and the almost "gravitational force that the inexpressible brings on scientific propositions."[86]

The Heideggerian investigation of the limits of language is different from Wittgenstein's logic, even if it belongs to the same twentieth-century obsession with language; it pertains to the realm of the words and their meanings—words being the very matter of which philosophy has been constructed. I would say that, beyond the vast literature and debates on his philosophy and his politics, Heidegger's influence in our time has been a mode of thinking, writing, asking questions, making endless distinctions—in short, the practice of deconstruction. It is well known how important this mode of thought has been for Derrida, and it is seminal for Cacciari's "Loos and His Angel" in the eighties. It would be enough to think of "Eupalinos and Architecture," where Cacciari follows and interprets in the light of the theory of the Metropolis the Heideggerian interrogation on dwelling and building.

In this Heideggerian sense, it would be logical to associate Cacciari and Derrida. But one should always keep in mind a major difference, not of philosophy, but of temperament (using Baudelaire's term for painters), which places Cacciari within a Catholic culture and the political activism I discussed above.

Introduction

Derrida contemplates language as writing and has a deep suspicion for the voice, whereas Cacciari is endlessly fascinated by the voice and oral language, precisely because of its instability, its precarious balance, its dazzling, fleeting, ephemeral character. Consider a passage in *Dallo Steinhof* on Schoenberg, where Cacciari comments on the presence of the text as a structural element in musical composition, and on the emergence of the voice and song.[87] Also, in the very moment Cacciari unfolds the Wittgensteinian conception of game, his natural tendency is to refer to the spoken word: "But such possibilities [of variants] cannot be described *a priori:* they proceed within the dynamics of language that is contingent in the intention of the speakers—intention that takes out of accumulated knowledge, testing, experimenting, transforming it, playing with it."[88]

Not a Home But an Adventure

The question of the multiplicity of languages cannot but be present for someone who has studied so deeply the moment of *finis Austriae,*[89] the end of Austria, of the Habsbourgs' Empire (of which Venice was part until the unification of Italy). In an essay on Hugo von Hofmannsthal, "Intransitabili utopie," Cacciari points out that the world and the language of the Austrian writer did not correspond to the cosmopolitan vision of the Enlightenment, nor to a totalizing idea of Europe, but to "the multiplicity of languages that turn around the great Habsbourg Reich."[90] Against a conservative reading of Hofmannsthal, Cacciari insists on how important is Hofmannsthal's vision of the poet as a seismograph, recording all the movements of the earth. This image shows that the poet does not invent a language but carefully listens to traditions, to their most imperceptible movements, without trying to fuse them in a mythical unity.

One of Hofmannsthal's themes as identified by Cacciari is that of things and time passing, which poses the problem of the past. How can one face this fading away? How can one look at it without falling into nostalgia?

Time goes by, ideologies and beliefs change, institutions, people, objects, and fashions disappear, endlessly. The metropolis itself is an image of the slipping away of everything, as Baudelaire writes in "Le Cygne": "Paris changes!" A true theory of

Introduction

the Metropolis ought to include the many voices of the passing away, and the only non-nostalgic way to look into it, which is a thought of transformation. The response of intellectual searches to the slipping away of things and time is probably a whole history that is yet to be written. A vast range of attitudes would come up, from the obstinate repetitions of the same themes, concepts, and forms to silence, or to the bold statement—such as Roland Barthes's—that "intellectual conversions are the very pulsion of the intelligence." [91] In that history, one could see melancholia and will to change, fear and bluntness, oblivion and memory, hope and regret—all those disquieting elements at the source of a blurred line between the conservative impulse and the thirst for the new.[92]

How should one face the changes in knowledge, institutions, parties, political lines? How can one achieve the refusal to change of all those very things that are changing? Where do we place our loyalty? The difference between Cacciari's (and Tafuri's) position and Asor Rosa's on these issues should be stressed. In Asor Rosa's 1988 preface of *Scrittori e popolo*, there is a chilling image of what I would call stubborn nostalgia for the past, the political life of an almost heroic past. He insists that the operaista position does not make any sense today because there is "simply" no class that would be able to assume that role—and that adverb "simply" is loaded with regret. Then, addressing the younger generation, he speaks, almost in spite of himself, of the everlasting validity of those past values, because everything is left still, as in a station where the train did not start moving.[93] In that immobility everything is waiting for the signal—to start all over again, to go where it was thought the world would go, twenty years ago or more.

Cacciari, on the other side, is loyal to the theory of the Metropolis, up to its extreme consequences, with no nostalgia for something which existed before and should be found again—because this nostalgia would be the ideology, not the theory of the Metropolis. The constitutive vigor and nervous life of the Metropolis implies continuous transformations. There are no still trains in stations waiting years and years for something that will never happen. As suggested by Simmel, Cacciari notes in part 2 that "modern Metropolitan life is but the force that drives things forward toward those *transformations* due to which a problem can be solved only 'by means of a new problem, and a conflict by means of a new conflict.'" And the Metropolis becomes the metaphor for the contemporary world, or better, it is the letter, the concrete reality of the contemporary world:

> We are in an era, says Foucault, in which the world is perceived as a network that simultaneously joins juxtaposed and distant points. This space alienates the "pious descendants of history," for whom the world was like a large street which developed different "meanings" through different ages. Neither does this space resemble the hierarchical space of the medieval city, where the juxtaposition of places referred to the "value" of their respective functions. The present-day space of the metropolis is made up of the non-hierarchical flow of information connecting disciplines and functions, of discrete aleatory currents, whose movements are not teleologically comprehensible but only stochastically analyzable.[94]

In the Metropolis of the present the notion of the political itself is changing: in a 1982 essay on the concept of the left with the emblematic title "Sinisteritas," Cacciari indicates that in our era the traditional vision of political parties cannot represent the concrete political forces of today. Cacciari started this investigation with the powerful Heideggerian questioning of words, their meanings and their visible and invisible implications. A major influence in his rethinking of the political is the controversial figure of Carl Schmitt, who after March 1933 became the ideologue of the Nazis.[95] Schmitt is one of the most important political thinkers who studied the relation between the concept of state and the concept of the political and stressed, as noted by Leo Strauss, that "all concepts in the mental sphere, including the concept of 'mind,' are in themselves pluralistic, and are to be understood only from concrete political existence."[96]

Against any abstract vision of politics, Cacciari proposes an immersion into the concrete, open, clashing, stochastic—in the statistical and musical senses of this term—situations of the contemporary world, which, like the Metropolis, is intrinsically unstable, continuously catastrophic. Neither the classic monolithic, substantialist language of politics—in which a party

Introduction

corresponds to a precise, stable ideology—nor the vision of a technocratic future based on a supposed common scientific language can describe the continuous transformations of the contemporary world. In its open and competitive system, there is an incessant "rapidity of transformation of directions" and an equally incessant "experimental mobility of strategies."[97] Even the modes of political commitment are changing: no existential dramas of the assumption of a credo, but an a-logical level of responsibility. Without any political sentimentalism, the same thinker who gave years of thought and struggle to the workers' movements and has been a Communist deputy dares saying in the eighties that the left could get rid of its foundational myths, such as that of "the working class and its Promise." May be what "the left" means today, Cacciari suggests at the end of "Sinisteritas," is the acute sense of the loss, the fading away of the myths of the left themselves. The pure political does not exist any longer, nor the "Great Political," but the "Great Opportunism" is possible. The political is limited by the individual loci, the contingent, the local, the plurality of the locals, the opportunistic—in the sense of grasping the opportunity—awareness of the changing of situations and programs.

The nervous logic of the unstable or transformable was an important theme for Simmel, with whom Cacciari started his own philosophy of the city, or theory of the Metropolis. In the preface to *The Sphere and the Labyrinth,* Tafuri quoted Simmel's essay entitled "Fashion": "The way in which it is given to us to comprehend the phenomena of life causes us to perceive a plurality of forces at every point of existence."[98] To perceive tensions, antagonisms, the plurality of forces, to feel the incessant transformation of directions, to listen to the multiplicity of languages uproots the idea of belonging to a home, of dwelling, in the physical and metaphorical sense. The architecture of the Metropolis, following Heidegger's interrogation, must be aware, beyond any utopia of urban planning, beyond that utopia that is the idea itself of urban planning,[99] that there are no more dwellers; the politics of the Metropolis must recognize the same condition of loss of place—as the local is not the rediscovery of a small organic community but the epiphany of the ephemeral, the contingent, the migrant.

Introduction

Simmel, although he had fully grasped the metropolitan condition of life, clearly showed in his short 1907 essay on Venice what Cacciari calls his ideological vision of the community. He opposed Florence to Venice and seemed frightened and at the same time fascinated by the impression of artifice he received from Venice:

> In Venice one can see realized the duplicity of life . . . Double is the sense of these squares, that, because of the lack of vehicles and the narrowness of streets, look like rooms. Double is the sense of meeting, pushing, and touching of people in the *calli* . . . Double is the sense of life in this city—now a crossing of streets, now a crossing of canals, so that it belongs neither to the earth nor to the water: and we are always seduced by what appears behind the Proteic shape of Venice, as if it were its real body. . . . Venice has the equivocal beauty of adventure which rootless floats into life, as a torn flower floats into the sea. That Venice has been and will be the *city of adventure* is just the most perceptible expression of the deepest destiny of its image: it cannot be a home for our soul, cannot be anything but adventure.[100]

Introduction

The

Dialectics

of

the

Negative

and

the

Metropolis

1. Metropolis

The problem of the Metropolis, as a problem of the relation between modern existence and its forms, is the point from which all of Georg Simmel's philosophy develops. In order to understand this philosophy, to isolate successfully its historical significance while not limiting oneself to impressionistic commentaries, one must start from this point—the import of which is best encapsulated in "Die Grossstädte und das Geistesleben" ("The Metropolis and Mental Life"),[1] a remarkable essay that resumes discussion of the essential themes of *Philosophie des Geldes* (the philosophy of money) and presents them in a new synthesis. Between this 1903 work and the appearance thirty

Metropolis

years later of Walter Benjamin's fragments on Baudelaire and Paris,[2] falls the entire avant-garde and its crisis.[3] But why is it that the limits of this historical period can be determined by two comprehensive historico-philosophical discussions of the Metropolis? What is meant by Metropolis?

The Metropolis is the general form assumed by the process of the rationalization of social relations. It is the phase, or the problem, of the rationalization of all social relations, which follows that of the rationalization of the relations of production. For Simmel, it is a determinant moment of modern existence; for Benjamin, it is a further moment of the dominion of capital as a structure of society. In either case, the form of the process is that of *Vergeistigung* (the process of the realization of the *Geist*) as a process that abstracts from the personal and rebuilds upon subjectivity as calculation, reason, interest. In this sense, the *Geistesleben* (life of the Geist i.e., intellectual life) can be understood as the life of the Metropolis itself. There is no truly developed Geist beyond the "metropolitan type," beyond the *Grossstadt;* nor any Metropolis that does not express the life of the mind—of reason, that is, in a fully developed form that has successfully integrated within itself the sphere of the social, in all of its ramifications. When the Geist abandons the simple and direct relations of production, it no longer creates the city but the Metropolis. It is the Geist, not the individual, that *of necessity* inhabits the Metropolis. This is the objective reason for the Metropolis.

Simmel presents the problematics of this historical movement in a precise manner. Inasmuch as the modern concept of Geist is a dialectical concept, the Metropolis has its base in the antithesis between *Nervenleben* and *Verstand* (life of the nerves and intellect, respectively), an antithesis that continually affirms and resolves itself. "The psychological base from which arises the metropolitan personality type is the intensification of the life of the nerves [*die Steigerung des Nervenlebens*], which results from the rapid and uninterrupted transformation of external and internal impressions."[4] However, this Steigerung des Nervenlebens, which is grounded in continuous "innovation" and is hence in direct contradiction with the traditional-mythical character of rural life, is "sublimated" in the creation of an "organ" to protect the individual from forces that threaten to "uproot" him (*Entwurzelung*), which come at him "from the currents and contradictions of his external environment . . . rather than reacting with the sensibility [*das Gemüt*], he reacts with the intellect [*Verstand*], with an intensification of his consciousness [*die Steigerung des Bewusstseins*]" (p. 228). The sensibility is henceforth an exclusively *conservative* concept. But the simple life of the perceptive discontinuity of irruptive impressions is not in opposition to it. This life is only the appearance of the Metropolis. The Gemüt, as the synthesizing foundation of social relations no longer in existence, finds itself opposed instead by the Nervenleben together with the Verstand. Hence, the Metropolis expands the scope of perception, increases the quantity of stimuli, and liberates, so to speak, the individual from mere repetition—but only in so far as this process is controlled by the "measure of the intellect," which comprehends these stimuli and discerns and articulates their multiplicity. The intellect, as the common measure of subjectivity, imposes itself on individuality. The "nervous life" of the Metropolis therefore does not by any means lead back to the "deep regions of the personality" (p. 229), but is rather the propellant force, the fuel of the intellect. There is no contradiction between the two, nor, strictly speaking, is it even a question of two different levels. The Nervenleben is a *condition* of the intellect—an internal condition of its power, its dominion, completely integrated within it. There could be no overall control of the evolution of the Metropolis without this "life of the nerves." The process of Vergeistigung is the same as that of the Steigerung des Nervenlebens, taken to its ultimate conclusions. The comprehensive rationality of the Metropolis, the system, is internal to the stimulus, which when received, developed, and understood, itself becomes reason. Thus we arrive at the first precise definition of the function of the Metropolis: it dissolves individuality into the current of impressions and reintegrates these, precisely by virtue of their constitution, into the overall process of Vergeistigung. In its first stage of evolution, the Metropolis uproots individuality from its conservative fixity; the process

Metropolis

5

begun by this uprooting will of necessity lead to the dialectical reasoning that governs, measures, and directs social relations, the interest (*inter-esse*) of the Metropolis.

The rational order that the Nervenleben assumes also affects the political sphere. In a Metropolitan situation, the revolutionary process itself is totally intellectual, as Tocqueville observed: "I spent the entire afternoon walking around Paris, and I was struck by two things: first, the singularly and exclusively popular character of the revolution. . . . the omnipotence of the people. . . . and second, the scarcity of resentful feelings—indeed, of any kind of resentful feelings whatsoever."[5] The geometric clarity with which, in the final analysis, class interest is posited, eliminates all possible teleological or ethico-sentimental synthesis and hence can inhabit only the Metropolis.

The system of this Verstand, its historical constitution, is the monetary market economy. "The monetary economy and the dominion of the intellect are very deeply connected," writes Simmel.[6] The abstraction from individuality, as well as from givenness (whether objective or transcendent), rules both this economy and this intellectual dominion. And confronted by these forces, everything that expresses qualitative relations falls by the wayside: what remains is a system of rationally calculated relations that preclude the possibility of surprises. The monetary economy formalizes economic relations, just as the intellect formalizes psychic relations and movements. It transcends use value, just as the intellect transcends the immediate stimulus, the quality of an impression. In this light we can see how the intellect and the monetary economy become inextricably interconnected in the Metropolis, and how the Metropolis is the place of exchange, the place of the production, and circulation of exchange value. And thus the whole cycle becomes clear: the Nervenleben corresponds to the continuous and relentlessly innovated transubstantiation of exchange value into use value—that is, it corresponds to the necessary instance in which exchange value becomes real value. The intellect, the *Verstand*, in turn abstracts from the appearance of use value the substance of exchange value; it extracts *money* from the process and thus correctly reflects upon the commodity as such—that is, it once

Dialectics of Negative and Metropolis

again produces merchandise. The Metropolis is the place of this whole cycle: it enables all of these instances to be reciprocally functional. We are still in the "city" as long as we are in the presence of use values alone, or in the presence of the simple production of the commodity, or if the two instances stand next to each other in a non-dialectical relation. Whereas we are in the Metropolis when production assumes its own social rationale, when it determines the modes of consumption and succeeds in making them function toward the renewal of the cycle. The Metropolis must set a Nervenleben in motion in order to realize, through the use value, the exchange value produced by the Verstand—and hence in order to reproduce the very conditions of the Verstand's existence.

This dialectic was described by Michelet in parts of his work *Le Peuple* (1846). When the textile crisis of 1842 reached its lowest point, an "unexpected thing" happened: the price of cotton fell to six sous! "It was a revolution for France . . . . We saw what vast and powerful consumers the people could be, when they set their minds to it." "Everywhere wool has come down to the people, and it has enlivened them." "Before, every woman wore a blue or black dress, and she never washed it for fear that it might fall to pieces. . . . Now, at the price of a day's work, her husband, poor working stiff, will clothe her in a dress of flower patterns. This whole throng of women now creating a bright rainbow of a thousand colors along our promenades, was only a short while ago in mourning." The Nervenleben of the boulevard, here impressionistic, concretizes the Verstand of the new industrial strategy; in no uncertain terms, Michelet understands it to be the decisive element of the overall reproduction of capital.

But this monetary market economy—which is, then, the economy in which the indissoluble relation between Nervenleben and Verstand imposes itself—penetrates individuality and shapes it. The process of the individual's internalization of the monetary economy marks the final and most important point of Simmel's analysis. Here we see the culmination of the dialectical process—and earlier definitions lose their general validity. When the *intellectualized* multiplicity of stimuli becomes *behav-*

Metropolis

7

ior, only then is the Vergeistigung complete, only then can one be sure that individual autonomy does not exist outside of the Vergeistigung. And in order to prove the all-inclusive validity of this conclusion, we must be able to demonstrate, in the most apparently eccentric behavior, the ascendancy of the form of abstraction and calculation, the offspring of the Metropolis.

The *blasé* type, most estranged from phenomena and least open to any experience of communication, epitomizes the Verstand's indifference toward the qualities of things, their use value. The blasé attitude exposes the illusoriness of differences. For Simmel, its constant nervous stimulation and quest for pleasure are in the end experiences totally abstracted from the specific individuality of their object: "no object merits preference over another."[7] The object reveals its historical essence as exchange value, and it is treated as such. The simple act of consumption is in constant relation to the equivalence of all commodities. And in this process, enjoyment itself is lost: one's relation to the thing and to the universe of things is completely intellectualized. Vergeistigung and "commodification" merge together in the blasé attitude: and with this attitude, the Metropolis finally creates its own "type"; its general structure finally becomes social reality and cultural fact. Money has in this instance found its most authentic bearer. The blasé type uses money according to its essence, as the universal equivalent of the commodity: he uses it to acquire commodities, perfectly aware that he cannot get close to these goods, he cannot *name* them, he cannot *love* them. He has learned, with a sense of despair, that things and *people* have acquired the status of commodity, and his attitude internalizes this fact. Universal equivalence expresses itself in *spleen*— but this spleen is only the product of the Verstand's omnipotence. The concentration of the life of the nerves, which seems to preside over the blasé experience, thus manifests itself "in the devaluation of the entire objective world,"[8] in the futility of the search for the *unicum,* in the desecration of the transcendent aura that once enveloped inter-subjective relations. Far from starting new myths of the Metropolis, the blasé type reduces all things to money and all experience to the measure of the Verstand, despite his despair at the integration of his Nervenleben

Dialectics of Negative and Metropolis

into the totality of the Metropolis as the end of the individual autonomy of his own situation. The city is the place of those differences that, as contradictions, still permit the existence of "magically" self-contained cultural entities; the Metropolis is the place of those differences that, as the measure and calculation of value, integrate every phenomenon into the dialectic of abstract value. In the first case, what emerges is a contrast; in the second, a necessary and functional relation with the calculation of the Verstand.

Simmel's analysis is important precisely because he takes the sociological description of the Metropolis to the point of isolating its specific ideology. The critique of the blasé type is no longer just a description of a particular manifestation of metropolitan life but the very symbol of its culture, of its self-reflection. Simmel's most outstanding perception is his recognition of the most appropriate expression of such an ideology *in a form of negative thought.*[9] If the blasé type fully reflects the structure of the Metropolis, it is not because he is fully consistent with it or because he is a mere reflection of it, but rather because he understands it from the perspective of his own inability to go beyond it, that is, from the perspective of his own negated individuality. Merely to reflect it would be to reflect it not at all: between the forms and modes of such a simple reflection and the specifically dialectical structure of the Metropolis, no consistency is possible. Only a thought that posits the ascendancy of the Verstand through the Nervenleben, or better yet, that understands the rational constitution, the legitimacy, of the Nervenleben—that is, only a thought that is able to see the subsuming of individuality not in terms of negation but in terms of use and functionality—can express the ideology of the Metropolis. This ideology arises wherever all "negativity"—that is, all the negative criticism concerning the traditional syntheses, the humanism of the city—bursts forth. It also arises wherever this negative is completely internalized, wherever the subject feels deep within himself the gravity of his task of "demystification," his task of acquiring a tragic awareness of the given.

This is where Simmel ends and Benjamin begins. Simmel's illustration of the ideology of the Metropolis through the blasé type is on the verge of leading him to the individuation, however indirect, of the indissoluble connection between negative thought and the capitalistic socialization process at a specific point in history. It is precisely negative thought (but only its dialectic) that can reflect the Metropolis as a structure of functional contradictions. Negative thought presupposes contradiction, and only for this reason is the former able to include the latter in the process of Vergeistigung, where contradiction as such assumes a function. To reduce contradiction "magically" a priori would destroy the whole rational fabric of the Metropolis. But Simmel does not utilize the perspective of negative thought, which would have allowed him to isolate the *theory* of the Metropolis by seeing the Metropolis as the fundamental system of the social integration of the growth of capitalism. Simmel uses the blasé type as a member of the Metropolis, not as a vehicle of a discussion of the Metropolis itself. He brings negative thought back to the Metropolis, but without explaining how this might signify the discovery of the negativity of the Metropolis itself. Only in this way can an ideology of the Metropolis become a viable proposition. But precisely because the function of the various terms of the preceding argument was not set down hypothetically, Simmel explains only the metropolitan form of negative thought, not the function of negative thought within the Metropolis; he explains the relation in the Metropolis between Nervenleben and Verstand, not the use of this relation. Simmel speaks of the ascendancy of the monetary and market economy as a phenomenon that concerns simply the level of the circulation of commodities. The Metropolis, in this case, still appears to be an "open place", disposed to ideological experimentation, rather than an instrument of political domination and a political function already ideologically, as well as economically, self-contained.

The rupture of the feudal social orbits, according to Simmel, made man free "in a spiritualized and refined sense." [10] This freedom is not subjected to criticism as in negative thought, and for the blasé attitude, it is no longer a formal freedom of rights but a concrete widening of personal freedom, an acquisition of real power. The widening of the horizon of the Metropolis,

Dialectics of Negative and Metropolis

which is the widening of the capitalist market, makes the Metropolis "the center of freedom," with freedom here meant as an "overflowing" of individuality and its material self-enrichment. Just as a man does not end "where his body ends or where the space that he fills with his immediate activity ends" (p. 238), in the same way the fact that the Metropolis consists of a chain of effects is symbolic of its dominion over a periphery, its specific will to power. For Simmel, this fact is supposed to indicate the maximum extent attained by freedom, the maximum power attained by individual freedom. By this logic, the division of labor awakens an increasingly individualized need for a personal existence. The resultant alienation is dissipated ideologically in the individual's liberation from the old "social circles." The very fact that Simmel can speak of the social division of labor in terms of mere "specialization" or contrast between "objective spirit" and "subjective spirit," enables him to glean from the division of labor a totally positive indication of relations of equality. The universality of the division of labor, having matured into a need for personal freedom, becomes a demand for equality— but for an equality within which the just-discovered personality is supposed to live. All of the economic-legal relations of the bourgeois society embodied in the Metropolis are understood by Simmel in their immediate ideologico-positive sense: the Vergeistigung of the freedom of bourgeois legal formalism is taken to be real freedom—the capitalist market, an intensification of personality—and the social division of labor, a foundation of equality, an individualized, "Goethian" equality. The ideology of the Metropolis that Simmel sets forth is therefore still an ideology of synthesis. Its form encompasses both the emergence of extreme individuality in the totality of the social and the constant internalization of this totality in the individual.

Through the "need for personality" created by specialization, human values return to the subject, but only insofar as this subject is precisely that of equality and the social division of labor. "The function of the Metropolis is to provide the arena for this struggle and its reconciliation." [11] Now it becomes clear how Simmel's treatment of the preceding elements of his argument was aimed at this result. The relation between Nervenleben and

Metropolis

Verstand serves this synthesis of the individual and the general, not the theory of the Vergeistigung of the capitalist relations of production. His very description of this Vergeistigung, which treats only the sphere of circulation, serves to reaffirm individual freedom at the specific level of the Verstand, not to critique legal-formal freedom. Simmel uses the relation between the negative and the form of the market not to pinpoint the historical functioning of this market, but to outline a synthesis between particularity (intended simply as negative, in a dialectical sense) and society. And this is made possible by his immediate obfuscation of the first fundamental conclusion of his analysis: the consistency between the form of the Metropolis and negative thought. Just when negative thought begins to point to the isolation or the perception of a historically specific form of capitalist domination, by presupposing this form as such—and thereby to break away from any nostalgia as well as from any utopia—Simmel immediately reduces this form to a simple expression of individuality in the Metropolis: an individuality that asserts itself, asks for the fulfillment of its rights, and demands freedom. The essay's final synthesis of "Die Grossstadt und das Geistesleben" answers this demand. But this synthesis is completely unrelated to the actual discussion of the blasé type and negative thought, and is not at all required by Simmel's concrete development of the material discussed. It is a synthesis that recuperates the value of community, of the *Gemeinschaft,* in order to reaffirm it in society, in the *Gesellschaft;* it recuperates the individualized freedom and equality of that Gemeinschaft and makes them the mainstay of the ideology of this Gesellschaft. But this synthesis is precisely what the theory of the negative would deny. Simmel's Metropolis is charged with an "aura," and it will founder, once again, in the myth of Weimar.

At this point Simmel's Metropolis can no longer be taken as a symbol of capitalist social relations. It is dominated by a Verstand that is still moving toward the values of individuality, in search of the human. It could not be further from the *Entwertung* (devaluation) effected by the negative—although, as we have seen, it is precisely this tragic, *wertfrei* (valueless) character of the negative that most accurately expresses the form and the function of the Metropolis.

Dialectics of Negative and Metropolis

Must we therefore conclude that Simmel's synthesis does not express the fundamental needs of the bourgeois analysis of the process of Vergeistigung embodied in the Metropolis? The problem is more complex than this, and perhaps it can help us to understand Simmel's original historic purpose and his place in history. Simmel follows the negative and its logic up to the point at which, by drastically reasserting itself in theory with respect to the conditions of growth, this logic cuts off all possibility of synthesis, control, and politico-ideological recuperation of the former social equilibrium—negative thought registers the leaps, the ruptures, the innovations that occur in history, never the transition, the flow, the historic continuum. And herein lies its formidable function, its value as symbol; it represents not merely a movement of crisis in the growth of capitalism but the very crisis serving a function within this growth.

But alongside this new aspect of crisis exists the tactical approach, the politics of ideology if you will. It is possible to carry the premises of the negative to their logical extremes, that is, to arrive at the essentiality of crisis as such; but it is also possible to limit these premises to the given historico-social situation, to make them function as instruments of an ideology. The first case involves a radical break with tradition: the task is that of finding a different resolution to the existing conflict. The second case involves the proposition of a renewal of the preexisting ideological synthesis, and this is the case with Simmel. As Lukacs pointed out, Simmel is truly a philosopher of *Übergang* (transition).[12] In radicalizing crisis, the negative looks for the necessary conditions that will follow the leap. In reconstructing the meaning of crisis as a nostalgia for synthesis, Simmel joins the search for these same conditions, but he is burdened with the aura of the past: he is allied with the past.

Metaphors aside, all this sheds light on the essential purpose of Simmel's overall position: he articulates an ideology of the *transcrescence* of the general conditions of capitalism's social dominion.[13] Simmel is a philosopher of Übergang in that he understands that the phenomenon of transcrescence is not only an indication of theoretical backwardness, but also expresses the class need to go beyond past syntheses dialectically, without denying them. In Simmel's argument, the persistence of the idea of Gemeinschaft in the Metropolis, of Goethian individuality in specialization, of the free mercantile personality in the conditions of the capitalist market, symbolizes this general, fundamental need. Capitalist dominion cannot exist historically except in the form of these alliances, nor can its all-inclusive rationality, except through transcrescence.

Simmel's argument is historico-political, whereas that of the negative is theoretico-analytical. But the fundamental importance of Simmel, for modern bourgeois ideology, lies in his having known how to use the negative for a decisive stretch, as far as its argument proved historically useful. This procedure, of adopting the negative and making it functional within the given conditions and political exigencies that an ideology finds necessary to articulate, would later dominate the entire tradition of modern sociology. This "assimilation" of the negative, which as we shall see more clearly below constitutes the real subject of Simmel's inquiry, has since become a broad and long-lasting methodological model. Its essential feature is a systematic resolution of the contradictions created by growth. Where there is rupture, there must be transition. This is how Simmel represents the transition from the city to the Metropolis. And this is how the values of both the city and the man of the city must be preserved in the Metropolis. But this work of *conservation*, which consciously makes use of the negative by reversing its sense, is not just a theoretical penury; it is a functional operation necessary to the system at a specific stage of its growth. It is precisely in those cases where the negative cannot be reduced to an analysis of the laws of the given, or where its tragic position in the face of the given as destiny has not yet been reduced to pure theory, that the concept of transcrescence has great ideological value. Indeed, this concept makes possible the definitive theoretical reduction of the negative. Transcrescence, by pitting the real multiplicity of forces and the will to conservation against the demystified tragicness of the negative, already begins to carry out this reduction: it situates the negative. And yet it transforms the mere assertion of the given into theoretical research. In the relation between Nietzsche and Weber, we find Simmel in the middle.

Dialectics of Negative and Metropolis

Here the function of Simmel's synthesis is explained by the historic impossibility of the capitalist Vergeistigung to express itself fully and in the first person. The problem lies in an unstable equilibrium between terms that tend to annul each other, terms that the negative had already set in open (impolitic!) contradiction with one another. Between Simmel and Benjamin, we have the rupture of this equilibrium. With Weber we have both the realization of the transcrescence of the Übergang, the affirmation of a bourgeois-capitalist theory on the negative, and the complete disregard, in essentially new, organizational terms, for the theory of the political contradiction between classes. The result, as far as our analysis is concerned, is precisely the breakdown of Simmel's resolution. On the one hand, his theory affirms the ascendancy of the Verstand and the laws that govern its system, the dialectical functionalization of the Nervenleben, and the existence of tragicness as the insuperability (or fate) of the given social relations. On the other hand, working against this theory are the beginnings of the mythic-nostalgic ideologies of pre-industrial man—but these no longer have anything to do with the Metropolis. If anything, they represent what the Metropolis ought to be, the teleological value of its history, but they no longer constitute an integral part of it; they no longer express its present ideological structure, as was the case in Simmel. Once its claim to direct synthesis is no longer valid, ideology refines itself and becomes duty. It becomes commitment. The values that Simmel singled out earlier still remain, but only outside the Metropolis—they can no longer be integrated into its present structure. The status of the real Metropolis is the same as that asserted by theory; but beyond this status lie the pure forms of what it "ought to be." Conservation masquerades as an alternative to the ascendancy of the Verstand. The substance of the reactionary argument goes so far as to pass off negative thought as a negation of the Verstand and a nostalgia for the human— or when the first attempt is not successful, as irrationalism pure and simple.

Banished from the Metropolis, the old churches find asylum in the memory of villages. Nothing smacks more of farce than discovering one by one the ideals of the Gemeinschaft in an argument that purports to be critical of the Verstand predominant in the Metropolis.[14]

But here I certainly do not intend to go into a discussion of the various "critical theories." Let us begin instead with the first consequence of the disintegration of Simmel's resolution: *the reduction of the negative to pure theory of the negative as a function of the life of the Metropolis.* Here of course the perspective of the negative reemerges. And beyond Simmel's ideological synthesis reemerges the possibility of constructing a theory of the Metropolis, just as it was seen from the perspective of the negative. It is a question of perceiving the Metropolis as a radical negation of the city's preceding form of existence and of perceiving its effects as useful to a specific class predominance. Thus one must start again from the negative, not with the purpose of reconciling it anew with the social in a general sense, but on the contrary with the purpose of stopping and examining the fundamental contradiction that its tragedy implies. Hence, our progression should be from the negative, to the Metropolis as an instrument of class, to its negativity as a contradiction of class: from the perspective of the negative to the perspective of class. This, in its essential outlines, is what Benjamin sets out to do. In this light the Metropolis becomes once again the comprehensive symbol of capitalist social relations. But all of the elements that in Simmel conspired towards synthesis (and aimed at establishing the "science" of the Metropolis) here become symbols of class contradictions or of contradictions in the functions of class domination. Not only does every ideology of the Metropolis as synthesis come tumbling down, but also all pretense to objectivity on the part of the scientific argument that integrates the negative within itself. The true status of such an ideology, like that of such an argument, proves to be irremidiably the same as that of the insuperable negativity of capitalist social relations. But we shall examine in detail how and to what point Benjamin develops this analysis.

According to Benjamin, Baudelaire's lyric and prose poems embody this internalization, through the negative, of the relations predominant in the Metropolis. The relation between *shock* and *Erlebnis* (lived experience), on which Benjamin bases

Dialectics of Negative and Metropolis

his analysis, derives directly from the Simmelian relation between Nervenleben and Verstand. In this dialectic, the threat of trauma implicit in shock is controlled and warded off by consciousness. The shock that is felt, registered, and finally ingrained in the memory takes on the character of a lived experience, of Erlebnis.[15] What we have here is a process of organization of stimuli and sublimation of the shock, a process immediately integrated into the larger process of the Vergeistigung, of which Simmel also wrote. But Benjamin derives his understanding of this process from the formation of the ideology of his time, and not from Simmel. If Freud sees in the organism's ability to shield itself from stimuli one of the foundations of his discussion of civilization,[16] then the entire experience of the modern lyric can be analyzed as a registering of shock. Anguish itself becomes a form of reception, a "sterilization" of the attack mounted by the external energy of the stimuli. The forms of the modern lyric appear as a broad symbol of the general process of the rationalization of existence. They attempt to bring the exploding of the Nervenleben back within the bounds of anguish, memory, and the lived experience.

These kinds of considerations had no place in Simmel: his ideological justification of the Metropolis (though functionally regressive) permitted only an analysis of the Metropolis still centered around the traditional values of historicist humanism. In Benjamin, however, the cultural forms of the Metropolis appear totally integrated into the overall functions and contents of its growth. The realm of the Verstand reappears intact in the poetic composition, and just as the multiplicity of stimuli, the danger of trauma exists in the poetic composition, so in the Verstand exists shock, and terror matures into anguish. But all of this implies the collapse of any culture that could be autonomous with respect to the mechanisms of the Metropolis; it implies the end of any Weimarian utopia—and not merely a widening of Simmel's investigation.

Benjamin's separate analysis of the terms shock and Erlebnis as a problem of the modern lyric, which is seen as a symbol of the culture of the Metropolis, may however cause serious misunderstandings. If these two terms were actually separate, the

Metropolis

17

fact would destroy whatever interpretative function they might have. A lived experience that is at its origins different from shock cannot relate itself to shock in order to overcome it—nor would any such overcoming be dialectical: it would be a simple negation. Shock does not appear within something else, nor does it reemerge in a consciousness or in an ego that waits for it to occur in order to systematize it and resolve it. Rather, shock produces by itself the energy necessary to resolve itself and to organize itself; it possesses a constitution of its own and therefore a *language* of its own. It is not thought, when it speaks of shock, that dominates Erlebnis—but the shock itself that speaks, reveals its structure, becomes subject. Only on this level, which seems to elude Benjamin, is one able to understand the work of true rationalization achieved by the modern lyric as culture of the Metropolis. An Erlebnis, already in itself rational, that dominated shock (as though it were a simple forest) would not in fact rationalize anything; it would lead to a tautology. The cultural-artistic proposition becomes integral to the overall process—to the general Vergeistigung—only when it discovers and directly expresses the organizational and structural laws of shock, in its own language.

In this sense, there is an important correction to be made in Benjamin's analysis, one which should not come as a surprise. We have already seen, in our discussion of Simmel, the indissoluble, reciprocal functionality between Nervenleben and Verstand—as though the Verstand were interpreted as the legal status of the particular Nervenleben dominant in the Metropolis. The relation between shock and Erlebnis, as explained by Benjamin and others as well, is consistent with the phenomenon of the Nervenleben's manifestation of rationality as functionality. Nor could it be otherwise, inasmuch as the image of shock is defined through contact with the crowd of the Metropolis,[17] and inasmuch as defining the Erlebnis presents the same problem as representational composition, the problem of the linguistic organization of its relation to the crowd as the existence of the Metropolis.

Anguish, even hopelessness, thus arise within a process of rationalization which, no longer restricted to the empirical forms

Dialectics of Negative and Metropolis

of the Metropolis, becomes cultural fact and in this way manifests its high level of socialization. Benjamin uses the negative as a theoretical instrument for the understanding of the social relations of the Metropolis, as the proper lens through which to interpret them. This theory is born out of a collision with the crowd and assumes unto itself the fundamental experiences of the life of the Metropolis, positing them as *inescapable tragedy.*

There is tragedy wherever shock has become Erlebnis, or better still wherever Erlebnis itself has revealed its fundamental constitutive laws, its quality of never changing, and sticks to them with heroic firmness. Nothing is further from the negative than dwelling on the image of shock and deriving from it a need for nostalgia or utopia, so that the shock will not repeat itself. The negative, on the contrary, constantly "presupposes" shock; that is to say, it seeks it, sees it, "desires" it precisely in order to construct the Erlebnis—and to turn it into tragedy.

For this very reason, therefore, the negative "presupposes" the Metropolis, inasmuch as the Metropolis forever repeats shock and constantly makes visible its function. But this implies a total Entwertung or devaluation. Indeed, the negative is such precisely because it is Entwertung. A discourse that completely demythifies shock, such as that of Baudelaire, does not allow for any kind of ideological recuperation. An image of shock that demands to be reduced to its own sameness and defined according to its own strictly immanent logic—to be, in short, presupposed—no longer has any relation to attempts to synthesize this existence of the Metropolis and the values of the human. The negation of these very values is presupposed by negative thought in its *hopeless* theoretical understanding of the early forms of modern capitalist society. This negation *is* rationalization, *is* Vergeistigung, and it moves in the same direction as this society, directly and knowingly sharing its destiny. But at the same time it lays bare the logic of this society, negates its possibility of "transcrescence," and radicalizes its aims and needs; in other words, the negative reaches the point where it exposes this society's internal conflicts and contradictions, its fundamental problematics or negativity.

Where Simmel looks for consolations in the face of this negativity, the negative assumes within itself, completely internalizes

Metropolis

"the tragedy of the given," and lets it speak for itself; where Simmel attempts to reconcile this negativity with the conditions of its past, Baudelaire assumes it to be not only the fundamental experience, but the only experience. But the shock's "loss of aura" implies that the representation of the Metropolis will henceforth serve to expose its specific historico-social constitution, the conflicts that shape it, and the culture that reflects and mystifies it. The negative stays within the limits of the Metropolis, since it has uncovered the Metropolis's negativity. But this negativity, once demythified, demystified, and thrust whole into Erlebnis and Verstand, presents an image of the Metropolis as symbol-place of the contradictions and functions of modern capitalist society. The negative, used correctly—that is, according to the terms of its own hopelessness, and not mystified as a requisite for synthesis, as a prayer for consolation—leads to this limit. And this is the point at which Benjamin resumes the discussion.

Of primary importance is the crowd. Simmel, when confronting it, is attentive to the "moral reaction" that it necessarily provokes. This is why his experience of it is in the end sublimated: the crowd becomes a unified whole of subjects, embodying the need for freedom and individual autonomy. There is no such sublimation in Baudelaire. As Benjamin puts it, the experience of the crowd is always an experience of catastrophe (p. 101). Within this crowd there is neither synthesis nor communication. The passer-by is not detained in any way, nor, strictly speaking, is he a specific apparition: the general equivalence dominant in the Metropolis is inexorably created by the always instantaneous and utterly undetainable emergence of the unicum. It is precisely because Benjamin theorizes the crowd in this way that the shock that it provides is able to reveal and express its logical constitution. Simmel's crowd actually much more closely resembles the feminine passer-by of Stefan George (whom Benjamin himself quotes), the woman not "borne along by the crowd" (p. 101n)—that is, it resembles an ideologized crowd brought back into the *civitas hominis*.

But the crowd that in its movement "internalizes" the overall circulation of commodities, thereby embodying the process

Dialectics of Negative and Metropolis

of the socialization of capitalist relations of production, cannot make room for a shock-Erlebnis unrelated to the structure of such a process. The problem we are faced with here is that of relating the image of shock to the actual productive functions of the system.

Benjamin confronts this problem through the schema of the game (pp. 109–113). For Benjamin, the futility, the repetition, and the sameness that form the basis of the game as the image of the crowd and of the shock-Erlebnis produced by the crowd resemble the labor of the worker in the process of industrial production. The formalization of the social relations within the crowd of the Metropolis—and the general equivalence of merchandise that they express—can be found in the "worker's interaction with the machine. . . . [which has] no relation to the preceding interaction precisely because it is an exact repetition of it" (p. 110). The crowd, as well as the Metropolis that provides its structure, thus both lead back to the moment of production, to labor, mirroring one another as each other's common foundation. This result of Benjamin's method of interpretation stands Simmel's perspective on its head. Rather than relating the factory to social types and to the laws of circulation, Benjamin sees the society itself as laying bare its own origin. The image of shock reveals its own class status.

The limits of Benjamin's argument, however, should not in any way permit us to overlook his impressive methodological intuition. It is true that shock is here reduced to the simple alienation of the worker's labor, in its immediate aspects and in those most conditioned by a certain production process. And it is true that the negativity of the Metropolis, manifested in this way, does not yet posit the modes and contents of the class conflict that breaks out in the Metropolis, for the Metropolis; however, in Benjamin the Metropolis becomes a complex of functions, interpretations, and machines of the overall system, together with all of its culture: such is the case in *Paris, Capital of the Nineteenth Century*.[18] In the face of the Metropolis, and within it, the ideology of the city—that is, the possibility of synthesis that the notion of *Kultur* implies—falls apart. No aura can survive in this Metropolis.

Metropolis

Haussmann expressed the Metropolis' will to power: he realized the Metropolis by destroying the ideal dialectic of the Gesellschaft as Gemeinschaft. He used the city directly as merchandise, opening it up to the speculation of great financial capital, and he alienated it completely from its former inhabitants, driving them out of its center. Haussmann conceived of the Metropolis, unlike the city, as the battleground of the class struggle. But his reason was not only the most obvious one, whereby the streets were widened to accommodate the cannon fire against the barricades; the more essential reason was a vision of the Metropolis from the point of view of capitalist interest, which sees the Metropolis in a sectarian manner and hence strives to make it the domain of big capital. In this instance, the Metropolis no longer expresses the ascendancy of one class seeking to synthesize itself with its opposite, according to the schema of traditional dialectical reasoning, but the ascendancy of a class that wants power: power that is imposed directly and constantly repeats its inherent violence.

Negative thought had foreseen and theorized such a result. Baudelaire's tragedy is Haussmann's victory. But the violence of Haussmann's vision—that is, the negation of synthesis as dialectic and its reassertion as might, which his Metropolis achieves— itself becomes a utopia. The "victory" over the people in 1848 and the liquidation of Paris's old, "rooted" class structure that his plan makes possible are completely ineffectual in the face of the new class contradiction, beyond the barricades, implicit in the mass conflict that now surrounds the Metropolis. In light of this contradiction, Haussmann's plan may be seen as a primary mechanism of accumulation, and its will to power a form of speculation, within which the contradiction re-forms itself in full. The solution of this negation is the utopia of capital. And this too had been intuited by negative thought. But not by Haussmann. Nor Simmel.

Dialectics of Negative and Metropolis

the treasures of his wisdom. But the fool spoke thus to Zarathustra:

"O Zarathustra, here is the great city; here you could find nothing and lose everything. Why do you want to wade through this mire? Have pity on your foot! Rather spit on the city gate and turn back. Here is hell for a hermit's thoughts; here great thoughts are boiled alive and cooked till they are small. Here all great feelings decay: only the smallest rattleboned feelings may rattle here. Don't you smell the slaughterhouses and ovens of the spirit even now? Does not this town steam with the fumes of slaughtered spirit?

"Don't you see the soul hanging like a limp, dirty rag? And they still make newspapers of these rags!

"Don't you hear how the spirit has here been reduced to plays on words? It vomits revolting verbal swill. And they still make newspapers of this swill!

"They hound each other and know not where. They overheat each other and know not why. They tinkle with their tin, they jingle with their gold. They are cold and seek warmth from brandy; they are heated and seek coolness from frozen spirits; they are all diseased and sick with public opinions.

"All lusts and vices are at home here; but there are also some here who are virtuous: there is much serviceable, serving virtue—much serviceable virtue with pen fingers and hard sitting- and waiting-flesh, blessed with little stars on the chest and with padded, rumpless daughters. There is also much piety, and there are many devout lickspittles, batteries of fakers and flattery-bakers before the God of Hosts. For it is 'from above' that the stars and the gracious spittle trickle; every starless chest longs above.

"The moon has her courtyard, and the courtyard has its mooncalves; to everything, however, that comes from

2. On the German Sociology of the City at the Turn of the Century

It is no accident that the attempt to reduce the negative of the Metropolis—or in any case to separate it from the Metropolis—is such a salient feature of Simmel's work. Tönnies had made this the central focus of his analysis of the city in *Gemeinschaft und Gesellschaft* (1887).[1] This approach is the exact reactionary counterpart to the Entwertung effected by negative thought; and it is the literal historical precursor of the present-day "radical" critiques of the Metropolis, their theoretical source. Overcoming the negativity of the Metropolis means reducing it again to city, to the Kultur characteristic of Gemeinschaft.[2] Tönnies conceives of the city as falling within the idea of the Gemeinschaft, a system of real-organic relations opposite the ideal-mechanical relations of the Gesellschaft. The city, a "self-sufficient domestic economy, . . . whatever its empirical origins might be," presents itself "as a whole . . . , as a permanent entity . . . assured of self-mastery . . . or of regular self-replenishment." It also devotes the full extent of its power to the most refined activities of the Mind . . . : all urban handicraft is true art." The city is the comprehensive system of "protection" of this art, and it impedes "the intermingling of social circles" that we find in Simmel: its ideal is the guild as a religious community. "Assuming this, the entire *economic* existence of a complete city . . . cannot be understood except by presupposing art and religion as the highest and greatest interests of the *city as a whole*."[3] This is the fullest possible expression of the reactionary myth of the polis: the dynamic-conflictual nature of the Metropolis, far from being presupposed as in negative thought, is reversed in the idea of community, in the idea of synthesis as the only solution. Here we are truly at the source of the contemporary radical humanist sociology of the city. But what in Tönnies is conscious reaction will later be mystified in the progressive critique of capitalist *Zivilisation*. History, when it repeats itself, always does so as farce.

Tönnies knows that the Metropolis has already answered the city. It has shattered the circles of traditional handicraft-familial life: "its abundance is the abundance of capital. . . . It is in the end the city of science and culture. . . . The arts cease to secure the means for subsistence and are themselves exploited capitalistically."[4] What we have here, then, is science-culture, or Verstand in other words, versus the organic totality of city life. Make no mistake: The utopian-reactionary character of this analysis lies not so much in its concrete proposition of the community model as such, but rather in the very idea of the *possibility of overcoming* the conflictual-dynamic essence of the Metropolis. And here we can also see the fundamental difference between Tönnies' analysis and Simmel's later arguments. Simmel seeks to capture, in whatever way possible, the instance of synthesis in the Metropolis, in its specific dialectic. This is the source of the paradox, and of the ultimate test, implicit in his argument: the regressive aspect is completely separated from the utopian aspect. And this represents the first step towards complete demystification—toward Max Weber, in other words.

But Weber formulated a response to Tönnies that came from afar. His attack on the Zivilisation of the Metropolis is a figure taken from Nietzsche's *Zarathustra*. The corporativistic-communal ideal was demolished, even as pure nostalgia, in

Dialectics of Negative and Metropolis

a decisive page of Nietzsche that preceded the publication of Tönnies' work. Weber, and his direct assumption of responsibility, should today be read in this light.

At the beginning of part III Zarathustra appears as a "wanderer" on his way back to the mountain.[5] Zarathustra is returning to his solitude, and during this return he fills himself with the images and symbols which, as explained in part IV, will constitute his teaching. He is biding his time, waiting for his moment. The first temptation he encounters is the spirit of gravity: "half-dwarf, half-mole, lame, making lame, dripping lead into my ear, leaden thoughts into my brain" (p. 156). Everything that rises must fall—you hurl a stone high into the air, and it will strike you—yet this pessimism, at bottom, is characterized by an ideal of perfect equilibrium. This pessimism regarding the direction of life's movements is only the equilibrium and the fulfillment of the Schopenhauer's nirvana, which we later find in *Parsifal*. This pessimism is countered by the idea of the eternal return.

It is essential to understand that the idea of the eternal return is the opposite of a synthesizing renewal. It is an absolute affirmation of the breakdown of the pessimistic equilibrium, an affirmation of the meaning of "casting beyond," of contradiction. There is a great difference between the hurling-falling equilibrium of the dwarf and the eternal return of Zarathustra. Strangely, the eternal return has almost always been interpreted mistakenly as the "circle" of the dwarf's time. " 'All straight things lie,' grumbled the dwarf. 'Every truth is curved, time itself is a circle.' "[6] This is precisely the opposite of the eternal return, which is a straight road, along which we stand in the space of the carriage gate, where Zarathustra and the dwarf converse, or in the time of this moment.

The path does not curve. At the gate, the road ahead goes on for an eternity, as does the road behind. The eternal return excludes the possibility of nostalgia, of our following the past road ever again. Its thought asserts, instead, that that which can walk, that which has reached this moment, must have already traveled the path behind it, must have already existed; and that this moment brings all things to come, because if we have walked up to this point, we shall have to walk once more (p. 192). The idea of

German Sociology of the City

conservation, of stasis, rules the dwarf. The idea of the perpetual return of the contradiction between the two paths, between the two eternities—now perceived as a whole, as a destiny—rules Zarathustra. To hurl oneself in the air is necessary. One does not fall back down—one surpasses oneself. And this surpassing is eternal, and it is at once the path ahead and the path behind. This structure of time works by effect: consumption with every step, and repetition of consumption and the obligation to consume anew. This thought can no longer be wrenched from the mouth of man. This serpent can only be bitten until its head is severed. Only then may we *laugh*.

Nietzsche explicitly illustrates the meaning of the eternal return. His demon, his mortal enemy, is the spirit of gravity, of falling, of equilibrium—the eternal return as indifference, as pessimism, as the instrument of the affirmation of nirvana.

Zarathustra suddenly encounters a disciple who has interpreted his thought in this way. Nietzsche is clearly aware of being stood on his head, of seeing his "abyssal thought" reduced to the categories of the Schopenhauer's tradition and through him, to the terms of European Kultur. For this reason, Nietzsche arranges for a test to take place precisely at the gates of the Metropolis (pp. 214–217). Zarathustra the wanderer "returned on roundabout paths to his mountain and his cave" (p. 214) developing within himself the idea of the return. No situation could seem more propitious to the dwarf than this. Zarathustra would appear to have started on the path of ascetic bliss, the path of "the interior transcendence" of contradiction—and this path would seem to have become confused with the path leading back, since Zarathustra is returning. Here, where the risks of misunderstanding are greatest, one must achieve the greatest clarity—the maximum *Aufklärung* (enlightenment). The idea of the return must be understood as the idea of destiny, and as the idea of *going beyond,* as well as the negation of nostalgia, as the culmination of the negative: in other words, as tragic theory.

At the gates of the great city, Zarathustra's ape, who has copied something of his tone and gestures, tries to stop the Teacher. "Have pity on your foot! Rather spit on the city's gate and turn back" (p. 214). Here we have the "eternal return" of the ape—which is identical to the dwarf's falling back down.

Dialectics of Negative and Metropolis

The ape hurls himself against the Metropolis. His argument is the epitome of the "Romantic": the Metropolis is the death of great thoughts and great sentiments; it is the tavern of the Spirit, filthy tatters of lives, a disgusting cesspool of words; the Metropolis is a *crowd* of pleasures, vices, and clerk's virtues. And above all, it is a negation of the freedom of the spirit: "I serve, you serve, we serve" (p. 215). We are well acquainted with this line of attack: the Metropolis as negation of organic form, as destruction of the "mind" of Gemeinschaft, as anonymous crowd. Zarathustra, who seems to be retreating into solitude, who affirms the eternal return, cannot live here. The ape interprets Nietzsche in the same way as the later essayists and littérateurs: Nietzsche as simple Romantic negation of Zivilisation, Nietzsche as elusive wayfarer. The ape's accusations, his complaints, his nostalgia, all live on, in negative or implied form, in every page of Tönnies. And they return, as we shall see, in the later sociology-philosophy of the Metropolis, but in a paradoxical form: under Nietzsche's name. Indeed, later still, the ape's own argument will be passed off as the later Nietzsche, Nietzsche the critic. And not only as regards the problem of the Metropolis. Nietzsche-Zarathustra, then, should spit on this Metropolis ruled by the merchant (the "monetary economy" of Simmel) and by the clanging of his tin can. And he should vent his spleen on the dregs of the crowd, the sewer of the Metropolis, and turn back. Is this not the path of solitude? Is this not the eternal return?

On the contrary, this is the spirit of gravity; this is being anchored to the given, able only to contemplate it; being unable to walk, to proceed, to go beyond; limiting oneself to spleen, without shedding light, without understanding; suffering one's destiny—not positing it; being the ape, the farce of Zarathustra—not his tragedy. The eternal return is not a turning back—but a repeating of oneself by going beyond. Solitude is not ascetic bliss—but preparation for repeating oneself. It is detachment in order to see, understanding oneself in order to teach. It is waiting for the moment of *power,* presenting oneself as actual, in the moment, in the destined instant. Solitude serves only as a function of this attempt to meet with destiny. Thus, the disdain of the Metropolis is of no importance. This disdain binds us to

German Sociology of the City

what we claim we want to abandon. The ape's squealing is a vain attempt to hide this servitude. Zarathustra, instead, gazes a long time upon the Metropolis, and remains silent (p. 217). His problem is to know the Metropolis: to see its time and destiny. To return to the time before the Metropolis, to retrace one's steps, is for dwarfs and apes.

The Metropolis exists. The criticism of the Metropolis is something else: it is interpreting the tensions and contradictions that will damn it, "the pillar of fire in which it will be burned" (p. 217). The ape contemplates the Metropolis as an insuperable given, as an end. Zarathustra, instead, situates it in time; it is the irreversible moment at which the road behind has arrived, stretching out forever at our backs, and which at the same time brings all the future. Indeed, we will have to know this future. In this sense, we will have to "go beyond" the Metropolis. And we must posit destiny, without any "spleen." Why hasn't the ape gone to plow the land, or into the forest? or onto one of those green islands so plentiful in the sea? (p. 216) Zarathustra knows that he belongs, in this moment, to the Metropolis—and he knows that his teaching can have the Metropolis as its only point of departure. The Metropolis is clearly a destiny—but it has a destiny of its own. It is this interlacement that must be known. This spider's web is the true, the actual problem.

But it is not enough. If Nietzsche had limited himself to this, his thought would only partially refute Tönnies and his "tradition." Tönnies did in fact "disdain" the Metropolitan spirit, as did Zarathustra's ape—but he made no pretensions of turning back. His was part of a body of work of mediation, transcrescence, and transformation, slowly emerging from the Metropolis and having the Metropolis as its subject. Zarathustra disregards this trend: "There is nothing to better, nothing to worsen."[6] The tragic vision illuminates a form, a structure, a destiny. A destiny cannot be corrected. But this is exactly the opposite of understanding the Metropolis as an absolute. The ape understands it as such, and he who pretends to transform it only reconfirms the intangibility of its essence; he who limits himself to disdaining it only participates in its life, leaving no trace of himself.

The tragic vision illuminates the destiny of the Metropolis. Zarathustra's pigs toil *around* the Metropolis—the center is

Dialectics of Negative and Metropolis

clear only to those who recognize the Metropolis as irreversible in all its contradictions, as a structure of time: only they will be able to negate the Metropolis, or rather, will be able to grasp the forces of its negation. But such a negation will be a total going beyond. All the attempts at transcrescence, at synthesis between earlier forms and those of the Metropolis, will fall like leaves. And after the Metropolis, nothing can be uttered. What we can utter, today, are the forces that posit the Metropolis as a moment.

If the Metropolis is posited as destiny and as time, it is a contradiction. Its history is a conflict. It is precisely that which is not in the ape's argument, which Tönnies' utopian assumption would like to overcome. And it is precisely that which any "essayistic" form mystifies. This is the point at which Weber resumes the discussion.

In Weber's *Die Stadt* (The city), which probably goes back to 1911–1913,[7] we do not encounter a specific discussion of the Metropolis. The formal clash between models, characteristic of Tönnies, is absent here. The perspective from which to trace the history of the city is naturally that of the realized Metropolis. The entire history of the Western city is part of the destiny of the Metropolis. The problem lies in understanding the role of the city's forms in the overall process of capitalist rationalization— the problem of the city must be seen in the light of the overall political problem of capitalist development. In Weber's analysis of the city, this political concept manifests itself in the rupture of the *tribus,* the liquidation of the classical agrarian city, the formation of the European medieval communities.

Here the city is not just an economic or military fact, but a new political organization.[8] The breakup of the previous organic system is the very origin of the process of *Rationalisierung* that the forms of urban organization set in motion: the original *coniuratio,* the organization of the *fraternitates,* the "ascent from servitude to freedom by means of economic profit" (p. 566). The recognition of one's fellow man in the pact of foundation and the collective movement toward a comprehensive social end formalizes relations in the city and brings into being a common language that is no longer that of the tribus, but that of political interest and political commerce.

German Sociology of the City

However, this is only the first shift that Weber points out.[9] There is a subsequent one that has been much less studied but that is essential to our purposes here. The real origin of the contemporary *political* problem of the city does not lie in the political formalism of the medieval coniuratio, but rather in its rupture, in the appearance of the "first consciously illegal and revolutionary political group." [10]

And this is, namely, the "people" who, not recognizing the sworn pact, break down the "walls" of the city and attack the "circles" of the fraternitates. The destiny of the Metropolis begins, in a concrete sense, with the people. The city tries desperately to resist this assault—but in so doing it already asserts itself as a locus of conflict, as a struggle: in short, as a dialectical structure whose solution henceforth becomes unthinkable within the city as such. The problem of synthesizing the conflict that breaks out in the city becomes subsequently a concern of the State. Thus we have an evolution from the *Stadt* to the *Staat*. At this point, having been integrated into the dialectical *ordo* of the new rational State, the Western-European city resolves itself materially in the overall orientation of the processes of rationalization. And therefore any discourse of the city in itself necessarily becomes at this point reactionary: the city *is* the State, the overall process of rationalization, the class conflict within the growth of capitalism. In Weber the analysis of the city directly precedes that of the rational State: "the bourgeois concept of State has its precedent in the ancient and medieval city." The *Bürger* as a man of *Besitz und Bildung* (property and education) is a historic product of the city: "The Bourgeois is always the Bourgeois of a specific city." [11] But the fundamental moment remains precisely that in which the rational system of the city as such becomes, due to the emergence of a specific conflict of class, a comprehensive capitalist system. This leap marks the transition from nonrational capitalism to rational capitalism. Creating a system, that is a State, from capitalism necessarily implies destroying the city liberties, the guilds, the fraternitates, the coniuratio of the medieval city. It implies moving toward the realization of the State, as absolute rational ordo, but the city of this ordo is already the Metropolis.

This impressive schema of Weber's not only emphasizes the

Dialectics of Negative and Metropolis

irreversibility of the form of the Metropolis; it asserts its very origin to be conflict: the negative character does not come to the Metropolis from without, but rather expresses its very foundation, its essence. The Metropolis is, from the beginning, the form of a synthesis irretrievably lost in time. It posits the new levels of conflict that rationalization implies—and it does not reduce these new levels to the dimensions of the city, but rather, knowingly consigns them to the absolute institutions of the State. A Metropolis without State, a Metropolis outside of a rationally organized State, is an impossibility—and so, therefore, is an analysis of the Metropolis outside of the analysis of the class conflicts within this State.

We find a complement to, and virtually a commentary on, Weber's analysis in the work of Werner Sombart, first in *Liebe, Luxus und Kapitalismus* (Love, Luxury, and Capitalism), and later in *Der moderne Kapitalismus* (Modern Capitalism).[12] In Sombart, the earliest form of the Metropolis—the "city of consumption," the Paris, capital of the seventeenth century—is both the State and the initial process of industrialization. The Metropolis is the center and the market of the luxury industry—and this luxury, by producing "love," destroys all sacred tribal ritual. The "legitimate child of an illegitimate love," luxury makes the Metropolis a milieu of consumers. In the mid-1700s, the truly industrial cities had no more than thirty to forty thousand inhabitants. London and Paris had more than half a million each. Beccaria and Filangieri in Italy, Quesnay in France, and the physiocratic and Illuministic currents were the first to attack this model of the "city of pleasures."[13] Classical bourgeois economics puts an end to this early image of the Grossstadt as a simple market, as the place of unproductive consumption, and (for Quesnay) as a parasite of agricultural surplus-value.

The contemporary Metropolis retains nothing of the large city of consumption. It cannot be confused with any specific type of large city, whether commercial, industrial, or consumption-oriented. Its essence lies in being a system, a multi-articulated urban type—a comprehensive service, so to speak, to the growth of contemporary large capital. It is an ensemble: a qualified organization of the labor force, a scientific reserve-supply for industrial growth, a financial structure, a market, and the all-

German Sociology of the City

inclusive center of political power.[14] In brief, the Metropolis, in order to be called such, must be a capitalist system, in the general sense: a city of the circulation-reproduction of capital, *Geist der Kapitalismus*.

Let there be no misunderstanding: with this formulation, Sombart asserts the exact opposite of the belief that the Metropolis must be a "city of industries."[15] He maintains that it must be a system perfectly integrated into the growth of industry and capitalism, or, a comprehensive, socio-political service of growth. The Metropolis coordinates, organizes, and socializes the forms of growth. This is the duty that its service vocation must fulfill: it must become a center of the political management of growth. Metropolitan Kultur, which Sombart sees asserting itself in these functions, is thus the Kultur of the capitalist program of planning.

Here Sombart's analysis of the Metropolis draws its final conclusions. The Verstand finally presents itself devoid of nostalgia, devoid of utopia. We have reached the point of defining the Metropolis' productive aspect—that is, the problem of qualifying, within a comprehensive economic plan, the optimal relations between metropolitan services and industrial growth. But this analysis, and its consequent ramifications, were of course already implicit in Weber's resolution of Simmel's problematics.

The political concentration of Sombart's Metropolis—in the middle of the Weimar era!—expresses an objective process of concentration and therefore presupposes a reciprocal functionality between the discussion of the city and that of the Rationalisierung that Weber himself outlined. For Sombart, the Metropolis is the spatial organization of the Weberian bureaucratization, in its fullest sense. And it is at the same time not static, but dynamic-conflictual in terms of its institutions, its continual political innovations, and its rationalization of the relation between the expansion of the labor force and political control. The Metropolis is the organization of the political control of growth, as well as the center of its continuous planning. In this sense, it endures as conflict and only as conflict. For Weber, the utilization of this conflict constitutes the very purpose of bureaucratization.

Metropolitan concentration was the result of economic process and political objectives. The years in which the *Verein für Sozialpolitik* was debating the structure of monopoly and the process of productive concentration and rationalization were the same years in which first Simmel, then Weber, were working out their analyses of the Metropolis.[16] And it was Weber who presented the synthesis of the two levels of analysis and proved their original inseparability.

All Sombart did was to complete this schema analytically. In Germany between 1882 and 1907 the degree of industrial concentration doubled. During this period, the number of workers in businesses with one to five employees increased by about 25 percent; the number in businesses with six to fifty employees almost tripled; in businesses of fifty-one to one thousand employees, the number more than tripled; and in businesses with more than one thousand employees, the number of workers quadrupled. The phenomenon of concentration is at the same time a phenomenon of the *massification* of capitalist relations of production: Höchster Farbwerke had five workers in 1863 and 7,700 in 1912; Badische Anilin, from 1865 to 1900, would go from 30 to 6,700 employees. In steel, the average number of workers per company went from 292 in 1880 to 618 in 1900. The electrical industry was born in an already concentrated and monopolistic form: in 1875 this sector counted 81 businesses with a total of 1,157 workers (of which 993 were employed in 56 businesses). In 1883, Emil Rathenau founded the Deutsche-Edison-Gesellschaft, later called AEG, whose capital in shares increased from five million marks in 1885 to sixty million in 1900. Between 1901 and 1911, four of the top seven German electrical companies were absorbed by AEG and by Siemens.

The same kind of internal concentration took place in the organization of financial capital. Trusts and groups of banks were being formed within the overall process of concentration, which was as vertical as it was horizontal. The Deutsche Bank, for example, was indissolubly integrated into the electrical sphere of AEG and Siemens.[17]

Since the first years of the twentieth century, these processes had begun to appear uncontrollable on the purely economic level. They themselves had created the question of the *neue Verfassung*, which was advocated by F. Naumann, Alfred Weber,

German Sociology of the City

and Max Weber. The theory of the Metropolis arises out of the same order of inquiry. The expansion of the industrial labor force also implies, insofar as it is considered a function of growth, the necessity of arranging for its placement, spatial organization, and mobility. The rationalization of the organization of labor is not enough; that is only the first stage of this process. The organization of labor is not the immediate reproduction of same: it is a general social fact. But the existence of the relation between financial capital and industrial growth—and between this connection and politics—is also a general social fact. And all this must be examined.

The Metropolis is either a response to these problems, or it is still a city; either it shall rise to the task of resolving them, or it shall fall into the "disdain" shown by Zarathustra's pupil, or into the transcrescence of Tönnies. In short, either it implies intervention in the destiny of the immediate social relations of production and renouncement of every idea of "freedom," or it shall once again be *Wille zur Ohnmacht* (will to impotence). "Weberian" politicians and industrialists such as Naumann and Walther Rathenau (son of the founder of AEG) went so far as to present this argument to the German artistic-architectural scene of the pre-World War I period.[18] The reactionary interpretation of this "mandate" was one of the decisive moments in the formation of the artistic-architectural ideology of the time. The birth of the Werkbund[19] in 1907, which followed the actual breakup of the *Verein* over such matters as monopolistic organization, occurred in the middle of the radical transformation of the German and European city. From the start, the Werkbund never seemed capable of offering any answers to the problem of the construction of that Metropolis which, as the place of the permanently controlled conflict of social forces, had already been implicit in the analysis of the process of concentration developed by the left wing of the Verein after the Congress of 1894, although it did not appear in defined terms until the late 1920s with Sombart's *type*. Did this "mandate" demand only a *Kulturarbeit?* or, as Schumacher put it, a *Veredelung*, an ennoblement of industrial labor? What was the significance of the demand for an actual *Zusammenwirken von Kunst, Industrie, und Handwerk* (art, industry, and handicraft cooperative) pro-

Dialectics of Negative and Metropolis

posed to the members of the Werkbund, and on the basis of which Walther Rathenau entrusted the "artistic supervision" of the AEG to Behrens? [20]

To set in order the processes of the massification of industrial labor, to rationalize, through artistic-cultural *form,* the destiny of metropolitan concentration; to be organs and instruments of Weberian Rationalisierung, intellectuals of Rationalisierung: this program aims at a result contrary to the reduction of Arbeit (work or labor) to Kultur—or to the synthesis of Arbeit and Kultur—emphasized in the Werkbund program. The Werkbund might have worked toward the construction of a factory—but not of the Metropolis itself. The members of the Werkbund had an ideal of Gemeinschaft that they thought they had to "save" from the concentration-massification of the social relations of production. And implicit in this was an image of the intellectual to be "saved," an image consistent with the organic "freedom" of Gemeinschaft and with its concept of form.

The demand, or rather the meaning and the direction of the Weberian political imperative, were inverted in a program of "assimilation," in a search for the organic tempo of labor as a culture within the confirmed, perfect instrumentality of the capitalist organization of labor. It was Scheffler who most coherently interpreted, on the critical level, this general tendency of the Werkbund.[21] He saw the Werkbund as a synthesis of freedom and the instrumentality of labor; a synthesis of the tradition of Gemeinschaft and the metropolitan revolution; and a synthesis of the spirit that produces and the spirit that creates and invents. Van de Velde is the key to this argument.[22] Here Arbeit ennobles itself as *Kunst* (art); however, all of the power deriving from the integration of this Kunst into the force of the process of production is withheld. It is necessary to "transform the modern, American meaning of life into an aristocratic and classical meaning." [23] A new *Klassizität*—a classical representation-resolution of the period of contradictions (the *Übergangsperiode*), which Simmel discussed and which Lukacs took up again—classicism as form-order-synthesis, the classicism that Dilthey, and later Simmel, believed characteristic of Goethe,[24] is what the Werkbund was supposed to have been. How all this was to be applied

German Sociology of the City

to the analysis of the Metropolis, and above all to its reconstruction, is easy to deduce.[25]

Like Simmel, Scheffler uses as his starting point the Metropolis, the monetary economy dominant there, and the rupture of community circles brought on by the Metropolis. But the rest of Scheffler's analysis is centered around the need to save the soul of the Gemeinschaft, *in* the Metropolis: the family, small property, the forms of transcrescence in the passage from country to city. The reasoning behind this program is disarmingly naive: this organization, this Metropolis that subsumes and preserves the city within itself, this form of international economics whose participants can cultivate their kitchen gardens after work hours, supposedly permits the total integration, the ubiquitous political division and the control, or rather the preventive repression, of all conflict. This reasoning sheds light on how the German intelligentsia of those years, or at least a large majority of them, interpreted the political-industrial "mandate."

According to this interpretation, the intellectual—in this case the architect—should "turn back," overcome the contradictions, resist the massification of labor in the factories and in the "services" of the Metropolis, and bring it back into the disintegrating "family". The intellectual is understood as a craftsman of synthesis, and hence as a *programmatic mystifier:* he looks for the forms of assimilation, points out perceptible, correct forms; he erases every leap and rupture; he reduces all contradiction to individuality and organicity. This intellectual is the anti-Nietzschean individual par excellence. The shortcomings of this ill-conceived argument are best revealed when it is uttered in Nietzsche's name! Here the spiritualization of the material, the new classicism, the intellectual's recuperation of the concept of *Beruf* (vocation) as the antidote to the instrumentality of pure *Arbeit*, are all claimed as the fruit of Nietzsche's critique.

This is not Nietzsche's thought, but rather the ideology of the Nietzschean "cults" initiated by his "accursed" sister, Elisabeth Förster–Nietzsche. This is not the Nietzschean tragic, but Van de Velde and the Darmstadt Künstlerhöhe. But if it is anti-Nietzsche, it is also in part anti-Naumann and anti-Rathenau. What these men called for was not the mystification of the instrumentality of labor. It was not the Metropolis as a ge-

Dialectics of Negative and Metropolis

neric form of concentration—as a space still open to invention and planning—that is irreversible, but the Metropolis as a political structure, as that place of contradiction between the bureaucratic and political, between finance and industry, between workers and capital, described by such critics as Weber and Sombart. The "left wing" of the Verein, the new industrialists united with the theorists of the new Verfassung and the new parties, did not call for a mystification of contradictions or for the elaboration of a regressive utopia, but for the exact opposite.

Their point of departure is the *inevitability* of all that Scheffler claims to go beyond: the mass organization of labor and its exigencies; the resultant, increasingly universal instrumentality of labor; and the breakdown of all microeconomic and city equilibrium, which makes the establishment of a world economy possible. But all of this must be given a *form*—and this involves understanding, representation, and oversight. One must give order to these necessarily alienated relations, just as one must control these necessary contradictions. To suppress them would be to suppress the entire system based on them. To suppress the instrumentality of labor would be to suppress the massification and rationalization of labor organization in large capitalist enterprise. To give an order to the absence of synthesis—to posit this absence and explore its implications to the end—was the real "mandate" and the real question. All other questions and all other answers are invalid and a priori irrelevant. This is precisely where the Werkbund failed: it was incapable of planning the Metropolis *of negative thought*, the social relations of alienated labor. That is, it failed to construe the Metropolis as conflict and as the functionality of conflict and was hence unable to systematize the imbalances among its various sectors. The Metropolis as synthesis is not Metropolis, it is city, family, organism, and individuality.

At the Congress of 1914 this was the real center of the debate, not the clash between Muthesius' *Typisierung* (standardization) and Van de Velde's "free, spontaneous creativity." [26] The clash between norm and form, as Scheffler would later summarize it, was in reality the clash between an idea of economic needs and a utopia of form as an all-inclusive "new style."

German Sociology of the City

The truth is that nobody grasped the real question posed, through Naumann's words, by capitalist growth. When Muthesius speaks of Typisierung, he intends a kind of classical ennoblement of the industrial product—its form becomes norm—a perfect synthesis of function and form. His polemical target is not the synthetical utopia of Van de Velde and Scheffler; indeed, he accuses them of leaving the synthesis incomplete, by keeping the figure of the creative spirit "autonomous." The struggle is thus one that takes place within a common set of goals.

Completely contrary are the goals implicit in Naumann's intervention.[27] Here it is no longer a question of the form-function relation, which is dissolved in the facts. The integration of form into the processes of capitalist growth is a destiny, in the Nietzschean sense of the term, where "there is nothing to improve nor to worsen." The only choice revolves around the amount of skill and theoretical energy expended in being integral to such growth, in proposing forms effectively consistent with the processes and problems of this growth. This choice therefore resides in the radical abandonment of all traditional or utopian perspectives. Here it seems we are listening to the Weber of *Wissenschaft als Beruf* (Intellectual labor as profession). But what exactly does this course of reasoning imply? The intellectual must recognize the modes and contradictions of growth as such. He must reflect them and set them in order as they are. Their synthetic-dialectical reformulation ceases to be valid precisely at the moment in which the microeconomic, marginal economy is transformed into a *Weltwirtschaft* (world economy). The fundamental character of the contradiction-functionality of the negative: that is what must now be explained. But this involves much more than a simple effort of consciousness. It implies the destruction of all professional status. Alienation, which must be recognized in the facts of existence, must be thoroughly internalized. The intellectual cannot be "free" except in the Nietzschean sense of the term: as *Freigeist*, free to contribute to and intervene in the direction of destiny.

The intellectual must stop mystifying himself as the agent of an "autonomous" labor, as the agent of Kunst versus Arbeit, as the symbol of all the possible redemptions of the instrumentality of labor. The fact is that the intellectual is radically alienated

Dialectics of Negative and Metropolis

and dispossessed. And only by starting from this given can he begin to acquire knowledge. His work can never overcome this given. And if it should claim to do so, it will be devoid of all meaning—a spectral existence, mere "hope principle." Only by acknowledging himself as alienated will the intellectual be in a position to speak of the actual social relations of production and assume the freedom necessary to integrate them.

Naumann develops this central idea in a way that is devastating to the entire debate of the Werkbund. "This Werkbund cannot in itself produce a single vase, since it does not possess a ceramics factory. It cannot produce a single teaspoon: it has to buy it." Creativity is the opposite of regaining lost autonomies. That which *produces* is the cycle of production—the contradictions on which it is based, its concrete agents, and their struggle. There is no need to add a form to all of this, or to mystify this struggle in a resolved, synthesized appearance. This appearance is not productive—to work at this appearance is not productive. The Werkbund would have to be transformed into an organizational and disciplinary instrument of the real cycle of production— that is, into an integral part of this cycle—in order to make the elements of this cycle as rational as possible and its products as competitive as possible. "We need German artists who are full of the American spirit of knowingly working for America, but as Germans for Germany." In other words, the need is for artists who are part of the structure of the processes of economic expansion, artists whose attention is completely and radically focused on the Weltwirtschaft that politicians and industrialists are seeking to build. Artists must be agents of the conquest of foreign markets, and agents of the domestic organization and rationalization of production necessary to this conquest.

Here there is no ennoblement of Arbeit, no spiritualization of material, and certainly no new Klassizität. The linking of art and industry implies a restructuration of the overall cycle in the new phase of growth: a restructuration of organization and of the science of commodities—but above all, a restructuration of society, a socialization of capitalist relations. This is what the artist should express to the highest degree in the construction of the Metropolis. The truly creative are those who can produce this outline of a *plan,* who can harmonize these requisites of

German Sociology of the City

rationalization and interrelation in a comprehensive structure. And those who know that, today, in order to produce vases and teaspoons, factories are necessary, and that it is necessary to comprehend the society in which vases and teaspoons are used, and in which their value is realized. Neither Muthesius nor Van de Velde were able, even on a simple level, to grasp the import of this argument. In the wake of Naumann's attack, their polemic recedes into the background.

At the opposite pole from Naumann, we find Endell and his work on the Metropolis, *Die Schönheit der grossen Stadt* (Beauty in the big city).[28] At first glance, the initial pages seem to be building a decisive attack on all Romantic hypotheses. The perspective of effective ethics borrowed directly from the most "Nietzschean" Schopenhauer; Rilke's eulogy of *Hiersein* (presence, or being here); the exaltation of *Arbeitsleben* and *Arbeitskultur*—and above all the technico-structural aesthetic, the analysis of artistic manufacture, which comes more out of the Austro-Viennese scene than from the German one, but can also be traced back to the Kunstwissenschaft of Dessoir[29] —in short, everything that is summarized in Endell's slogan of the Metropolis as destiny, would seem to situate this author outside of the norm-form conflict that Naumann would eventually consign to oblivion.

Indeed, the only problem that Endell sets forth at this point is the improvement of metropolitan Arbeitskultur through the "beautiful form" of a *Genusskultur* (culture of pleasure). It is essentially a question of reducing the problem of the Metropolis to the criterion of a "beautiful, living architecture," as Scheffler said when exalting the genius of the creator of the Gabinetto Elvira. Endell's entire book aims at teaching one to see the Metropolis as the new Beauty, and at assimilating the intellectual of the Gemeinschaft into the Metropolis—it seeks to reveal to the intellectual the Metropolis' most familiar aspects.

But this goal also involves a precise program: the design of the Metropolis must be wholly based on the precepts of "good form" and on the need for synthesis between beauty and functionality, and between individuality and Gesellschaft. The work of "educating" perception will be followed by a work of planning: the new hedonism of the Metropolis. Endell shares the per-

Dialectics of Negative and Metropolis

spective of synthesis, and the view that the architect-intellectual should be the center of this synthesis, with the rest of the Werkbund. Endell's originality consists in having successfully exploited, in this program, a nascent psychology of the form given to the Impressionist image of the Metropolis. Impressionism, which Lukacs found in Simmel, might also be found in Endell. Endell shows the same exaltation of the metropolitan *Erleben*, but his is directed towards the new form, towards the new Cezanne. This is Impressionism as transition and nothing more: the throng has to be set in order, and its life, its movements, are to be analyzed and reconstructed. It is clear that what is lost here is the central fact of the Impressionist Metropolis: that is, precisely, the breakdown of good form, and its irreversible decline—the fact that it is the culminating and final stage of the Sombartian Metropolis of *Genuss* and consumption. And this, of course, is what Proust saw in the gardens of Paris: the era of the paleo-Metropolis evaporating, and with it the *consonantia*, the *ordo rerum et idearum*, between mind and social circle—which Proust himself declared definitively terminated and irretrievable.

On the other hand, an interpretation of Impressionism as a transition toward new forms, new syntheses, inverts its whole meaning and scope. At this point, the only attainable dimension remaining is that of the essay. Such essays are remembrances of the Metropolis, images of the city. Things are said only in so far as they can be internalized. The problem of the Metropolis is systematically excluded. Not even Simmel's arguments can be resumed here. The problem of the functionality of the Metropolis is reduced to the problem of its subjectivity, that is, the problem of its *consonantia* with the Gemüt. The apologia for the Metropolis becomes an apologia for the "beautiful soul" that derives pleasure from life there. Such an apologia is totally unproductive, as we have seen, for Naumann and Rathenau.

This same set of problems reemerges in the work of Spengler. In *The Decline of the West* (1917), Spengler faithfully recapitulates Simmel's analysis: he goes from the breakdown of tribal organization to the emergence of money and spirit (*Geist*) as the new powers that be.[30] But what served in Simmel as the conclusion to an attempt to grasp the irresolvable contradictory-

German Sociology of the City

negative substance of the Metropolis, reappears in Spengler as a new, perfectly resolved spiritual order: Simmel's transitional solution here becomes a direct apologia for the city of capital, for the city in which ownership is constantly transformed into capital—the Metropolis. This Metropolis is the new synthesis, the new Beauty, just as Endell had "sung" of it. Spengler transforms manifest ideology into nothing less than the image of its own impotence. Spengler's Metropolitan type says nothing about concrete political structure, real conflicts, or the effective internal articulation that the Metropolis must produce; in other words, nowhere does he perceive the functionality of the Metropolis. Spengler's totally ideological apologia is already in the past tense of actual Metropolitan growth. Simmel's perceptions were no different. Spengler's absolute scholasticism serves only a posthumous faith in the functions of the old style intellectual as the one who will "overcome" the "ugliness" of capitalist growth. It is no accident that Spengler would be read and commented upon at such length by the architects and urbanists of the avant-garde.

3. Merchants and Heroes

The Soul "is God's mirror"—thus resonates the beginning of Walther Rathenau's *Breviarium Mysticum,* which he composed under the spell of his first visit to Hellas in 1906.[1] The opposition he sets up between *Seele* (soul) and Geist (mind) derived from the German philosophy of life in the period between *Wilhelmzeit* and Weimar and characterizes the Kultur we are examining here.

Dialectics of Negative and Metropolis

The mind (Geist) is intelligence that aims at a specific end—in this case it is the spirit of the rationalization and mechanization of the world. But does this not produce endless conflict and disunity? And by this very fact does the mind not fall short of its essential end, that of building an effective power embodied in the State as value? If the essential forces of an epoch are left to the Geist, not only will there be no synthesis, no Kultur, but, with the failure of every possibility of building on the notion of Fatherland, the State too will fail, as will the possibility of directing economic forces toward their essential ends. The Geist must for this reason recognize the primacy of the Seele—pure intelligence must go beyond itself in recognizing this primacy, if it is to guarantee its own effectuality.

Since capitalism exists in the sum total of these relations, it cannot by any means be reduced to crude materialism. For Rathenau, capitalism is instead the dramatic history of the conflict between Seele and Geist, whose end result, however, is the *Aufhebung* (sublation) of the Geist. The Kultur of the age of capitalism is a direct expression of this teleology. Capitalist Zivilisation has a "providential history": and this is manifest in its driving forces' "nostalgia" for synthesis in the State as organism and in patriotic language. Rationalization and mechanization do not constitute ends in themselves—but are the price paid daily for the renovation-transformation of economic-productive relations, for the broadening of man's power. In Rathenau, capitalism is passing through a purely mechanistic period (*Maschinenzeitalter,* or machine age), whose import lies however in shattering the old social circles, the ancient cultural hierarchies.[2] Mechanization is the technical means employed in imposing new ends and policies. Rathenau, unlike many "romantics," sees the absence of soul, *Seelenlosigkeit,* as a necessary but only transitional phase in the movement toward Fatherland and State: it is necessary to the destruction of the old communities and to the desecration of the aura of ancient bonds. The Geist of capitalism is necessarily counter to the ancient Seele, but in its becoming the Geist does not only perpetuate itself, it also manifests the need for a new Seele. His polemic against *Sicherheit,* certitude, and the image he presents of its collapse are characteristics that Rathenau shares with the basic

Merchants and Heroes

currents of German culture at the turn of the century. The disappearance of all bourgeois certitudes, a necessary consequence of the impetuous process of rationalization, is also a *dynamis*, an enrichment of needs, a pro-ductive impulse. The "revolutionary" fever of renovation-transformation, however, also contains within itself the need for a new Kultur, a new Seele. Its incessant growth in the end makes form and order necessary. It is important to understand that here ideological need coexists, inseparably, with functional need. The growth of capitalism cannot be reduced to mere calculating intelligence, and by extension to the divided interests of its subjects. It must bring forth, for its own self-preservation, a new Kultur, new forms of synthesis capable of embodying the legitimate *auctoritas* of a State. This State must have the value of a Fatherland, and the Fatherland must at the same time exist as a real State. (This same schema also informs Rathenau's discussion of Judaism: *Judentum* speaks of a promised land—but today, says Rathenau, this must be considered to be Germany.)

Mechanisierung is a destiny—and it has a mission to fulfill.[3] It lies in the expansion of political and economic life, in the increase of needs and of the means to satisfy them, and in the development of the intelligence and the Nervenleben that accompanies it. In modern capitalism this mission has been fulfilled, its end has been attained. The means employed by capitalism to "obey" its destiny—that is, the division and conflict among the classes, the political domination of one over the other, the politico-economic expropriation of the workers' movement—are of no further use. There is room for only the immediate conflict between contrasting interests (and therefore only *Zweckmenschen!* [functional men]) in the age of pure mechanization. The existence of this age cannot be denied by a return to the past; but to go beyond it, we must understand how it reached its goals. The socialization of economic life, the oligopolistic organization of capital and labor, and the new form of State intervention, compel (*Verantwortung*) us to perceive the very richness of the economic as an instrument-means to educate the Seele and to form (*Bildung*) new social relations and a new Verfassung.[4]

Rathenau of course is not Weber—nor Simmel. While keeping

Dialectics of Negative and Metropolis

a clear distance from reactionary anti-capitalism, he nevertheless continues to think of politico-economic history in teleo-
logical-organic terms. The notion of Kultur that he puts forth—
the same pairs of opposites that he seeks to set in dialectical
relation to one another—derive from a specific tradition: the
intersection of the Weimarian-classical myth, the Tönniesian
utopia of the Gemeinschaft, and the ideologies of the *Volk and
Preussentum* (Prussianness). However hard he may try to re-
work it from within and in all the aspects that we have covered,
this tradition finds expression in Rathenau's work, occasionally
with a rhetorical or scholastic emphasis. It is a feature of his
that reappears in many written remembrances of him by his
colleagues. Kessler remembers his friend's "virtuousness," and
saw in his behavior a mixture of vanity and bitterness.[5] Friedrich Meinecke speaks of Rathenau's overly "artificial" methods,
"like those sometimes employed by cultured, brilliant Jews."[6]
And yet these methods, like those of Ernst Troeltsch and Max
Scheler,[7] were able to grasp the reality of the problem that "af-
flicted" Rathenau. Rathenau recognizes, in a manner perhaps
more lucid than that of his "teachers" that capitalism cannot be reduced to the simple notion of Zivilisation; that the
transformation of capitalist social relations will have an un-
usual politico-institutional impact that cannot be managed only
technically and intellectually, since it seems to pose universal
questions of culture and value. In a more acute manner than
his "teachers," Rathenau realizes that when mechanization-
rationalization has reached a certain stage, a new State plan
becomes necessary, a new Verfassung based on a global vision
of policy—whether industrial, commercial, or foreign policy—
and that cannot be reduced to the canons of the old liberalism.
He then goes on to analyze, in a more concrete manner than
even Weber, the articulations of this new State, the forms that
the socialization of the capitalist *ratio* will assume, the *Verstaat-
lichung des Kapitals* (the socialization of capital). This projec-
tion of Rathenau's thought remains fundamental, even if his
ideology still adheres to the cultural climate of Wilhelmian Germany. Of all of Rathenau's commentators, Robert Musil most
clearly understood these aporiae in his intellectual base, as evi-
denced both in the 1914 review of *Zur Mechanik des Geistes*[8]

Merchants and Heroes

and in certain sections of *Der Mann ohne Eigenschaften* (the man without qualities). Rathenau's "fall" into the meanders of Parallel Action itself pitilessly symbolizes his unresolved tension with regard to the new Seele, and the inexorable transformation of this tension into rhetorical ideology.

Naumann and Sombart are perhaps the figures who come closest to Rathenau in the attempt to define the features of a Kultur of social capital. An examination of some of their works might help us to explain more satisfactorily the failure of this "mission". Naumann's idea of a democratized *Kaisertum* of harmony between the individual and the hard necessity of large capitalist enterprise, and the political function he assigns to the Protestant message (especially with regard to social democracy, which he calls "the great heresy of the Protestant church") shows how Naumann interpreted his own Beruf. He viewed it not only as Weber saw it—that is, as going beyond all utopianism and dogmatism—but also as defining and expressing the fundamental "synthetical qualities" of contemporary life. This life must be transformed to encompass a greater sense of solidarity, a fuller *Staatsleben*. This life possesses a vast moral and aesthetic potential waiting to be acknowledged, educated, and put to good use. The real responsibility of the *Bürgertum* (bourgeoisie), as Brentano had already indicated, lies precisely in leading the whole country, the *Volk*, to this acknowledgment. The endeavor of the Werkbund, to which Naumann passionately devoted himself, cannot be understood outside the context of this politico-cultural program. The activity of the Werkbund should not be perceived as a simple model presented to the contemporary world but as an effort claiming to express the inherent artistico-cultural telos of this world. The syntheses that the Werkbund brings about are in keeping with the fundamental goals of Zivilisation and mechanization-rationalization. The champions of the Werkbund do not set themselves up as exponents of an artistic-cultural trend, but as an embodiment of the destiny of the transition from Zivilisation to Kultur. This mode of procedure is expounded upon in a clear manner by Naumann in numerous essays, and in particular in *Die Kunst im Zeitalter der Maschine* in 1904.[9]

Dialectics of Negative and Metropolis

The title of this work echoes *Der Christ im Zeitalter der Maschine,*[10] written by Naumann ten years earlier, one of the more involuntarily, of course, anti-Christian works, together with the famous *Briefe,* of Wilhelmian culture. In this work, Christ's "recognition" of the machine precedes and legitimizes its recognition by Art. Naumann begins with an examination of the artist's social relations, which were transformed from personal dealings into impersonal exchanges. Until the emergence of the machine age, the artist depended on a specific clientele. His works were intended for social circles whose inclinations, taste, and culture were easy to know. And this Kultur had firm roots in tradition, which the artist's works protected from the *Nervosität* (restlessness) of fashion. Clearly this situation changed with the advent of the *Zeitalter der Maschine*. The artist henceforth must depend on the market, like any other manufacturer. But the real question is, are we dealing simply with a social transformation that affects artistic production from without, as it were, or does this transformation actually affect the essence of the work of art?

To respond to this question, one must analyze the relation of art to commercial and social policies. In the pre-World War I era that we are examining, the prosperity of Germany depended on the continuous growth of its market. This goal can be pursued not only quantitatively but also qualitatively, by enhancing German labor. The product of labor does not in itself make possible global commercial policies. "The future of our industry depends, for the most part, on art, which *gives value* to our products . . . The most important movements of contemporary artistic sentiment are, in their specific natures, determined at least in part by the machine."[11] On the one hand, then, art is a determining factor in the process of valorization; on the other, it is the expression of the machine age. Art is not added to the product of the machine, but together with it forms a new synthesis. Naumann speaks of a "national-popular German style of the machine age," (p. 16), whose ideal is an "artistically educated and trained *Maschinenvolk*" (p. 17). The organic synthesis of machine and art is a symbol of the capitalist Kultur, of the possibility of producing a Soul of capitalism. This "production" is

Merchants and Heroes

the fruit of a highly complex labor: worker plus artist, simple producer plus Seele.

Artistic intervention does not add to the machine's product the nostalgia for past forms or for its former "independence". Rather, it gives expression to the machine's other side; it fulfills its profound cultural purpose. In other words: artistic labor must give form to the contemporary mode of production and to its merchandise. Art is the maieutics of the Seele of capitalism: "in the best commodity there is always Soul in some form" (p. 12). The process that leads to this result—which Riemerschmid, Fisher, Muthesius, and Osthaus all tried to achieve—is a long and difficult one. At its beginnings, the machine age presented itself as crude materialism. The new materials and machines began their march without form and without taste. In Naumann's day, one was still surrounded by these products. Only slowly does our vision become sensitive to the aesthetic potential of the new machines and materials. Gradually we learn how to recognize their beauty. Naumann's thought, in this instance, has the same emphasis as Endell's: the Metropolis is transformed before his eyes into a grandiose natural spectacle or into a pure artistic landscape. Streets, factories, and so on, become "minarets of the West"; the Eiffel Tower is compared to the Acropolis, to St. Peter's, to Hagia Sophia, and to Balbeck.[12]

This rhetorical effusion, however difficult in itself to accept, nevertheless has its own self-justification. Naumann's task—like that of the entire Werkbund on this matter—lies in proving that artistic labor in the machine age can have no value as a style that descends from above to ennoble the products of industry. Artistic labor must express the tendency toward *Gestalt* (form) that is triggered by the process of mechanization itself. For this reason, art must not hinder the functional expression of the product, but on the contrary must give this expression a form, a bearing. In this light, we begin to see the reasons behind Naumann's harsh polemic against all ornamentation[13] and against the "autonomistic" tendencies that were emerging within the Werkbund itself with regard to the economic-industrial end.

The development of this polemic can be traced from the *Deutsche Gewerbekunst* of 1908,[14] a veritable manifesto of the

Dialectics of Negative and Metropolis

Werkbund's original goals, to *Der deutsche Stil* of 1912, up to the Werkbunds of 1912 and 1914, where as we have just seen, Naumann intervened with particular firmness and clarity. The target in these cases was the *Eitelkeit* (vanity) of the ideology asserting itself in the Werkbund with regard to the hegemony of artistic form over the utility-functionality of the object. Here, finally, there was no longer any need to see boats, bridges, workshops, and railway stations as examples of a new nature, or to compare them to temples or minarets. If the new ends and the new materials, in their active reciprocal relation, produce new forms and new styles, then these will become embodied in the actual relations of production and circulation. The new gestalt can exist only in the area of the relations of production. If, together with Naumann, we assert that it is these relations that determine new forms and new styles, then all that contradicts these relations also contradicts the possibility of the existence of these forms and styles: for this reason, defining the end, defining what is useful and seeking to attain it by the most economical means, therefore coincides with the pursuit of the new gestalt. If, on the other hand, the inference of a capitalist Kultur, obtained in this manner, appears to be an empty apology for development, and the irreducible difference between artistic production and industrial production is reconfirmed—or if one attempts to "train" the latter in the requisites of the former—then the very notion of *Gewerbekunst* (industrial art) itself is invalidated and must be abandoned. The way in which Naumann, in opposition to Muthesius and Van de Velde,[15] decides the question—which left its mark on the entire history of the Werkbund, at least until World War I—in itself demonstrates the very pointlessness of the question. If indeed, as Naumann asserts, the Werkbund must henceforth become an organizational and disciplinary instrument of the real cycle of production, abandon all "auras," and "know how to work for America, but as Germans for Germany," what sense could there be in repeating the other side of the Werkbund ideology: the great goals of the spiritualization of labor, the elevation of German labor? Here we are simply *Im Reich der Arbeit* (in the realm of work): what matters and what it boils down to are the conditions necessary for the maxi-

Merchants and Heroes

mum productivity of labor, not the "beauty" of the product, which would supposedly redeem its subordinating-alienating character.[16] As much as *Arbeitsideologie* remains an essential component of the thought of both Naumann and Rathenau,[17] its possibility of success, starting with the first decades of the Werkbund experience, became more and more uncertain.

Nothing could be more misleading, in an analysis of German culture around 1914, than to assert these themes to be a natural outgrowth of a vague *Dilettantismus*. In his *Kunstgewerbe und Kultur,*[18] Sombart does exactly this. He begins by creating a problematics of the concept of the autonomous end of the work of art (art only as *Selbstzweck,* as an end in itself), in order to analyze, in terms of economic and social history, the various relations that have existed between Kunstgewerbe and economy. In the spirit of *Der Moderne Kapitalismus,* he distinguishes two fundamentally different epochs: that of the rich and happy consonantia among the handicraft and small-shop economy, the high culture of the art buyer, and the autonomous work, on the one hand; and that of the capitalist dispossession of *Handwerk,* of the artisan, and of the handicraft organization of labor, on the other. It is in the latter period that the artist, bereft of his "natural" economic environment, begins a time of "absolute misery" (p. 45). Capitalist industry rejects his forms as idle play; the capitalist-bourgeois art clientele is totally uneducated; the *Leadergeister,* they who set the tone of artistic endeavor, begin to venture into areas completely foreign to *Kunstgewerbe:* the artist becomes *pure* artist. But according to Sombart, this purity bears witness to precisely the misery of the artist's real socio-economic situation. This rough analysis of the social destiny of art was predominant in German culture (and elsewhere) up until the First World War and beyond—and it was from this premise that derived the theory of the fundamental mutual exclusiveness, or opposition, between Kapitalismus and art. With the epoch of capitalism assumed as an essentially anti-artistic one, art then becomes, in a certain way—if it is conscious of its destiny—a revolutionary force with respect to capitalist social relations. Many of the "great" modern aesthetic theories cannot be understood outside of this sociological framework, however modest its origins.

But Sombart, like Naumann and Rathenau, does not stop at the contradiction; he aims at delineating the possibilities of a new synthesis between art and industry. For him, too, the Werkbund is the *exemplum* of such an attempt: its artists are so many St. Georges fighting to free the princess *Kunstgewerbe* from the thousand dragons of the present-day economic relations of force (p. 45); they are fighting against capital, whose only aim is profit; against mass demand, now become "democratic"; against technique, whose sole aim is utility-functionality, and which so far has been unable to develop any kind of aesthetics. How can the artist survive and "e-ducate" the princess in such an environment? The answer to this question is right out of Naumann. It is impossible to carry on this battle by radically opposing modern technique.[19] No one has anything to gain by reversing the tide of technique, whose organization and purpose are dictated by capitalism (p. 84). But this technique has, in a latent state, its own aesthetic, its own beauty. The task of the artist lies in recognizing this beauty, "e-ducating" it, and developing it. The modern artist whose gaze is not nostalgically fixed upon a utopian past must realize the potential aesthetic of technique. That is to say that while he does not identify with the given organization of society and production at all, he discovers and reveals its values: its tendency toward formal purity, toward "naturalness," toward, one might say, rational sincerity (p. 90). But in addition to this, the large-scale organization of industry opens up great new opportunities to the artist such as the invention of technically reproducible forms, the organization of highly specialized group labor, the increase of available materials, and so on. The artist must confront these new problems and dimensions by producing the new aesthetic implicit in them. This aesthetic is indeed the modernist-rationalist *Glaskultur* (see part III), here transposed onto the level of applied art. If the artist succeeds in this endeavor, he will be able to say that he has found the way to educate and prevail over the factors of production: labor, the businessman, the public. On this artist, says Sombart, "rests all our hope" for a modern Gewerbekunst

Merchants and Heroes

(pp. 117–118)—the symbol of the possibility of a capitalist Kultur, of a new harmony between Seele and Geist, of a labor all the more productive and commercially "penetrant" as it becomes more noble and "artistic". As we can see, Sombart is no more aware than Naumann of the aporiae in Werkbund thought.[20]

In many ways, the figure who best understood the needs of capitalist organization and its objection to the ideology of the Werkbund was Walther Rathenau. After 1907, his presence as a great industrialist became one to be reckoned with. Between 1907 and his death, he would have a hand in the administrative councils of over sixty firms in countries as varied as Germany, Italy, England, and Spain. He emerged as a true Leadergeist of German capital's phase of domestic concentration and international expansion. In 1912, after having absorbed such companies as Felten & Guillaume, Lahmeyer, and Union, his AEG encompassed a complex of two hundred firms, with total assets of a billion and a half gold marks. The AEG's activities spanned ten countries. This process of assimilation and concentration had been made possible by a scientific division of the world market, first with Siemens, and later with General Electric and Westinghouse.[21] The classic "Manchesterian" businessman certainly could not represent a world-wide group such as this; nevertheless, there was in Rathenau a persistent, subtle, impossible nostalgia for the "heroic age," a nostalgia that Musil very poignantly captured in his dialogue between Arnheim and his black valet Soliman *The Man Without Qualities*. Arnheim remembers the "old man" who "did business by intuition," the age when "the use of intuition was customary for all those who were unable to answer for their actions through reason." He sees that "the primitive force" of this talent has now become almost incomprehensible.[22] And this is not so much because natural talent must be succeeded—according to worn-out theories—by reflection, intellect, and calculation, but because the management of world-wide business affairs in itself necessitates a political perspective, the relations and dimensions of a large-scale policy. Industrial management itself becomes henceforth a problem of collective negotiation, of political relations with

Dialectics of Negative and Metropolis

mass-based organizations, and of diplomacy with regard to the State and to foreign states: a problem of domestic and foreign *policy*. The monopolistic form of organization adopted by all the forces of mechanization-rationalization imposes the problem of the political and the State—and of their new Verfassung. The head of the AEG can only be, henceforth, a *politician*.

This image of the new entrepreneur, beyond the "colorfulness" that is often assigned to it, is essentially a sober one, without illusions. To a certain degree, Rathenau even adopts the ideology of labor as promulgated by the Werkbund—which, as we have seen, is inextricably part of this image—but he develops precisely those aspects most bound up with the spirit of the organization of labor and capitalist aims. It was this spirit that was supposed to be expressed in the new constructions executed by Behrens for the AEG (fig. 1), and not the "message of beauty" that, according to Van de Velde, the Werkbund was addressing to the world of industry and the engineer. These constructions were not supposed to be a testimony, but rather the real products, the strongest and most powerful result, of a new European *constructive* spirit. Even the wariest critics of the time bore witness to the classical brilliance of Behrens' solutions. In Gropius' words: in our age, "perfectly moulded form (*Prägung*), clarity in contrasts, the order of the elements, the sequence of the equal parts, the unity of form and color—all this corresponds to the energy and the economy of our public life." [23] The importance of Behrens's contributions lies not in having overcome or removed or "embellished" the presence of the "engineer", but in having openly presented the function and the purpose of this presence in the new structures, in the use of materials, and in the arrangement of interior space, where everything is ordered and controllable. There is a strict correspondence between the architectonic gestalt and the functionality of the organization of labor. The irruption of air and light inside the factory makes all angles, all divisions, all opacity disappear; it is an Aufklärung in the physical sense of the term: understanding and control— a perfect reduction of the space to place of production, and a perfect specialization of the space in accordance with this use. The interior of Behrens's turbine factory is comparable to the

Merchants and Heroes

"cleanest" pages of Naumann, Rathenau, and Sombart. There the artifices of Arbeitsideologie (ideology of labor) really cross over into a new *Industrienwissenschaft,* (science of industry) where engineer, politician, and technician (with the "artist-as-producer" implied in the technician) seek paradoxically to reconcile themselves with one another.

But in Behrens's industrial buildings, there is also a play of exterior and interior that expresses the irresolvable tension with regard to the Seele, the impossibility of the industrial Aufklärung to manifest itself purely as such. This tension is explained in everyday terms by Paul Jordan, the man who originally brought Behrens to the AEG: "A motor must be as beautiful as a birthday present." [24] But it is Behrens himself who gives this tension its most culturally self-conscious expression when he charges the imagery of his buildings with visible monumental significations. The factory is supposed to serve as the *sacred place* of labor; and although on the inside this sacredness at first resembles functionality and clarity, on the outside it is supposed to act on the senses, provoke pathos in the observer, while representing in his heart and intellect both the grandeur and the solidity of the enterprise. The facade of the Kleinmotorfabrik on the Voltastrasse symbolizes the perfect rationality of the labor carried out under its roof (the factory as the home of labor) as well as the value of this labor, the fact that it is not pure mechanization, and the particular relation established, in this way, between labor and its urban context. This latter aspect is particularly important to an understanding of the ideology that we are analyzing here. Clearly the facade, given rhythm by the monumental pilasters, encloses a space that is set up as separate from the urban context. The activity that goes on behind these walls must appear to be *exceptional* and hence set apart from the anonymous labor of the large city. What takes place within such buildings is labor par excellence, whose very repetitiveness (this is precisely the signification behind the sequentiality of the facade) assumes a ritual, sacred value. Here repetition is much more than a mere symbol of the Metropolis. It actually expresses the stability (*Festigkeit*) and permanence (*Dauer*) of the power that is founded on labor and emanates from labor. Like all monuments,

Dialectics of Negative and Metropolis

the factory stands out from its urban context, but at the same time it maintains a singular relation with it: and this relation is one of *dominion*. Behrens's form is supposed to emphasize that the factory governs the hustle and bustle, the kaleidoscopic multiformity of life in the Metropolis. Gropius understood this point well and saw it as a characteristic of the factory *heterotopia*[25] in the modern Metropolis: Behrens, he wrote, has built "buildings of truly classical bearing, which dominate their environment with a sovereign air."[26] These monuments, at the very moment in which they let air and light pass through to the inside—which are necessary for the full specialization of the space as a place of production—govern the life of the Metropolis as a whole, dominating every view. In this factory, the life of the Metropolis recognizes its very foundation and not just another element of its flux, of its Nervenleben. The place of productive labor is made sacred in the heterotopia of the factory. It becomes the substance, the real, the new subject of the life of the Metropolis, of its intelligence, its impressions, and its unceasing consumption and reproduction. In the factory, the metropolitan Nervenleben assumes its own specific gestalt.

Here the symbol of the soul of mechanization (which cannot be reduced to the "crude materialism" of its original "Americanness") seems to emerge; here capital and labor together express the new ethic ruling the Metropolis, whose church is the factory. No doubt Behrens' factory is still an example of *Preussentum,* but it is inextricably linked to the clarity-transparence of industrial calculation. And on the other side of the coin, Mechanisierung is no doubt the *dynamis* of this building, but it also embodies at once the single, unifying Bildung of capital and labor, and their common Fatherland. This is why the awakening of 1914 was that much more difficult for those who, like Naumann and Rathenau, had never shared in the spirit that led to the war.[27] While for many proponents of the new liberalism, apart from the circles of the "conservative revolution", 1914 was an apotheosis of the themes that we have been examining, the entry into the War forced large industrial capital to come to terms, in a radical manner, with its own Kultur—a Kultur destined, like so much else, "to die in Weimar."

Merchants and Heroes

4. Negative Thought and Artistic Representation

Benjamin's analysis of the Metropolis becomes historically comprehensible only when we see how, between the time of Simmel's *Die Grossstädte* and Benjamin's essays on Baudelaire and
Paris, the synthesis of Vergeistigung and ethical individuality—
a synthesis attempted by Simmel himself—comes to collapse.
What does it mean to assert that Simmel's perspective is still
that of Kultur? It means that his thought is totally determined
by the definition of the modes and forms by which thought can
dominate "being." *Cogito ergo sum:* the cogito *must* be.[1] This
perspective can be explained only on the basis of an ego that
is still autonomous, still individualized and in a state of relative
freedom—an ego still able to free itself from the energy or the
force of the given, and therefore still in a position to dominate
it—that is, still above the tragedy of the given. If this is the case,
the ego can then become the center that determines the tools of
understanding and the perspectives of value by which to judge,
measure, and direct knowledge and action. Duty is only the most
formalized ethical expression of this general perspective. Duty
embodies the typical aim of thought's dominance over being,
inasmuch as this aim of all-inclusive rationalization does not
present itself immediately, but is constructed precisely through

Dialectics of Negative and Metropolis

56

an *ergo* charged with ethical intent and responsible for "civilization". Duty must be upheld as long as this ergo exists. In spite of the admonitions of many of his critics, Kant insisted, to the point of tedium, that practical reason is totally integrated into the schemas of theoretical reason. The great ethics of classical bourgeois philosophy, far from being an instrument for the mystification of epistemological problems, always contitute their logical continuation, their maximum extension and radicality.[2]

We shall see how this perspective presents itself in Simmel in terms that are already problematic. Simmel makes the asserted form of duty, and value defined on the basis of thought, change constantly according to the relative assumption of the negative. But this moment of suspension or transition was to be very short-lived.[3] Already Benjamin's thought no longer has any direct or explicit connection to it. The process of the general Vergeistigung can no longer be reduced or justified, in any way, on the basis of the transcendental structure of the ego, inasmuch as the rational status that seemed the ego's exclusive privilege has now become a social phenomenon—that is, the duty of integrating being implicit in this status has become a real process, an actual, teleologically articulated tendency. The collapse of duty is already a fait accompli in Nietzsche, from a theoretical point of view, and in Weber, from a political point of view.[4] But this is only one step in the process. What followed were the analyses of the transcendent relation between thought and being, which would later find their full flowering in the linguistics of Saussure and his intellectual descendants. Language does not dominate any *thing;* it exists in relation to *nothing.* Its structure, the laws of its rationality, its form, have no specific *significations;* they do not communicate directly with anything. The rational is no longer a state of being to be gained, the goal of a duty, the thing to be attained or dominated through a transcendental relation—it is given in the very structure of language, in its immanent constitution. As such—and not as a signifying communicator—language is rational. Here the collapse of duty is the collapse of the whole structure of values: values become precisely that about which one is unable to speak.

These conclusions necessitate a whole new discussion of the negative and of the avant-gardes. Simmel fairly shrinks from a

Negative Thought and Artistic Representation

direct analysis of these phenomena, precisely because he feels them to be totally alien to his perspective of synthesis, his reformulation of Kultur. Benjamin's treatment of them—as manifesting the hopelessness of the capitalist state, making them thus consistent, within the laws of its form, with the very reason of the system—still does not say everything. What is lacking in Benjamin is a clear perception of the functionality of the relation between the negative and the results of the Vergeistigung that we have outlined above. That is, he fails to see how the negative is in reality representative of that formidably destructive critique of the privileged status of the ego, of duty, of value, and of the transcendent word-thing relation, the critique on which the Metropolis is based; he fails to see how the negative aims directly at such results, precisely insofar as it senses them and expresses them as destiny. This type of critique should now be re-examined, at least in an illustrative manner, so that we may draw some general conclusions.

With E.T.A. Hoffmann emerges the great theme of the dissolution of the "classical" bourgeois "I." But the "multiplicity" that results does not yet reveal its own linguistic status. In reflecting, the I no longer succeeds in dominating being and the thing, but only reflects itself, splitting itself in two. Hoffmann grasps and gives precise expression to the immediately negative side of the Fichtian-Romantic argument. In Hoffman's world, it seems that no reason can exist other than abandoned reason. His odd fancies and irony are born out of this situation of powerlessness. The fantastic reveals the shock of a rupture not yet rationalized—and irony the impossibility of synthesis, all travels and apprenticeships notwithstanding. And yet, the void that remains in the place of such synthesis lies unconcealed. Even in the absence of synthesis, synthesis still rules.

The aesthetic of the fantastic, asserted in this manner, must be clearly distinguished from the aesthetic of the imagination. Fantasy pursues the image, which the imagination posits. The fantastic wanders in search of its own form, in search of the new laws that govern the subject-object relation—it seeks a language that might express the substance of the I's becoming object through splitting. The imagination is able to define this language as *Einbildungskraft* (the power of the imagination): the ability, the power to give form, to posit something in a formed image. This implies the ability to express the dissolution of the ego's contitution within the general process of rationalization, to express it as Vergeistigung. Imagining implies the construction of a model—that is, the construction of a language rational in itself, a *system* of signifiers. Fantasy (like that of Hoffmann, for example) can be considered the first form assumed, in the realm of artistic representation, by the shock resulting from the conditions of modern society.

The imagination, on the other hand, is the shock that has already assumed a form of self-expression and become a system, a structure: it is the further, decisive maturation of shock within the processes of rationalization that invests the artistic forms themselves, and that these forms integrate in a functional way. Of course, here we are no longer speaking of the imagination as a schema between thought and being, word and thing. Fantasy is also the dissolution of this kind of theoretical imagination, which plays such a fundamental role in Kant. Now it is no longer thought that imagines. Rather, it is shock that becomes image, and hence, language: shock no longer in search of synthesis, as in the previous schema, and which, unable to find it, disperses itself in fantasy and irony—but also shock that matures to the point where it constructs itself as structure, where it makes manifest the laws of its own sign, where it imagines itself. Imagination is not a wandering or an endless duty, but quite the contrary: it is the analysis, the postulation, and the construction of the abstract-formal model of shock. The tale tends inevitably toward calculation; the narration toward the combination of signs; and contradiction and splitting toward the unfolding of an equation. When Hegel destroyed the relation between artistic form and signification, as a result of the process of Romantic art, he believed that in so doing he had grasped the fact that artistic representation was condemned to mere ironic-dispersion or fantastic individuality. Instead, in this century, it is precisely by virtue of that destruction, that rupture postulated by Hegel, that modern art has salvaged itself as rationality.

By totally internalizing the absence of signification to which Hegel had condemned it, modern art tends to become the imaginative process of shock, the most comprehensive symbol of the

Negative Thought and Artistic Representation

Vergeistigung of the overall social relations, precisely inasmuch as it turns the negative moment itself into language. But it should be added that only negative thought can reach this limit; only art that counters Hegel, by assuming the entire negative charge of his judgment; only thought that destroys its own claim to dominion over signification and transcendence—thought that understands, if you will, being-in-itself as the status of the thing as a rule; and only that artistic representation capable of constructing itself as pure imagination. And this is precisely the case, after Hoffmann, with Poe.

Language, in Poe, is already a thing among things.[5] The radical alienation of language from its "privilege" constitutes the immediate rupture that must be explained and developed. Poe's tales all reveal the same structure: contradiction, shock, and madness itself, as a constant starting point, slowly unveil their own language. The image of madness, which in Romanticism would imply the simple negation of subjectivity, is indeed rational in Poe, not rationalized, not cured from without. In an analytical manner, passage by passage, without leaps, without discoveries, madness—by recovering its past and coordinating it with the present and by planning a series of specific resolutions—reveals its own logic.

This process is embodied in the maximum formalization of relations. What matters are not the givens, things, the story or the turn of events. That is all just appearance. What matters are the relations, the functions, the laws that govern the movements and the interest of the quantities of energy posited in the story. Character is all the more important, all the more plastically conspicuous, as it expresses this logic and approaches the model, set up by the imagination, of the radical "mathematization" of discourse.[6] The tale must for this reason be of a serial nature. The interest lies in the posing of the problem, in the determination of other variables, in the enrichment or complication of the terms of the equation, and in the nature of the unknown quantities; it can never lie in the upsetting of the tale's fundamental laws, in "surprise." The abolition of adventure is total; the mode of procedure is reversed to the reduction of an apparent inexplicable to an understanding of its signs. What is presented is a signifier that must be deciphered.

Dialectics of Negative and Metropolis

In order to understand the structure of signs set forth at the beginning of the story as the problem to be resolved, one must remain extremely firm with respect to their immanence. One must heed the signs-clues, travel through them, and finally understand their constitution.[7] The difference between the analytical search of Poe's "Gold Bug" and the search in Robert Louis Stevenson's *Treasure Island* is immense. Between these two searches lies the difference between imagination and fantasy, as we have defined them.

Perhaps nothing expresses Poe's mode of discourse more explicitly than "The Murders in the Rue Morgue": here the interpretation of the given, the analysis, the choice of the method of procedure, and the solution become so interconnected that they make the "mathematical game" an all-encompassing rule.

The "absurd" establishes itself in the intelligence: this is precisely what Baudelaire seized upon in Poe and made most profoundly his own.[8] And not in the banal sense in which the absurd is explained and understood by the Verstand—but rather in the sense that it is madness itself that speaks. Madness is not the object of a thought or of an ego that speaks of it; it is the subject itself: hence the crime, the contradiction, the *exception,* as a rule. All of Poe is for this reason a powerful symbol of the process of rationalization. This process no longer appears as something imposed from without—it is the voice and language of all the elements. It is no longer an objective domain, so to speak, but an intersubjective structure—and hence all the more actual. There is perhaps only one work, among all the novels and short stories of the nineteenth century, that compares to this symbolic aspect of Poe, and that is Melville's *Bartleby the Scrivener,*[9] written ten years after "The Murders in the Rue Morgue"; but in this story the signs are not unveiled, and the clues blend together, providing no single outcome. The alienation between language and thing is on the verge of becoming internalized within the language itself: the signs enclose themselves within the same reticence as the character Bartleby himself: they prefer not to be understood, not to become rational, not to unfold their subjectivity. The sign of shock is as though fixed on itself, thus preserving its exceptionality, its mystery. But this is a totally ineffectual loyalty, a death sentence indeed.

Negative Thought and Artistic Representation

Although it cannot be penetrated or rationalized, it can be manipulated and mystified from without (hence the function of the bourgeois narrator!) Thus, what we are dealing with is not a madness that eluded Poe; but rather the most radical and desperate conclusion that can be drawn from his discourse: the rules of the game must be respected in whatever way possible; outside of this form nothing else exists.

Baudelaire already sees in *this* Poe the poet of the Metropolis. The serial element and the repetition form the anguish that wards off fear and shock, and express the universal equivalence of the throng to which the dandy belongs. The formalization of discourse attempted by Poe finds in the lyric a propitious terrain in which to take root. Mallarmé is the first to speak explicitly of poetry as a "game of twenty-four letters." [10] Poetry is no longer a vase of images that transforms or ennobles a given material— it is now an ensemble of effects strictly and uniquely tied to the possibilities of language itself. Signification has become totally irrelevant; it is the formal interrelation of the signs that constitutes the work. The realm of experience-Erlebnis exists only in the discovery and the definition of such a form.

In brief, Melville's *Bartleby,* like Poe's tales, like Baudelaire's *passante,* like Mallarmé's inescapable game of signs, allow for neither therapy nor recovery. The sign cannot be redeemed. To decipher it is to sink into it, without any means of escape—to sink into the status of sign that dominates, hermetically, the Metropolis. The negative is indeed in force here, since it negates the existence of alternatives to this process, and since it postulates this process as being without consolation.

There is no justification or indirect apology offered for this postulation. At the same moment in which the negative grasps the absoluteness of the sign and internalizes the overall Vergeistigung—that is, at the same moment in which it comprehends the mystification of nostalgia as well as the ineffectuality of hope—it thoroughly adheres to the alienation that dominates this system. Like Baudelaire's dandy in the world of the universal equivalence of commodities, Poe's detective Dupin is totally, and consciously, alienated in the universe of signs, in the universe as sign. The universal status of the sign is the same as that of universal alienation—it is the premise and the base of the

Dialectics of Negative and Metropolis

process of the production and circulation of capital. Arriving at the sign thus implies not only defining a new rationality, beyond the transcendent thought-being relation, but also defining the very rationality of alienation, the logic of alienation. It is only because the negative is able to perceive and express this point, that it is a total symbol of the Vergeistigung and inseparable from it. The Vergeistigung finds total expression only in the mirror of its own misery. The more the negative assumes the Vergeistigung to be insuperable—precisely because the negative is desperately aware of the impossibility of opposing it, and because it sees it as henceforth inextricably bound to artistic and ideological form—the more the Vergeistigung reveals itself in all its fundamental misery and lays bare the relations of alienation that constitute it. With the collapse of its image as all-inclusive synthesis, the Vergeistigung does in fact become fully actualized but only within its own contradictions and on the basis of the unresolved problem of its own permanence. Thus, its rationality is one that does not reconcile, a rationality consisting of differences that are insuperable for the time being. But it is sick: the negative's own emphasis on illness is in this way the highest symbolic manifestation of its demystified theoretical strength. Such is the case in Poe and Baudelaire, as well as in the Nietzschean sense of tragedy.

Benjamin takes what is probably the first step towards interpreting the negative in this vein in a letter to Gerhard Scholem of June 12, 1938.[11] The subject of the letter is Kafka, and in a few decisive pages Benjamin destroys Max Brod's interpretation of his friend and colleague. Benjamin sees in Kafka the experience of the modern Metropolis; but the critical perception of the most lasting importance here is the connection that Benjamin establishes between this experience and the findings of contemporary physics. Benjamin then has us read a page of Eddington with this in mind: "I am standing at the threshhold, with the intention of entering my room. This is a very complicated undertaking. First, I have to struggle against the atmosphere, which presses against my body with the force of one kilogram per square centimeter. Then I must try to set foot on a floor that is traveling at a speed of thirty kilometers per second around the sun. . . . Indeed, it is easier for a camel to pass through the eye of a needle than for a physicist to get beyond a threshold" (p. 761). The incomprehensibilities of Kafka's discourse are a perfect analogy for the aporiae of modern physics.

Here, alienation within rationality becomes complete. This threshold, with all of its possibilities rationally calculated, is precisely the insuperable threshold, the door of the law. Rationality, as a law of alienation, finds herein its most complete symbolization. It is the maximum formalization of discourse that impedes all action, and at the limit, all comprehension. In Poe, analysis still finds solutions, the clues still explain themselves. In Kafka, the clue finally discloses its logical nature, presenting itself totally as pure form, but it is for this very reason that no analysis of it can find the solution. Perfecting the logic of the sign to its very core means that this core will never be explicable.

In Poe, the method is repeated, equation by equation. In Kafka, on the other hand, repetition results from the impossibility of resolution. Being totally and in itself rationalized, the sign rejects any further analysis. Relations are clear, the discourse unequivocal, the functions explicit—but the alienation of and within their universe is so total that they present themselves and repeat themselves without any further movement. Judgment is analytical and nothing more. The situation is perfectly tautological. And yet, as Benjamin points out, one can get a glimpse of the meaning, the solution, but he who makes an effort to see it only shows that he does not see.

The difference between sign and thing is thus presented, in Kafka, directly within the sign itself. In Poe, the sign could still construct itself as a complete presence resolved in itself and hence could present its alienation as a premise: given this premise, the sign was perfect. In Kafka, the difference is totally inherent in the sign. In the sign, it is the difference between language and being itself that is expressed.

The emphasis is no longer placed on the expression of the sign's logic, but on the expression of difference. Carried to its logical extreme, the rationality of the sign traps the sign within itself—as signifier without signified, fact without object, contradiction and difference. The Kafkan novel is peripeteia condemned to difference, but is a visible peripeteia, since difference is a given from the start. The meaning of the novel is precisely the total

Dialectics of Negative and Metropolis

difference that separates it from all signification. Meaning no longer lies in the analysis of a clue toward a solution, but in the analysis of a solution presented directly as difference. The directly given solution is the condemnation to difference: the breakdown of all "presence". The "story" is only the description of this sign, a sinking into the already given.

As Bense has definitively explained,[12] shattering all the various idiocies that have been said about Kafka, the Kafkan novel is nothing but an investigation of the initial *weder-noch* (neither . . . nor) of *The Castle:* "The 'No' of the answer was audible even to K. at his table. But the answer went on and was still more explicit, it ran as follows: 'Neither to-morrow nor at any other time.' . . . But being pressed, he replied quickly: 'When can my master come to the Castle?' 'Never,' was the answer. 'Very well,' said K., and hung the receiver up."[13] All the rest is a development of the tautology; and it shows the same "rationality" as the behavior of that physicist unable to cross the threshold. Trapped within the unbending logic of the sign, K. can only make variations on the theme of weder-noch, get entangled in it, and develop it into a chain of syntactical structures. All the anguish is here. Never is this anguish expressed (as in the various *engagements* of the literature and the "neo-Christian" ideology of decision and choice) in the representation of something— rather, it is itself the sign. The anguish lies in the inability to do anything but posit this sign and translate it mathematically, without the possibility of breaking it apart in any way, without the possibility of looking beyond it, without the possibility of signification. The collapse of the transcendent relation—the collapse of the intentional structure of consciousness based on the privilege of the ego—is therefore also the collapse of utopia, in all of its various meanings.

The Kafkan novel is an analysis of the various modes of being that coincide in the explanation of difference. According to Bense, all of these modes are expounded in juridico-objective terms (p. 85). In Kafka's language, there is never a moment of respite, of open possibility. Every sentence is a juridical pronouncement: a conviction. The unity of Kafka's language lies in its absolute closure. That which lies beyond these pronouncements, that which one can only glimpse, does not exist. Lost

Negative Thought and Artistic Representation

time, the past, is no longer; the future, not yet. Possibility, in the final analysis, is unreal.

The cosmogonic dimension characteristic of the novel up to Proust, the causal or imaginary concatenation of events, and the use of memory (as in Baudelaire) all collapse in Kafka. The novel appears to be simply a "fragment of an analysis," (p. 115–120) but a fragment all the same, not the resolved analysis of Poe or the successful game of Mallarmé. The Kafkan novel is an equation begun elsewhere and subsequently broken off. What we see is perfectly logical; his language is utterly objective—but we can know neither its premises nor the solution.

Bense is therefore correct when he sees Kafka as one who gives coherent expression, within the avant-gardes, to the reduction of the object to language, to form—one who completes the process of the mathematization of being, from *Sein* to *Dasein*, from nature to the *künstliche Sphäre* (the realm of the artificial) (pp. 90ff.).

But Bense does not see the original conditions that alone permit Kafka to express this "art" as "signifying-structure," as *Form des Discours*. Bense presents in directly apologetic terms what in the negative thought of Kafka is despair and alienation. Bense obscures the essential fact that Kafka might very well be the definitive embodiment of the Vergeistigung, precisely because he expresses its fundamental contradictoriness and lets it speak openly in all its misery—because he sees the all-powerful structure of the sign as alienation, and the comprehensive logic of the system (though it is obvious since neither illusion nor utopia exists, and we know that language cannot go beyond it), as grounded in the *use* of this alienation.

Thus what we find in Kafka is not the neutral sign of technological art suggested by Bense's aesthetics, but rather the desperate sign of difference and contradiction. The acceptance of the new physico-technological rationality obscures the Kafkan inability to do otherwise; it tends to assign a character of choice and free decision to what in Kafka is the ascendancy, existing before all will or words, of alienated relations. Bense posits a synthesis between the theory of the negative and the analytical positivity characteristic of the system, the positive functionality of analysis within the system. Of course, this use of the negative

Dialectics of Negative and Metropolis

is inscribed in the system's logic, in its destiny. Benjamin is well aware of this, if indirectly.[14] And all of the negative's despair is a despair of this known outcome. But precisely where this position made it possible to perceive that the entire Vergeistigung was in the end grounded on the necessity of contradiction—and where this awareness, however impotent, ineffectual, and even silent, revealed a point of suspension and rendered impossible the affirmation of any future whatsoever (whether for K. or for the Castle)—Bense presents the contradiction as resolved, the suspension as simple methodological doubt, and the solution as implicit in the mechanism and in the correct use of the "whole machine."

On the Nature and Form of the Essay

A Letter to Leo Popper

My friend.

THE ESSAYS intended for inclusion in this book lie before me and I ask myself whether one is entitled to publish such works—whether such works can give rise to a new unity, a book. For the point at issue for us now is not what these essays can offer as "studies in literary history", but whether there is something in them that makes them a new literary form of its own, and whether the principle that makes them such is the same in each one. What is this unity—if unity there is? I make no attempt to formulate it because it is not I nor my book that should be the subject under discussion here. The question before us is a more important, more general one. It is the question whether such a unity is possible. To what extent have the really great writings which belong to this category been given literary form, and to what extent is this form of theirs an independent one? To what extent do the standpoint of such a work and the form given to this standpoint lift it out of the sphere of science and place it at the side of the arts, yet without blurring the frontiers of either? To what extent do they endow the work with the force necessary for a conceptual re-ordering of life, and yet distinguish it from the icy, final perfection of philosophy? That is the only profound apology to be made for such writings, as well as the only profound criticism to be addressed to them; for they are measured first and foremost by the yardstick of these questions, and the determining of such an objective will be the first step towards showing how far they fall short of attaining it.

The critique, the essay—call it provisionally what you will—as a work of art, a genre? I know you think the question tedious; you feel that all the arguments for and against have been exhausted long ago. Wilde and Kerr merely made familiar to everyone a truth that was already known to the German Romantics, a truth whose ultimate meaning the Greeks and Romans felt, quite unconsciously, to be self-evident: that criticism is an art and not a science. Yet I believe—and it is for this reason alone that I venture to importune you with these observations—that all the discussions have barely touched upon the essence of the real question: what is an essay? What is

1

5. Essay and Tragedy

The terms into which Simmel translates the difference exposed by the negative would later remain typical of the culture of "late Europe." The problem of negative thought becomes that of the relation between the realm of life and the realm of forms. It is within this relation that the effort is made to reduce the difference between sign and thing, as well as the ineffectuality of the sign and the aporiae of its "reason." In reality, the contradiction between form and life only emphasizes the fact that contemporary existence eschews a transcendental structure of thought: the breakdown of the given equilbria, the phenomenon of innovation, the category of the "leap," all become constitutive and essential elements of life as a *dynamic,* beyond any possible a priori synthesis. And all this happens at a fundamental moment in the restructuration of bourgeois thought, where such thought tries to keep up with the new dimension that the productive and social processes are assuming. It discovers that not only do Kantian formal categories prove to be constitutionally static and hence inapplicable at this level, but the Hegelian dialectic itself can no longer prevail over the concrete substance, the emergence of real contradictions that now constitute this life. To treat the relation between form and life as problematic implies an awareness of this crisis, but from a perspective that already in itself attempts to formulate a resolution in traditional terms. If the problem lies in the fact that life as dynamic shatters the former equilibrium between thought and reality, then it will be necessary to discover and define new forms of categorization proper to this dynamic, forms that derive directly from life as a dynamic and that are intrinsic to it. With the problem put in the terms of life-form, there can only be one task or commitment to be fulfilled: that of reestablishing the forms of this life—a task proper to *Philosophie als Kultur.*

This illusory perspective, however, is possible only if one continues to think of form in its traditional sense, as something defined and ruled by thought, and treated in accordance with the pure perspectives of value and duty. But once the process of formalization *within* the thing itself—or, if you will, the process of the universalization of subjectivity—has been postulated, as is precisely the case with negative thought, then the Simmelian contradiction can only appear to be either overcome before it has even been formulated, or ideologically aimed at reestablishing form on the "privilege" of thought, in the domain of the subject.

In other words, the very postulation of the contradiction between the terms "life" and "form" implies, unambiguously, a specific will for synthesis in the traditional terms of Kultur. Even though this contradiction may be developed and explained in an apparently "tragic" manner, it must in any case remain trapped

Dialectics of Negative and Metropolis

within this position and fundamental aim—especially since this contradiction, as such, directly obscures the source of the real despair of the negative: that the contradiction between form and life no longer exists, that the multiplicity of this life is condemned to the Verstand, that shock is language, madness a sign, love a repetition. To posit contradiction here is thus to seek to liberate form once again, to make it once again autonomous with respect to life and hence superior to it, at least potentially, as a privileged instrument of understanding and action. Thus this contradiction is actually a liberation from the burden of the despair posited by the negative—and, as we shall see, it is a *consolation*.

In this general discussion, however, a fundamental distinction should be made in regard to Simmel: in the early stages of his thought, he explicitly adopts the synthetical perspective of the contradiction between form and life; in historical inquiry as well as in the theoretical field, he insists on the possibility of overcoming the problem. In a later, much briefer stage, whose only result was probably *The Conflict of Modern Culture* (1918), Simmel, while not abandoning the terms of his previous analysis and for this reason remaining ever distant from negative thought, sees the impossibility of the earlier synthesis as a "demystification," and therefore indirectly sees also the reactionary-ideological nature of the "nostalgia" that posited such a synthesis. The terms that were supposed to function toward synthesis are here trapped within themselves and analyzed in their perfect ineffectuality. They are in fact still "etymologically" charged with *Sehnsucht* (longing), with hope, and with consolation, yet they are inserted into a context of total demystification, total disenchantment.

The profound difference that sets Simmel apart from the various philosophers of value lies precisely in this critical awareness preventing him from drawing any sort of synthetic-transcendental conclusion from the ideology of the contradiction between form and life. Simmel's true prominence in the German philosophical environment of the first two decades of the twentieth century lies paradoxically in the *illogic* of his conclusions: there can be no question that from the contradiction between form and life, one can only draw conclusions that synthesize

Essay and Tragedy

69

new transcendental forms and a new transcendental logic—but Simmel's inability or unwillingness to do so can only mean, objectively, that he has intuited that the original contradiction presents itself in completely different terms and that it is completely alien to the rules that have until now determined the relation between subject and object, thought and reality.

The great myth of Simmel's first period is Goethe. Simmel was the first to present a unified image of him, whose fundamental features would endure at least until Meinecke's *The Origins of Historicism.* [1] And Lukacs himself was anything but immune to this illusion.[2] Wilhelm Dilthey had provided the premises of this process of mythification, on the one hand with his general interpretation of the eighteenth century, and on the other with his works specifically on Goethe.[3] He sees the entire eighteenth century as the formation of *Individualität* within and beyond Enlightenment analytics. Goethe is the individual who has in time become his own law, a perfect and self-contained autonomy— an Erlebnis become *Dichtung,* an existential multiplicity ruled by measure and by the "rhythm" of subjectivity.

Goethe is the *organism* that at last finds Kultur modern— it is no longer mere duty disembodied, but a synthesis of the part and the whole, of sensibility and reason, of being and duty.[4] All of Goethe takes on this symbolic value: in every instance of his work "lives the God," at every moment "one is at home." Goethe's theoretical supremacy over the contradictions of Enlightenment thought, his awareness of the contradictory-negative character of bourgeois-capitalist growth and the general problems that this creates for cultural forms, is stood on its head in the notion of a realized synthesis, a resolved contradiction, a negative that has been overcome. It is as though the introductory dialogues of *Elective Affinities* really described a spiritually resolved situation, where action and reaction, aggregation and disaggregation, obey rationally planned and controlled laws. The failure of synthesis is totally cast aside in the interpretations of Goethe given by Dilthey, Simmel, and Meinecke. According to them, Goethe is the one who finds at once problem and solution, question and answer, lack and fulfillment.

This Goethe is the foundation of the form-life contradiction itself, the general import of which I described above. He is the

Dialectics of Negative and Metropolis

life that, in its longing, destroys the former stasis of the spirit, but at the same time finds new forms in which to represent itself fully; he is the new synthesis of form and life required and sought by the contradiction itself, a synthesis indeed presupposed by the contradiction itself. By this logic, Goethe is one who averts the tragedy of the negative, and not, as in certain pages of Kafka's diary, one who singled out its causes and contradictions.[5] But what is of interest to us here are the consequences that result from such an interpretation of the historical moment expressed by Goethe.

Although Goethe symbolizes the Individualität that subsumes circumstance and universal law, this synthesis is no longer the same a priori, purely rational stasis as before, but a synthesis determined by and manifested in the tangible concreteness of Erlebnis, a synthesis that occurs in life as it is experienced and seen: *Erlebnis und Lebensanschauung* (lived experience and life perspective). Thus Goethe serves not only as historical myth, but as a solution to the present aporiae: he represents precisely that dynamic form, the premise of that transcendence of becoming and of life, that is posited by the same contradiction between form and life. And herein lies the functionality, the usefulness of this interpretation of Goethe—as well as the reason behind this interpretation's mystifying character. It understands Goethe from the perspective of the Schillerian utopia, and hence from a perspective that Goethe himself had thrown into crisis and destroyed by the end of the eighteenth century.

This Goethe of the philosophy of life "positivizes" the longing that would otherwise risk falling into an abstract form of imperative, and overcomes the errant Romantic irony by means of a *cogito* which is no longer that of pure thought, but that of the intellect united with sensibility—a cogito of the intellect that lives and in living takes form, becomes, transforms its context—a cogito that is *effective*. This Goethe is therefore also the basis from which to begin the reestablishment of that duty that the negative had radically denied. With form restored—as form-life together and no longer as pure instrument of the cogito—we should then possess the means to posit ends and values to be achieved; and we should possess once again the means to develop our existence on the basis of the superiority

Essay and Tragedy

of our being as subjects. But where Goethe poses questions, he posits anguish: where is this synthesis between life and form, between existence and law, between inquiry and solution?—This interpretation asserts that there is a solution to the contradiction; where Goethe posits the crisis of the past syntheses (from that of the Enlightenment to that of Kant to even that of early Romanticism), this interpretation provides the new answer: the positivization of Goethe, his consolation, his "repose". The repose that Goethe could find only by constructing a public image is here treated as theory, as critique, as the cornerstone of the new Lebensanschauung.

Goethe thus "functions" as the recuperation of the "subject of thought" within the historic conditions contemporaneous with life as dynamic. Rather than representing the first formidable problematicization of Kultur (as is in fact the case), Goethe here becomes the model and foundation for Kultur. He answers in full to the contradictions set up by Philosophie starting with Dilthey and Simmel: without Goethe, the thread between form and life breaks.

Goethe is the bridge, the door, the window of this connection. He is the duty of the synthesis that is the direct result of the contradiction but at the same time the goal of this duty. *Sollen* (duty) has finally a purpose, defined as it is inscribed in Erlebnis. Its object is no longer the "never-given," but the reactualization of a given, of a historical experience. Although Goethe is thus mythified—inasmuch as the image presented here represents an ideological resolution of the problematics he embodies—the function served by this interpretation is anything but mythical: on the contrary, it is a question of inscribing Sollen into history, of insinuating the synthetical teleology of thought into the ambit of real possibilities. Simmel even goes so far as to attempt to force negative thought into this schema, by once again interpreting its difference as the difference between form and life and hence seeing it entirely as Sehnsucht, as a longing for the reestablishment of form, duty, and value.[6] According to this perspective, the negative is such because it is powerless to attain the synthesis that Simmel posits on the basis of the "symbolism" of Goethe's life—and not because it is in fact the negation of such a plan of synthesis.

Dialectics of Negative and Metropolis

But the entrapment of the contradiction, by means of which Simmel elaborates his inquiry, in itself shows how Goethe's assimilation and his search for synthesis appeared in his own mind as completely sui generis phenomena. Even while remaining within the limits of the contradiction between form and life, he without question understood the contradiction in its most radical sense.

If the duty is to rediscover the form of life and of life's dynamic, then this life must be understood precisely in its most fundamental sense, that is, in all of its primary manifestations. It is the multiplicity of existence, the variety of its modes of being, and even its contradictoriness, that must be formally systematized. The reduction to form cannot be understood on the basis of an estimated impoverishment of directly lived experience in its immediate features. If there is a form to life, then there must also be a form to the Nervenleben and to the tiniest irrelevancies that make up everyday life. The two terms must initially be placed at the greatest possible distance from one another, so that the eventual synthesis of life and form will have an effective meaning. This schema renders any continuation of the analysis problematic. The task of fully exhausting the meaning of the multiplicity, of mastering its particular value, so that the general synthesis can be realized concretely and not mythically, necessitates a perpetual postponement. The synthesis is turned into a regulative end that lays the groundwork for the method of concrete analysis, but it is never a concrete part of this analysis, nor can it ever be concretely verified. Moreover, the direct assertion of such an end or of such a method almost always assumes the form of a *petitio principii*. Nor can this contradiction be resolved: if life is understood as this actual life, as the Nervenleben of the Metropolis, then the radical conclusions that can be drawn from it are those of the negative; then the life-form contradiction should be abandoned and the entire structure of the philosophy of values brought tumbling down.

It is not possible, without contradicting oneself, to follow the negative for only a short spell and then to use it to re-establish a transcendental form of subjectivity. This form can be applied only where this life is reduced to its categorical and cultural elements. In other words, the despair of the later Simmel, the

Essay and Tragedy

Simmel of the *Conflict,* is already implicit in the way in which he treats the contradiction of form and life, and in the way he consequently relates to the German philosophy of his time. And here, precisely, lies his exceptionality, in wanting to define synthesis in terms that are not schematized, not imagined from the start. Hence, his investigation is in fact constantly divided between the simple assertion of the duty of synthesis and the hopeless analysis, the circular wanderings through the "forest of givens," with no issue in sight. This forest offers only postponements, and barely comprehensible ones at that. The sought-after synthesis appears there at moments, but without ever speaking. Such moments are the first visible *Holzwege* (paths), but there are no woodsmen around who might know which one to take.

In his important essay on Simmel, Lukacs seems to have grasped this problem. For Lukacs, Simmel's limitation lies in "the lack of a center, in an inability to reach final and definitive verdicts."[7] Simmel was indeed the first to render transparent the relations between the things and the facts of everyday life—but he never succeeded in extending this process to their essential form. Thus he remains an *Übergangsphilosoph.* Lukacs outlines the actual historic situation of Simmel's thought (though in terms that leave no doubt as to what should have been, even then, the focus of his research: the definition of categories capable of com-prehending life—in fact, Lukacs goes so far as to speak of deficiency in regard to the greater critical and self-critical merits of Simmel's philosophy), and attempts to give it a general definition: Simmel, for Lukacs, is the philosopher of Impressionism. "Impressionism feels and judges the great, solid, eternal Forms to be a violent menace to life, to its domain, to the multiplicity of tones, to its fullness, to its polyphony;" but with this, "the very essence of Form has become problematic." Indeed, form must now cease to be "self-contained, self-controlled, and perfectly whole." But if this happens, does not the very idea of form cease to exist? "A Form that serves life, that is open to it, cannot be a given." If what is valued is the polyphony of life, how can the concept of form be recuperated? If life is maintained to be an *effective* value, how can form have any effect? Impressionism seems condemned to an Erlebnis that is not yet Dichtung, or to a Metropolitan Nervenleben that is not

Dialectics of Negative and Metropolis

yet Verstand. Although Simmel remains within this contradiction, Lukacs goes on to outline its broader perspective. In spite of their "unending problematics, new, eternal and ineradicable values are developed in the works of the great impressionists." Impressionism opposes those forms that want to rigidify the flow of life in all its richness, that petrify the apperception of life, that "reduce" life purely and simply. Impressionism shatters static form, but it does so in order to recuperate form as gestalt, as form in the apperception of life, form in Erlebnis.

There can be no doubt that Simmel also shares this tendency: "to prepare a new Classicism that will eternalize the richness of life by putting it into new, solid, exact but all-inclusive Forms"; but it is also just as certain that this tendency cannot be consistently inferred from the way in which Simmel sets up the initial contradiction. Having posited life without any schemas whatsoever, without translating it into "images," Simmel can only be, in fact, part of the transition—constantly tending, of course, towards the new Classical, but constantly pushed back by every possible realization of this duty, into, precisely, the pure form of Sollen. Simmel is, then, a Monet, but one who can never be followed by a Cézanne, and it is useless for him to expect this.[8] But his "preparing" the classical in a perfectly ineffectual manner is not a failing, but rather the culmination of his critique— it means that he has tested the synthetico-historicist ideology of values to the point of his own crisis, that he questioned it in precisely the area where it was incapable of providing an answer. Implicit in all this is the demystification—indirect but nevertheless objective and decisive—of his own synthesis. It is thus Lukacs, if you will, who is "deficient" in his essay on Simmel. He sees perfectly well that Simmel is the philosopher of form become completely problematic, but he also interprets this situation as a resolvable one, precisely where the concrete method with which Simmel confronts it proves instead its very irresolvibility. And this Simmel demonstrates even before the matter becomes clear in the *Conflict,* where the ineffectuality of duty with regard to form, and the maximum formalization of the latter (although within a still-ethical context), prevent it from having any relation to life.

A certain sense of tragedy constantly underlies this situation of

Essay and Tragedy

Simmelian impressionism—a radical impressionism, inasmuch as it is restricted to transition, aimed toward synthesis and the development of form by *Lebendigkeit* (vitality), and prevented from achieving this because of its very premises and the conditions it imposes on the process. The ineffectuality of duty and the impossibility of the goal make necessary a repetition of the problem which, as such, comes to manifest itself as a tragic situation.

But this tragic situation is a drastic reduction of the idea of tragedy predominant in Nietzsche and Goethe. In Goethe, the tragedy is the impossible utopia of the artistic representation's total ascendancy over modern social relations. The unredeemable immanence of the Bildung, which becomes the principal structure of the bourgeois novel, can be overcome only through the consciousness of destiny that is tragedy. And what would be overcome in this case are all the contents and elements that make up the Bildung: the moral imperative that, directly or indirectly, acts as its motivating force; the ethical and aesthetic judgments that measure and interrelate its various levels and justify their value; the dominant perspective of subjectivity, of the subject of thought, which is always the work's true protagonist. Having developed a tragic subject in the form of the novel, at the cost of forever confusing the two realms and forever relinquishing the possibility, even in utopia, of liberating tragedy, is perhaps the highest, most problematic and complex achievement of Goethe's oeuvre. Hölderlin, too, was taken in by similar aporiae. But only with Nietzsche is the utopia of tragedy defined in full and its radically alternative nature contrasted with the cultural and artistic forms of the time. In Nietzsche, tragedy as *theory of utopia*, as a direct and perfectly whole vision of the contradictions and unresolved problematics of life, is set in opposition to the art of the Bildung and subjectivity, to the "dialectical" art of the clash-assimilation in the world. And perhaps even more radical is tragedy's opposition to the argument of the form-life contradiction, which is the basis of this art.

Experience and tragic poetry lie completely outside of this contradiction. As we have seen, this contradiction is posited on the basis of its resolvability—and if it happens that it cannot in fact be resolved, it is the ethical forms of duty that are assumed as the result and value of the process. But that is not all: the very movement of this contradiction is from life toward form. The truth that it projects or determines is still that of thought's dominion over being. The truth that Nietzsche speaks of as the basis of tragedy arises and unfolds as an explicit struggle against such conditions. Truth is the negation of substance as subject. Truth is the emergence, the speaking, of substance as it is. But this substance is not in any way form, the product of thought functioning for its domination over being; it is not a category, but life itself, as it is given, in all its contradictions, its struggles, its sameness of contradiction and destruction. Within it, there are no different levels such as appearance and substance, contingency and necessity. There is no categorical separation between existence and essence. Tragedy lets life speak as an indivisible unity; it is the negation of the reduction of life to form, and thus the negation of the very difference thought to exist between them; it is a representation of necessity as all, as given in the text of the world. Sehnsucht does not exist in this tragedy—nor, therefore, do Bildung, search, nor becoming—all relations are directly given. But not given in a calculation or a category, but as life, as nature—as destiny.[9]

Lukacs's 1910 essay, *The Metaphysics of Tragedy*, [10] although it attempts to draw radical conclusions from Simmel's premises, falls far short of doing so and does not even approach Nietzsche's negative. When Lukacs speaks of the disappearance of all existential relations, the elimination of all "atmospheric elements," the "sharp mountain breeze," as the substance of tragedy, he is actually radicalizing the form of the *Trauerspiel*, [11] and he does not even touch upon the truly negative utopia of Nietzschean tragedy. His understanding of tragedy as the pure form of essence, as the life of essence, constitutes a direct response to the historicist-Simmelian problem of the synthesis between form and life as the goal of duty, the fulfillment of the Sehnsucht—it implies a conception of tragedy as the structure of this synthesis—but it is a betrayal of the Nietzschean perspective, an abandonment of the real problem of tragedy as it had first emerged in Schiller and Goethe and was later developed by Hölderlin and presented in all its negativity by Nietzsche. The problem, indeed the object, is not to imagine essence, but

Essay and Tragedy

to destroy its entire history and tradition. Lukacs does not venture beyond the reductive conception of the tragic. Nietzsche makes tragedy the instrument of the negation of reduction as the basic method of Western thought. The object is to destroy all ontological stratification of life and to rediscover it whole as substance, to let it speak, without seeking to reconcile it with the subject, with thought, or with Sehnsucht. The problem of tragedy is that of representing the fact of the inviolability of sameness.

From this perspective, there is no tragedy of essence or of form, but, on the contrary, the tragedy of life as destiny—as a destiny that does not represent a categorical reduction of life, but life itself as it is given, in all of its fullness, in all of its energy. Lukacs, in the manner of Simmel, postulates a Trauerspiel of form in opposition to the sentimental or historical Trauerspiel, the bourgeois-Enlightenment Trauerspiel. Paul Ernst, regardless of the artistic merits of his work, expresses this opposition perfectly. Lukacs' choice of him as an example is by no means accidental. All of Ernst can be seen as an illustration of the Lukacsian motto: "Naked souls converse alone with naked destinies." [12] Here tragedy consists entirely of aura, despoilment and reduction of all life, with life understood as "dross." The "summits" and the "irresponsibility" of the Nietzschean milieux, on the other hand, indicate that we have arrived at the point where life no longer permits syntheses or escapes; that we have arrived at the destructive power of life—and hence at the negation of aura, at the postulation of the insuperable negativity of life.

Of course it is clear that in this light, this form, and this life of essence cease to have any relation to the radical character of the Erlebnis as it is presented in Simmel (and Lukacs). And the contradiction between form and life remains. But it is the focus and the direction of the inquiry that completely distinguishes this notion of tragedy from Nietzsche's—and that makes it only Trauerspiel. The contradiction that one is left with at the end of this inquiry is hence a contradiction of Kultur and its "will to survive," and definitely not an attack on, or a destruction of, its premises, its tradition, nor its goals. Simmelian tragedy ends with the same failure with which Nietzschean tragedy begins. Neither Ernst himself, nor the impossibility of his ideas—which

Dialectics of Negative and Metropolis

Lukacs, however indirectly, comes to prove—have anything to do with the theory of the negative.

However, there is an important, if not always explicit, difference between Simmel and Lukacs. Though Lukacs defines tragedy as the contradiction of form and life and as the attainment of the life of essence, he keeps closely to the problematic arising from this position and does not compromise it with edifying ethical considerations. If the relation remains problematical, this does not mean that the human mind is always and happily productive, but that its "productivity" falls short, or rather that man is compelled to produce. If the synthesis is totally problematical, this does not attest to our profundity and richness, but to our endless misery and indigence.[13] Although his terms remain those of the philosophy of values and he still considers tragedy a possible overcoming of their aporiae, Lukacs's intention is to test the effectuality of such a perspective at the limits, to cover all of experience, without compromises or schemas of any sort. Seen as a whole, Simmel's argument seems much more malleable. The notion of consolation plays an important role, especially in his later works, where the burden of the contradiction between form and life makes itself felt more acutely in its radical irresolvability. But all of his philosophy can be seen as falling within the perspective of "consoled tragedy." To posit tragedy in the terms that we have just analyzed is already in itself a desire for consolation. Lukacs himself, objectively speaking, seeks it, even if in the end he makes an effort to renounce it (whence originate the gravely mistaken conclusions about his connection with Nietzsche). This is evident in the fact that such consolation emerges when the forms of duty, of intersubjective relationships, and of Sehnsucht are thrown, as contents, into the void between the two terms of the contradiction. To fill this void is to seek consolation for tragedy, even though what we are really dealing with here is Trauerspiel. Moreover, only Trauerspiel is consolable. Tragedy has no need to renounce consolation, its world is not that of *Trost* (consolation): it knows of no contradictions to resolve, no voids to fill—its life is all. Trost arises where there is becoming, where there is a subject that decides, where alternatives exist, where necessity acts together with thought—or rather, where thought rules being or has the

Essay and Tragedy

possibility of ruling being. Trost arises where indecision, fault, and error are possible. Hence, it must be of an ethical character. After man discovers the contradiction, he discovers its universality, and feels "sympathy". The ethics of intersubjectivity is born out of the sharing of the common burden of contradiction. *"Der Mensch ist ein trostsuchendes Wesen"* (Man is a creature that seeks consolation).[14] Note well that consolation is not help (*Hilfe*)—but ethical sympathy, human solidarity. "Man cannot help himself," since there is no one who can make his fellow man overcome the contradiction that is everyone's.[15] Tragedy is hence not resolvable but consolable. But in all of this we can see an ancient Christian pessimism blended with certain suggestions of Schopenhauer: the whole conspires towards an explicit negation of the foundations of Nietzsche's argument. This Trauerspiel is the alternative to Nietzsche, in that it usefully implements some of its themes and goes along with the negative, as we saw earlier, for only a spell. Consolation in this way brings the tragic experience back to ethical duty, brings the solitude of the tragic hero back to the community, and the totally demystified theory of the negative back to the aura of the ideology of the Metropolis.

But what is the form of the "consoled tragedy"? What is the form of this contradiction that constantly repeats and surpasses itself within the ethical perspective of Trost, in an ineffectual Sehnsucht? How might the problematic of the life-form relation be expressed in authentic and original terms (that is, in such a way as to reflect even the aporiae and the ideological charge that our critique has assigned to it)? In connection with this we should point out that Lukacs's idea of the essay, which one finds developed in the letter to Leo Popper introducing *Forms and the Soul*, has its origins in Simmel.[16] Simmel does not confront the problem of the essence and the form of the modern essay as a specific theme, but he provides its first basic model in *Bridge and Door,* which antedates the Lukacs letter by seven years.[17] The inseparable connection between *Trennung* and *Verbindung* (separation and connection), *Lösen* and *Binden* (loosening and binding) is the theme of the essay. The disintegration of unity and the reunification of opposites, the constant self-declaration of the elements as united or divided, find their form in the essay.

Dialectics of Negative and Metropolis

The bridge and the door are only symbols of this dynamic of the contradiction between form and life, since this, after all, is what is at stake. The immediacy of life presents a place, two places, with a "forest" in between—the will to connection makes its imprint on this void, on the intermediary road. The will to connection becomes form in the road, it transforms life into form; but it also turns into form the mere movement initially necessary to cover the distance. This movement has become solid form; it has become value. In this way, the essay unifies the various shocks of immediate experience, brings their tones, their polyphony back within a framework, and discovers or lays down the road that takes them back: "the simple dynamic of movement . . . has become something visibly long-lasting" (pp. 2–3). The "natural" contradictions, "the passive opposition of the separateness between elements in space," (p. 2) are reconciled and overcome by our Bridge-form. Thus the essay not only opens roads "over solid matter," but unifies what is really divided by the void. It aims to prove that Trennen and Verbinden "are just two sides of one and the same action" (p. 3). To measure a fragment of space, to illustrate it, and to set it up as a limit, is thus to give form to the uninterrupted unity of being, to articulate it according to a meaning, according to a value.

The essay also works in the following manner: in the part, in the "seperate," it sees the self-contained unity through which it may penetrate into the whole and command an overview of the entirety. In sum, the essence and the form of the essay is: to give form to movement, to "imagine" the dynamic of life, to unite what is divided within our own ends by means of precise teleological structures, and to distinguish what is directly given as uninterrupted unity, such as space, time, and natural being.

The form of the essay functions toward the re-proposition of the plan for synthesis. But now the problem is that of defining the synthesis *of* life itself; which is not pure transcendental synthesis, but a synthesis sought within the actual dynamic of the elements of life. The essay seems to provide an answer to the painful question: is there a form to life, is there a form into which life, in its sensible visibility, consolidates as solid creation, as real Dichtung? The essay is the final appearance of the ideology of synthesis, the final attempt to refute the negative,

Essay and Tragedy

to refute contradiction as negativity. Of course, the Sehnsucht remains after this synthesis: unity breaks apart and this rupture can find only indefinite resolution.

The Sehnsucht, therefore, is not negated. The mystification enacted by the essay does not lie in such negation, but rather in the fact that it transforms what originally presented itself as a radical problematic—the very contradiction between form and life—into a principle of synthesis, a value. The contradiction, thus reduced to the perpetual succession of Binden and Lösen, finds itself entirely dominated by the teleology of thought and its quest. Thought can always construct a door to define the limits of its home and hence, at the same time, a perspective from which to measure being, and in conformity with which to build its own roads and bridges. At this point, the Sehnsucht itself is reduced, by virtue of the problematical status of an impossible quest, to a will to make and construct according to its own forms and powers. The essay in this way emerges as tragedy's most radical consolation.

If Simmel's *Bridge and Door* concludes with the image of the rush toward freedom by those who have created their own door, thus internalizing once again all contradictions and all limits (and his essay on the Metropolis, as we have seen, ended in much the same way, with the overthrow of the abstract dominion of the Verstand leading to the growth of individuality, freedom, and equality), the framework is not much different in Lukacs's "On the Nature and Form of the Essay: A Letter to Leo Popper."

Lukacs's point of departure might at first appear quite different from Simmel's. The essay, for Lukacs, deals with the multiplicity of forms and moves toward life. "It is true that the essay strives for truth: but just as Saul went out to look for his father's she-asses and found a kingdom, so the essayist, who is really capable of looking for the truth, will find at the end of his road the goal he was looking for: life."[18] The essayist cannot reduce the multiplicity of forms, provided by the works of others and by his own knowledge, to the "essence of things," to Truth; he can only illustrate life by traveling through it. In Lukacs, every element of the essay is treated as a clue to this voyage, and hence it would appear that the essay form itself must embody a general problematic. The essay supposedly posits the unrepresentability of

Dialectics of Negative and Metropolis

substance. Its grasp of life would then be indicative of the impossibility of using forms in any transcendental manner or toward the comprehension of being. "When something has once become problematic—and the way of thinking that we speak of, and its way of expression, have not become problematic but have always been so, then salvation can only come from accentuating the problems to the maximum degree, from going radically to its root" (p. 15). There is no doubt that Lukacs's reconsideration of the Simmelian form of the essay is problematical: the very fact that he begins his inquiry by positing forms as multiple and as totally homogeneous with the multiplicity of life—and thereby dissolves their transcendental function—is proof enough of this. But this does not constitute a radical change of perspective.

A Simmelian Sehnsucht also dominates Lukacs's essay. The terms of the inquiry have not changed. If anything, a radicalization of Simmel's original problematic demands a synthesis in even more explicit and defined terms. In Lukacs, the essay's plunge into the multiplicity of forms and hence into life, cannot be separated from the Sehnsucht that this very act awakens: a flight from the "relative and the inessential" (p. 44). Hence, immediate life remains, as in Simmel, relative and inessential—and it is clear that where there is the relative, there is also the substantial, and where there is the inessential, there must be essence. Life here is still expressed in terms opposed to the tragedy of the negative.

And life here is still the counterpart of form, in search of consolation. Of course, synthesis can no longer exist, as in Simmel, within the essay form itself; the essay itself can no longer serve as the sought-for synthesis. In Lukacs, it "roams" through multiplicity and is definitely not an instrument that unifies and divides, that "imagines" multiplicity and safeguards against the inessential. But by this very fact, it keeps to the Simmelian perspective; it may reject Simmel's solution, but certainly not the problem itself, nor the Sehnsucht. For Lukacs the essay becomes the sheer idea of synthesis, its categorical imperative. In revolving around multiplicity, without a solution, it constantly refers to the form that might comprehend it. In its very misery, it always describes the happy days to come.

But there is more: this essay gathers materials for this synthe-

Essay and Tragedy

sis, toward this end. It functions, as it were, as a kind of schema, a preliminary organization, still in time, of the phenomena that form will later comprehend totally. It matters little whether this end is considered more or less attainable. In any case, it is clear that this end functions as a regulative idea. And it is clear that the essay itself could not stand without the Sehnsucht emanating from this idea and for this idea. "The essayist is a Schopenhauer who writes his *Parerga* while waiting for the arrival of his own (or another's) *World as Will and Idea,* he is a John the Baptist." [19] The essay thus moves entirely in the direction of synthesis, toward a system. Its internal problematicity tends and functions entirely towards surpassing itself. If the essay, as such, finds itself to be impotent, it certainly does not find its idea of synthesis to be ineffectual; in other words, it does not critique, much less dissolve, the idea of synthesis or the contradiction of form and life aimed at the affirmation of form.

The death of the essay, or more precisely its impotence, is not of course the death of value. Here the death of the inessential and the apparent does not eliminate, as in Nietzsche, the essential and the substantial as well; quite the contrary, "this Sehnsucht for value and form, order and purpose does not end, as does everything else, after it disappears and becomes a pretentious tautology" (p. 46). The end of the essay comes with the actualization of the value that it proclaimed and anticipated. Moreover, if in the end there should be such an actualization, then the road that the essay has traversed will also be salvaged. This road is no longer mere inessentiality, mere impotence. In itself nothing, the essay finds its whole reality in the synthesis that could not exist without the essay and its schema: "the end is unthinkable and unattainable if the process is not carried out in a new manner." "The essay thus justifies itself as a necessary means for the attainment of the ultimate goal" (p. 46): and this goal is the system, *The World as Will and Idea* that follows the *Parerga,* the "great aesthetic" that will follow the "freshness of impressionism" (p. 46).

Hence, what had initially appeared to be a treatment of Simmel's argument as problematical proves, at this point, to function toward an even more complete recuperation of the Kultur

Dialectics of Negative and Metropolis

of synthesis. In seeking such Kultur exclusively in the form of the essay, Simmel "trapped" the problem of synthesis, negating the very possibility of the idea of a system. In Lukacs, on the other hand, this idea governs the Sehnsucht itself. Where Simmel's duty is forced into a hopeless resignation of the formalization of the inessential, Lukacs still proposes a duty of the substantial, a tending toward an effective imperative. Hence, by this token not only is the perspective of duty-value reintroduced in full, but it is done in positive terms. The essay is not the sentence itself, but an implementation of the process of judgment; it is not the system itself, but it anticipates it by necessity (and in this way escapes being transitory);[20] it does not embody the system, but derives it from its own Sehnsucht. Moreover, the essay is valid precisely inasmuch as it does not negate within the system its own "acquired" multiplicity, but rather, step-by-step, prefigures the system and brings it to life in the multiplicity of forms, making it grow "parallel to the pulse of Life" (p. 47)— with the effect that this essentially ethical relation between essay and system also tends to fulfill Simmel's requirement that form be a concrete form of life. In sum: the Lukacsian essay is prefiguration and anticipation, synthetical Sehnsucht, the duty of dying in order to be redeemed in the system that has already been brought to life, from the intellectual perspective of the idea, in the slow maturation of the system's dominion over the inessentiality of the forms of life. The essay is not this dominion itself, just as Kantian duty is not holiness, but rather expresses its idea, sets in motion its duty, and begins the reduction of life to substance.

This notion of the essay never frees itself, in its substance, from the form and contents of Simmel's notion, nor does it even come close to the negative. Nothing could be more mistaken than to confuse it with the Nietzschean aphorism.[21] The aphorism is a line from a tragedy, the essay a fragment of an analysis. The aphorism comes after the system, and within the collapse of the *ordo-connexio* between ideas and things; the essay is the Sehnsucht for such an ordo. The Nietzschean aphorism is the word of one who proclaims the death of God; the essay is the word of the Baptist announcing His return. Moreover, as tragic quip, the

Essay and Tragedy

aphorism is also living proof of the unattainability of the utopia of authentic tragedy, since between one quip and the next, between one aphorism and the next, the Chorus is absent. The aphorism is fallen tragedy—not reduced, not consoled—but fallen into the powerlessness to explain itself as a whole, to grasp life and destiny as inextricably connected, to affirm the certitude of its own despair. Its direction is exactly the opposite of that of the essay. As affirmation of the absence of the Chorus, the aphorism explores contradiction and difference, whereas the essay is by nature analysis toward synthesis, difference toward unity, an abyss requiring a bridge. The aphorism dissolves and negates, or else it leaps by will and power; the essay ties things together and dialecticizes, or else it transforms or initiates a transition through the forms of thought. In the essay, the analysis is desired and carried out by thought—and constantly determined by its ends and hence teleologically disposed. The aphorism is an isolated quip, after the dissolution of the difference between form and life, and hence after the Sehnsucht for Sollen. Of course, the aphorism, too, is an Aufklärung; nobody felt this contradiction more deeply than Nietzsche himself. Unable to attain the status of tragedy, but rejecting any kind of Trauerspiel, the aphorism is by necessity relegated to isolated differentiation, to radical analysis.

But this is the Aufklärung characteristic of the negative: the dissolution of tradition, of the history of the ideology of the synthesis based on the subject. The Aufklärung of the essay, on the other hand, is that of the restoration of duty and value. In both cases, the intellectual structure is insurmountable: but in the first case it is experienced as an inevitable fate and in the second as an instrument of potential liberation. The importance of Simmel lies in having found a definition of contradiction that makes it possible to overcome contradiction without abandoning life in the process. Lukacs proceeds in the same direction, pointing out the shortcomings in Simmel's formal solution, but in so doing he re-establishes its value as a symbol of the intellect's potential for freedom. In both cases, there is an attempt to alter the import of Nietzschean tragedy, to assimilate it—and having done this, to move toward a new criticism, a new aesthetics, a new Kultur: toward the ultimate adventure of reason.

Dialectics of Negative and Metropolis

6. The City as Essay

The city, too, can be comprehended only in the essay form. As
the goal of metropolitan life itself proves to be the synthesis of
individuality and freedom—the rupture of community circles as
well as the emergence of the Geist—its representation falls entirely within the formal laws of the essay as we have defined it
above. The value that the city must embody—the attainment of
freedom, the effective formation of Individualität—is the same
as that of the essay: it is the Verbindung of *Bridge and Door*, the
Lukacsian angelus. With a different sort of "ponderousness,"
Scheffler was pursuing the same idea in his effort to preserve
the Gemüt of community in the Geist of the Metropolis. The
essay form "revolves" around the same crux: to seek consolation for the tragedy of the Metropolis—which Nietzsche had
already imposed as a premise—in the memory of the synthesizing form characteristic of city life. This is why the essay becomes
necessary. The search for synthetical relations, for the forms of
continuity and duration, for moments of transcrescence—the
recuperation of the individual within the social and the assertion
of idea and duty as contemporary life's horizon of meaning—
all this can only belong to the essay. The analysis of the city becomes, then, a symbol of the essay form itself. This form attains

The City as Essay

its fullest expression in such analysis and in this way fulfills its real function.

This connection—between essay and city—also finds its first representation in Simmel. In his 1898 essay on Rome,[1] the city itself is used as a demonstration and concretization of the aesthetico-philosophical principles that *Bridge and Door* and subsequent essays would clarify further. The very notion of the city here is inferred from an aesthetico-philosophical principle. The value of the city is seen in its tangible realization of gestalt. But the confirmation of the supremacy of the whole over the separate parts—the ascendancy of the perspective of the totality—comes with the synthesis of the various functions of the city. The harmony of the individual parts implies a harmony in the methods of understanding the whole. This further transition is essential to an understanding (and a chronological situation) of the discussion that was to follow—which we outlined in chapter 2.

The a priori synthesis by which Simmel understands the city is a synthesis of form and function. Practical ends are understood as form and vice-versa. The "original unity of apperception" is the original unity of value.[2] Inasmuch as the image of the city succeeds in achieving these syntheses—in embodying the supremacy of the whole over the parts, in reconciling the intellectual opposition between function and form, and in showing itself to be a divine plan—it is value.

In Simmel, the city is called upon to concretize Kantian teleological judgment. Here, the themes and key problems of neo-Kantian philosophy all reappear. The regulative idea of the harmony between reason and nature becomes an effective measure of judgment, a criterion of the city's existing structure. But this is a total reversal of the Kantian notion of tragedy: Kant's ideas are turned upside down into values of judgment, into effective ideals, which supposedly manifest themselves tangibly in the structure of the works themselves and in the life of history. And for Simmel, in the city above all. And after Simmel, for Endell, for Scheffler, and for all of "urbanistic romanticism," these principles will not change.

The reduction of the process of history to duration (*durée*) concludes Simmel's analysis of the city as essay. And this was the particular nucleus of the neo-Kantian problematic that sought the *form* of becoming. As long as the value of the city is simply the synthesis of form and function in the original apperception of its totality, the temporal dimension will remain absent—and it can at any time contradict the essayistic search for truth of which Lukacs speaks. Time, as well, must be reconciled. And for time, there must be a form. Not for Kantian time, whose tragic character it seems only Hölderlin understood. But for the time of Erleben, the time of the actual products of history. And the form of this time must be the city.

The city overcomes the negative implicit in the structure of absence characteristic of the true Kantian form of time, since it is a synthesis of actual times, and both the form and the reality of such a synthesis. The a priori form of space, first attained with the unity of form and function and the unity of the separate parts, is united with the a priori form of time: the diversity of the various epochs becomes duration—the negativity of relations is annulled—and all leaps are negated.[3] On the city's terrain the form of time is realized—and it is duration: ubiquity of the whole, synchronicity in the face of the Erleben of Individualität. And all this serves as end, value, idea. The realization of this duration (and the resultant reduction to duration of the entire dialectical relationship, which had been made to function together with the more specific problematic of Kantian gnoseology) confirms the value of the city as the realization of the teleological judgment.

To the synthesis of the parts, the synthesis of form and function, the synthesis of time in duration, Simmel's essay on Florence adds the synthesis of nature and art.[4] Here the conflict of modern Kultur seems finally resolved. The city must be thus: an overcoming of the Romantic Sehnsucht. The essay on the city is hence the Lukacsian essay itself; it is the same idea. To pursue the city is to seek those values that lead beyond Sehnsucht. The essay begins with the city, in order to go beyond it. It revolves around the object in order to perceive which of its possible tendencies and perspectives are aimed at form, at the new classical. In this manner, Simmel's essay revolves around Florence. It starts with the conditions of the divided Kultur in order to seize upon the possibility and the idea of synthesis—of an extreme

The City as Essay

synthesis, one that will crown the forms already encountered in his essay on Rome: an understanding of nature *as though* its end were a reconciliation with the Geist—and an understanding of the Geist as though its work were necessary, destined, like the products of nature.

The city lives on these organic relations: on the organic exchange between nature and spirit—between the time of the individual and his Erleben, and the time of the structure and the works of the city itself. The city is such inasmuch as it is an organism. This is the real center of Simmelian analysis, and it finally becomes explicit in "Florenz." The city can be essayistically described only because it is able to grow, through "transcrescence," from the split between nature and spirit, from the absence of Kantian forms, from the discordance between time periods, to the synthesis that we traced above through its various articulations. The city can do this and must do this. The pure form of the idea shows itself to be a *possible* utopia in the reality of Rome and Florence. The essay form could not stand for an instant without the primary consolation of a fact on which to base itself. Without a miracle to begin with, there would be no essay.

In this way, the image of the organic city appears to be the solution to the conflict of modern Kultur itself. No work could be more totally a gestalt; none could more fully give the sense of both the multiplicity of time periods and their synchronicity; none could be more closely connected to the individual Erleben; and none more fully reconciled with nature. For the subsequent aesthetics of neo-Kantian derivation, the importance of the analysis of the city lies in these above-mentioned conclusions —which will also serve as the aesthetico-philosophical foundations of the subsequent anti-Weberian sociology of the city.

In such cases, there is a decisive reversal of the bearing of the Metropolis on the idea of the city. Once again, the object of discussion ends up being the city. Simmel uses the Metropolis as his starting point: it constitutes the original situation. But its contradictions, its conflicts, its negativity, must be overcome. The essay is nothing but an expression of precisely this movement—from the Metropolis, to the image of a *given* city that overcomes metropolitan conflicts, that is, that embodies the form of synthesis, to the idea of the city as organism as an objec-

Dialectics of Negative and Metropolis

tive hope; or to the idea of the recuperation of the city as such, the idea of the *recapture* of time past. This understanding of city and Metropolis as forms between which transcrescence is possible—that is, the quest aimed at exalting, within the Metropolis itself, the characteristic values of the Erleben of the city—will become the basis of all the utopianism of *Stadtplanung* in its more profoundly regressive manifestations.[5]

Once again, we must point out the bridge between Simmel and Benjamin. If we take Benjamin's *Images of the City* (published 30 years after Simmel's piece on Rome) at face value, we can only conclude that their respective positions came to a complete convergence.[6] Benjamin's Recherche is entirely aimed at asserting the value of the synthesis of Erleben and Gemeinschaft— at demonstrating that true Erleben is possible only where the values of community assert themselves in the city as organism. There are passages in this work that seem to refer directly to Simmel, and even to Scheffler and Endell. One need only think of the symbolic value that the street, not yet emptied out, assumes here: it is the meeting place of the various Erlebnisse, it is the life of the community, at once Individualität and Humanität. Even the theme of the beauty of the city's sounds, a theme so dear to Endell, re-emerges in this context, (pp. 9, 28). The contrast between the symbolic character of the nordic Sehnsucht and the lively organicity of Mediterranean cities, typical not only of the analysis of the city but of Simmel's entire aesthetics, is fully revived by Benjamin. The North Sea is contrasted with the "Neapolitan" vision of Moscow—and the exuberance of the street, the chaos of commerce, the playful instinct is contrasted with the cleanly marked boundaries of the houses of Bergen (p. 69).

But for Benjamin, as for Simmel, it is above all the specific form assumed by time that characterizes the Erleben of the city community. The absence of an objective time is continually underscored in the image presented of Moscow: Erleben fills and transforms every hour and every day, preventing repetition. By preventing the consumption of time, it makes time duration: "every life a flash" (p. 27). The games of the streets, of commerce, the errors in procedure, subjectivize time. Individualität reappropriates time. This, at bottom, was the very goal of all neo-Kantian research: to reconcile the a priori form of time

The City as Essay

with the lived experience of the subject. Moscow, Naples, and Marseilles, all appear as examples of this "miracle," which is exactly the opposite experience of the Metropolitan blasé. Here the city serves as a negation of the monetary economy and its form, which Benjamin will later present as dominant in his essay on Paris.

Moscow, Naples, and Marseilles are unaware of Baudelaire, just as Simmel's Rome and Florence are unaware of the Metropolitan Geist. Like Simmel, Benjamin finds the epitome of Gemeinschaft in the image of Tuscany. Here the contrast with Nordic symbolism is at its most radical. Everything in San Gimignano is *homeland;* everyone is "in close touch with the land, its traditions and perhaps its divinity" (p. 66). Discordances between time periods, as well as conflicts between individuality and urban structure, are absent. Everything lives inextricably in "this overcharged reality" (p. 66). The unity of historic time and subjective time is the fundamental feature of Gemeinschaft.

That Benjamin's Recherche is here directed towards the city— and that the forms of the city as an organic community, already defined by Simmel, constitute the dominant tone—there can be no doubt. Moreover, these forms are blended together with the themes of the German sociology and anti-urban literature from the period before the First World War. This is especially clear in the essay on Moscow. The value of Gemeinschaft expressed in the image presented of Moscow is a judgment passed on the "heroic" Soviet experiment, from the Revolution to wartime communism, up to the NEP. And it is exactly the same as the "literary" judgment passed by the radical German intelligentsia: the exuberance of the streets, the chaotic variety in commerce, the Neapolitan summer—in sum, the sense of play that pervades time in Moscow—this is socialism, this is the Revolution.

The Revolution concretizes Gemeinschaft in as much as it embodies an anti-bureaucratic, anti-repetitive, and preeminently anti-Metropolitan spirit.[7] Every line of Benjamin's image of Moscow clearly reveals the presence of Lukacs's and Karl Korsch's critique, as well as that of the entire cultural tradition of this critique: from neo-Kantian Kultur to Simmel, from Tönnies to Roberto Michaels. But it is precisely at this point, where the cultural and political parameters of Benjamin's argument—that is, where the very import and function of his recuperation of Simmel—come to light, that Benjamin reverses the overall perspective of his analysis. The Moscow summer is a *childhood:* it is an absence, just like the Berlin he presents in the autobiographical essay, written after 1930, which concludes the parable of the *Images of the City* and sets the stage for *Paris, Capital of the Nineteenth Century.* This summer, this infancy, ends with the establishment of the NEP. The revolutionary game has been completed. The Russia papered over with revolutionary posters, the Russia of taverns and theaters and churches, the Russia that symbolized the *spielerische Utopie* (playful utopia) of the German radical intelligentsia, is now only *Recherche*—an object of Recherche. The miracle is over—since it has now been explained. About this explanation, Benjamin can say nothing. Benjamin's Kultur can only speak about childhood and its games. German radical Kultur knows only consummated communities.

But this is precisely what Benjamin affirms, in the real focus of his essay: to reduce the forms of Gemeinschaft to the status of memory. The Gemeinschaft is thus totally undone. Withdrawn into the word, it can only be spoken about. It was believed to exist, and yet it consumed itself. The Recherche does not, in the end, lead to the discovery of effective criteria—but to time past. No mystification of this condition can stand up any longer. The Erleben of Simmelian Individualität, the basis of philosophico-aesthetic syntheses, which dictated the direction from essay to truth taken by the Lukacs of *Soul and Form*—this Erleben no longer judges, it only searches through history. It is itself a force of the past: it inhabits the cities of the heroic age of socialism, the open skies of Tuscany, the Mediterranean communities—only to present itself completely transformed in the Paris of Baudelaire, at the origins of the Metropolis. Benjamin undoes, voids the structuring capacity and effectuality of the a priori neo-Kantian forms applied and tested by Simmel in his images of the city. He presents in fact the same argument on the city, the identical irreversible tendency towards the value of individuality and its games, that characterize the Simmelian *Übergangszeit,* but *without duration:* he presents it not in the Bergsonian form of *durée,* but in the Proustian form of the consumption of time.

The City as Essay

Proust is the real author of these *Images*. In these essays, the utopia of the city is entirely in the past tense. Benjamin's essay on Paris shows a critical awareness of, and an ability to draw conclusions from *Die Grossstädte und das Geistesleben,* and his Berlin essay shows an indentical relation with Simmel's vision of Tuscany. It is the same kind of relation that Benjamin had elucidated between Bergson and Proust. The object, of course, is always the city, but a city that one can no longer posit—whose form has irreversibly run its course. Inasmuch as he is still unable to recognize any value other than that of the urban structure synthesized with Individualität—inasmuch as the object of the analysis is still the values of Gemeinschaft—Benjamin too writes essays, essayistic images of the city. But the real center around which the essay here revolves is not the possible utopia, the objective hope of Simmel and later of Bloch. However moving the memory of Moscow may be, it is still memory. There is no room for any kind of project, on top of the ruins of the urban organism; "The places we have known do not belong only to the realm of space, which is where we situate them for the sake of facility. They are but a thin slice from the sequence of impressions that constituted our life at that time; the memory of a particular image is but the regret for a particular moment; and the houses, streets, and avenues are as fleeting, alas, as the years themselves." [8]

However, there was a moment in Simmel where the forms of the city structure did not hold up, where the image of the city came dangerously close to the style of Benjamin and Proust. The essay form assumed the absolutely problematical tone that only the Benjamin of *Elective Affinities* has been able to confer upon it successfully. In the face of Venice, every value of the city—the essay form as the path to truth, the synthesis of nature and spirit, interior and exterior, the tangible realization of the harmony of the whole—becomes useless, uncomprehending, silent.[9]

In Venice, the philosophico-aesthetic categories that appeared to represent Rome, Florence, and the entire Mediterranean as opposed to Nordic symbolism, cease to hold water. And yet in Venice, too, there is no allusion, no symbol, no Romantic Sehnsucht. Here other forms come into play, forms that definitively throw the utopia of Gemeinschaft into disorder. And these

Dialectics of Negative and Metropolis

forms are tragic forms, the very forms that the essay sought systematically to eradicate: the split between exterior and interior, the loss of the root of being, the autonomy attained by appearance. Venice has no signification. Its being-as-game indicates that it is language only. The image it presents embodies the crisis and conflict of Kultur—not its utopia or its form. Venice symbolizes the tendency that broke loose in Baudelaire's Paris, the history of which we have already traced through Benjamin: language without signifieds—a signifier—a structure of signifiers. *Hiersein* (being here) and nothing more—as is proclaimed, moreover, in the *Duino Elegies*.

Twenty years before Benjamin critically consigned all city *Erleben* to the past, Simmel had already come upon the total paradox of the city. And he had found it in the use of place in Mann, in Rilke, in Hofmannsthal, and in Nietzsche above all—as well as in Proust. Here our discussion comes full circle. In Venice the double meaning of life becomes a destiny. There is no more synthesis among the dissonances. All appearance exists in itself and for itself—a perfect mask that hides being, or rather, reveals the loss, the absence of being. Here, every instance of familiarity, every appearance of Gemeinschaft is a lie—since nothing has roots or direction. Venice is a symbol of the loss of homeland—the same radically anti-city symbol in which all of Rilke's lyrics are contained. Here Simmel and Benjamin cross paths once again, and in the work of Hofmannsthal. Indeed, Simmel's image of Venice is identical to that in *Andreas oder die Vereinigten.* [10] They present literally the same impressions. The city is masked—there can be no interlacement, no interrelations of signification. The form of the Bildungsroman is so constantly proffered and withdrawn that it becomes an expression of the absence of direction itself. There exist only movements and moments irreducible to one sense or direction. This is why Venice is the city of adventure. And Andreas's experience will be an adventure, precisely the opposite of Bildung, just as tragic form is the failure of the Bildungsroman. The same figure of adventure will return in Proust. And Aschenbach's "adventure" comes only four years after Simmel's "discovery" of Venice.

In his *Voyages,* [11] Hofmannsthal repeatedly tries to achieve a Simmelian synthesis, in individuality, of nature and spirit and

The City as Essay

of the diversity of objective historical time periods. In Greece, his despair in the face of "impossible antiquity" and the "futile quest" (pp. 279–280), seems that it could still be resolved with the miracle of reappearance, with a resurrection of the past. This duration, this continuity, these miracles, all vanish in *Andreas oder die Vereinigten,* just as Simmel's Rome and Florence are annihilated in his "Venice." The voyage has stopped reactualizing—now it divides, it reveals the absences. The metropolitan experience is born out of this original and radical difference.[12] The essay form is utterly unable to explain it. Only the language of Hiersein and of *its* adventure (which, as Benjamin explains in his discussion of Baudelaire, involves repetition), only the *theoretical* direction implicit in the Nietzschean form of the aphorism, will be able to comprehend the tragedy of this experience.

Dialectics of Negative and Metropolis

Part II

Loos
and
His
Contemporaries

7. Loosian Dialectics

The Vienna of Loos, *Loos-Wien*, is primarily important for having demolished the general ideological foundations of the German Werkbund and the Vienna *Werkstätte*. Loos's most significant essays towards this end—as well as his first key works—all appear during the main period of the crisis of Viennese culture.[1] And it was in this same area that his work coincided with the more authentic currents of negative thought: that is, in the critique of historicist-synthetical Kultur and of the Weimarian image of the classical.[2]

In many ways this critique anticipated the later internal dissolution of the Werkbund—in particular, Naumann's attack on its ideology.[3] As we have seen, for Naumann, the "quality" that the Werkbund is supposed to produce should be totally indistinguishable from a maximum potentiation of the use value aspect of the commodity.[4] There can be no quality except as use value. If, therefore, this quality is not totally integrated into the overall needs of the circulation of commodities, if it does not become an effective agent of circulation, it will cease to be usable in any way and will become, on the contrary, an obstacle to the socialization of capitalist market and productive relations. There is quality that "enriches" the use value of commodities—a "productive" quality—and there is also quality that limits or annuls use value. This second kind is the result inevitably produced when the quality aspect of the work is made to derive from a priori spiritual concerns, from forms—whether they express the "good old" social relations of production (handicrafts, and so on), or an intangible future (quality as utopian form). According to Naumann, the task of the Werkbund is instead to ally itself firmly with what Brecht called the "bad new."[5]

The essential features of this critical position had already appeared in Loos. It takes the form of a *logico-philosophical* attack—the opposite of an aristocratic critique of taste. The ideology of the Werkbund operates in two basic directions: on the one hand, it distinguishes, in terms of value, quality-use value and exchange value in the commodity produced; and on the other, it transposes, in progressive-historicist terms, earlier forms of productive relations into the contemporary socioeconomic context. The initial distinction clearly functions toward the subsequent transposition. If the quality of the product is seen as a characteristic in itself implicit in the totality of commodities—of capitalistically produced commodities—then it will always be possible to assert, at least in principle or as a "real utopia," a continuity between pre-capitalist and capitalist forms of production. The tools and concepts of the Werkbund find their function in this area of utopian transcrescences: they transpose Muthesius' notion of "dwelling" onto the Germany of Rathenau,[6] the "socialism" of William Morris[7] onto the situation of 1905 or 1907, the quality of handicraft labor onto the quality characteristic of use value and embodied in the use value of capitalistically produced merchandise. This latter transposition can be seen as having two distinct aspects, or rather, two distinct phases: the first concerns the possibilities of the immediate use of merchandise; the second concerns the transformation of the

Loos and His Contemporaries

value of immediate use into pure value corresponding to precise a priori forms, forms constituting artistic creativity. Here—in the Werkbund as well as in Olbrich and Hoffmann—we find a reaffirmation of the artist's function of effective emancipation-liberation from the pure relations of exchange dominant in the Metropolis; art is conceived of as an expression of a de-alienated work-time and hence as a full expression of freedom itself. And this image of de-alienated labor and freedom is secured in the product through the "absolute" distinction between use value and exchange value and the subsequent transformation of use value by artistic creativity. Handicraft labor represents, in one way or another, the language of this creativity, its necessary technique of application. The quality implicit in use value ceases to reflect a condition of the entire capitalist mode of production and becomes as it were the remnant of a vanished form of labor, nostalgically tending towards its reactualization—memory *and* duration.

This position can and must be criticized, particularly from an economic point of view. This is Loos's essential purpose in "Ornament and Crime." This economic line of reasoning functions like Ockham's razor, that is, as a general criterion: it is manipulated in the same way as in the "future" pages of Wittgenstein's *Tractatus*.[8] There is no quality dissociable from the actual totality of the modes of production and distribution of merchandise. All quality must correspond to the overall demands and functions of these modes of production. All historicist claims of continuity between the qualitative characteristics of handicraft labor and the quality of the use value of capitalistically produced merchandise are based solely on appearance and are hence illusory. The analogy asserted between the two terms (quality and use value) obscures a violent rupture, a leap, a radical and irreversible difference. Use value, in its capitalist sense, has no "autonomous" quality to manifest. Nor can the quality of a particular merchandise be abstracted, even hypothetically, from the amount of time socially necessary for its production—that is, from the cost of its production. And it is not possible to reduce this amount of time, to reduce this cost, except through the progressive simplification, massification, and functionalization of the modes of production and organization of the

Loosian Dialectics

work itself. Hence, Loos's anti-ornamental "ethic" is directed in reality toward the mode of production: far from being a "question of taste" or simply an aesthetic policy, anti-ornamentalism is for Loos the overall tendency, the "destiny" of Rationalisierung, of capitalist Zivilisation. The concept of ornament in Loos hence goes well beyond the facade—it boils down to a concern for the ends of construction, production, and communication. For Loos, as for all the other "great Viennese masters of language,"[9] ornament is every word that goes beyond the conditions of its meaning, beyond the formal laws of its grammar and syntax, beyond the limits of its function. (In Schönberg, ornament is every repetition and every voice not included in the basic compositional idea). Ornament in Loos is also every "mystified" continuity, every simple duration opposed to the nullifying memory of Altenberg and that of Klimt, in many respects. Every teleologico-synthetical "judgment" is ornamental because in the end it cannot be represented or verified, and because it is applicable to nothing. Lastly, ornament is the expression of alleged creative subjectivities forming a priori the substance of the relations of production and exchange. Quality is inherent to the relations, embodied in them: it is their use value "aspect," just as this latter is concretely determined by the given processes of production (by their degree of socialization) and by the given market relations (by a given structure of demand).

As Loos understands it, the historical development of handicraft contained within itself this process of simplification-rationalization, which saves labor, material, and capital, and through which the quality of merchandise becomes its fully manifest use value. If handicraft is "left alone," "uncontaminated" by the ideas of architecture, it will "naturally" express the historic tendency towards maximum use value. But if handicraft labor is mystified as a simple technique to be redeemed-exalted through the ideas of poetic subjectivity, or as a language of the pure quality to be stamped into the substance of exchange relations, then it will tend towards the minimum use value: it will become anti-economic, ornamental. In this way, Werkbund handicraft belongs to no verifiable age or historical period but rather aims at representing a form of the spirit: the creative autonomy of the subject that wants to ex-sist, that must realize

Loos and His Contemporaries

itself as such in the "substance" of the relations of production. This is exalted handicraft—unnecessary labor. In the historical development of handicraft as a materialistically manifest form of the organization of labor, Loos, on the other hand, sees only the symptoms that point to its eventual end, and the conditions that will lead beyond it.

The real conceptual focus of Ornament and Crime is its critique of every linguistic hypostasis intellectually dominating the substance of the individual premises. More specifically, Loos's emphasis falls on the impossibility of a schematic resolution between *langue* and linguistic "technique." The meaning of the premises cannot be sought in the absolute unity of an ideal and eternal syntax. This meaning cannot be redeemed or exalted; in the same way, handicraft labor cannot be transformed into an expression of the poetic freedom of the subject, and its language cannot be reduced to a technique of the artistic langue. According to the ideology of the Werkbund and the Werkstätte, these two moments (langue and technique), in their unity, supposedly constitute the qualitative aspect of a commodity necessary to its realization as commodity and as use value. This aspect may be expressed in varying degrees of "attractiveness," representing to varying degrees of effectiveness the Nervenleben characteristic of the metropolitan relations of exchange: the signification of the "syllogism" does not change. For Loos, on the other hand, the language of the relation of exchange is inherent to the structure and modes of exchange. The relations, demands, and functions of this epoch determine its "style." But this perspective is not even reminiscent of Semperian positivism: here not only is the purely functional aspect included in a broader vision of the basic economic relations, but the very teleology of the Werkbund and the Werkstätte (which is in many ways similar to nineteenth century positivism in its more progressive tendencies) is now challenged from a more generally logical perspective. This teleology expresses a fundamental concern for synthesis, one certainly not foreign to Semper. Loos, on the other hand, bases his critique on the discovery of the decisive and irreducible mechanisms of the division of labor and the radical differences that make up the universe of languages.

Zivilisation is not synthesis: it is not industrial handicraft nor

Loosian Dialectics

industrial art, but rather art *and* industry, art *and* handicraft
—music *and* drama, painting *and* music. There is no totalizing *Harmonielehre* (harmonics), as Kandinsky had hoped[10]; no
"musical drama": Loos's Wagner is the same as Schönberg's.[11]
The general ideology that underlies the musical drama collapses
at the very point at which it seemed to unfold in all its effectiveness: at the Matildenhöhe of Darmstadt dreamed up by Olbrich.
A clear separation, a radical negative, marks the beginning of
the process of rationalization. And separating-dividing also implies understanding the specific linguistic form inherent to the
production and circulation of commodities, from the totality
of which no autonomous value can be extricated. The Werkbund is for this reason superfluous. The questions that it was
supposed to have answered but did not answer were: does its activity effectively strengthen the language of the circulation and
distribution of commodities? does it reduce work time? does its
debate over production lead to real savings? does it develop the
products market?[12]

The emphasis of Loosian Aufklärung does not in any way fall
on art's "transcendence" of handicraft and industry, but on the
mutual "transcendence" of all these terms: that is, on the functional multiplicity of the languages. To separate means to set
in conflict; not to establish abstract hierarchies of value but to
measure-calculate specific differences, on the basis of specific
functions as well as specific histories and traditions. Where the
Werkbund imagines bridges, Loos posits differences. And this
holds as true for the general difference between art and handicraft as for the internal differences that make up the structures of
the various languages of composition: the languages that figure
in the composition of dwelling and the home, the experience of
which constitutes the base on which Loosian *Baukunst* (architecture) is defined. A fundamental difference exists between the
wall, which belongs to the architect, and the furnishing, the
overall composition of the interior, which must ensure maximum use and transformation by the inhabitant. This is a difference of languages, which no aura of universal syntax will ever
be able to overcome. The wall is form, calculated space-time—
it is "abstract." It would be absurd, "Wagnerian," to attempt
to reconcile it with this interior, this lived experience, with the

space of the multiplicity of languages that make up life. Therefore, the bourgeois, philistine concept of the home—the concept of a totality of dwelling, of a reciprocal transparence between interior and exterior—on which every *Stilarchitektur* has been based up to this point, is intrinsically, logically false. The home is in reality a plurality of languages that cannot be reduced to unities by the deterministic logic of nineteenth-century positivistic utopianism. The home is not in its entirety formally calculable: we cannot reduce from one of its levels to the next, nor infer from one language to another. The exterior says nothing about the interior because they are two different languages, and each speaks of itself. Indeed, one must take the greatest care to ensure that nothing from one linguistic level alludes to the other or tends toward the other, creating irresolvable nostalgias that would prevent the conflicts from appearing in all their reality as irreducible and primary, forcing them back within the limits of a kind of "suspended architecture." [13] The architect remains true to his calling as long as he gives maximum voice to these differences and lets them appear in full.

But whoever understands this tendency as an example of compositional eclecticism is on the wrong track altogether.[14] What is most important here is not the variety of languages but their common logical reference: the need for every element and function to formulate its own language and speak it coherently and comprehensibly, to test its limits and preserve them in every form—to remain faithful to them, not wanting idealistically or romantically to negate them. Equally foreign to Loos's argument are pan-artistic tendencies of an aristocratic character, *l'art pour l'art*. His strict limitation of the meaning of the production of use values is at the same time a harsh definition of the meaning of the artistic act, as we shall see below. The confusion of the two levels is, logically speaking, non-sense. The search for synthesis continually reveals its own ideologically *regressive* underpinnings: the desire to confirm the privileged status of the ideal langue of the subject, the efficacy of the schematic relation, and the "free" character of the quality aspect of the commodity. This is an aristocratic attitude. In fact, this attitude of mind asserts the feudal privileges of the ego, absorbing all premises and relegating economic structures and process to a

Loosian Dialectics

state of empty potentiality, where they can only wait for forma-
tive intervention. Loos's aristocracy, on the other hand, is merely
the isolation of one who has unmasked this false Zeitgeist.

The ideology of labor finds ultimate expression in the dialectics
of the Werkbund. The artistic act comes to be labor's teleologically destined end. Here artistic form does not merely intervene
in industry, since one aspect of the commodity, as use value, is
free. It also serves a comprehensive ethico-ideological function
in industry: it shapes and influences all labor, in its concrete
organization, toward artistic discipline. A totally "redeemed"
place of labor had already appeared in the Mathildenhöhe of
Darmstadt.[15] Matildenhöhe's "cry of life" was supposed to signify the liberation of labor: the transformation of labor into
creation. The introduction of artistic forms into industrial production hence did not have as its goal the circulation, in the area
of consumption, of de-alienated objects, but the de-alienation of
the producers themselves. Moreover, one must bear in mind that
this extreme ideology of the recoupment of labor is no longer
based on the leftist neo-Ricardism of the nineteenth-century
utopian-socialist currents, but rather on a Fabian interpretation of neo-classical tendencies: the level of the structural relation between capital and labor is of no interest whatsoever to
the Werkbund or to Hoffmann's Wiener Werkstätte—the emphasis has been shifted completely onto the need to direct the
cycle of production-distribution towards the satisfaction of the
consumer. The economic relationship is here reduced in all its
aspects to the function of supply and demand. The very role
that the synthesis of art-handicraft-industry is expected to fulfill
within this function is characterized by its intrinsic opposition
to the most advanced forms of massification and industrial concentration (just as in the leftist currents of marginalism): that
is, its opposition to all that hinders the affirmation of the "sov-
ereignty of the consumer." The Werkbund position regarding
the organization of labor, "industrial art," and the essentiality
of consumption in the economic cycle can only be situated in
the ambit of marginalist neo-classical analysis. It is no accident
that the crisis of this analysis—the beginning of its crisis—
coincides with the ripening and the exploding of the crisis of
the Werkbund. These are the same years in which Schumpeter

Loos and His Contemporaries

published his *Theory of Economic Growth*. Earlier, Weber and Sombart had already thrown into crisis the general philosophy of the neo-classical doctrines.[16] It is within this same process of critical dissolution that Loos's critique must be situated historically.

Every synthetical approach to the problem of the handicraft-industry relation is clearly and explicitly reactionary. Such an approach does not question capitalist Zivilisation in any way, but on the contrary represents its pre-history—its ideal prehistory, to be exact. The actual process of capitalist Zivilisation is made up of contradictions and conflicts. Within this process, two irreversible trends emerge: on the one hand, the instrumentality of labor, and on the other, artistic freedom as a totally sui generis phenomenon. Instrumentality means necessity and functionality; the modern organization of labor aims at the elimination of all superfluity, at reducing all labor to necessary labor and reducing accordingly the time involved in such "necessity." This development of the mode of production is functional both economically speaking and in terms of the qualitative characteristics of use value, which in the end should correspond to those requisites of simplicity and comprehensibility proper to the structure of the socio-economic relations of this life. Labor implies power, but only in so far as it integrates itself into this process and this context—only in so far as it becomes integral to it. It comes down to a reactualization of the Nietszchean argument.[17] The new power of labor lies precisely in its instrumentality—and in this instrumentality lie the conditions from which its products emerge "naturally" in the style of the times.[18]

This position regarding labor corroborates the preceding one regarding the difference existing between the various languages —regarding, that is, the crises intrinsic to composition. Indeed, this position transforms the preceding one, by generalizing it into a recognition of the division of labor and its role in the historically specific growth of the forces of production. The obfuscation carried out by the Werkbund in this area is a radical one (and in this case it derives from post-Marxian utopian-socialist currents): the division of labor is reduced to disciplinary socialization, and the interdisciplinary question, as a consequence, is reduced to the idea of overcoming the division of labor. The art-

Loosian Dialectics

handicraft-industry relation, as a synthesis of instrumentality and labor, is itself supposed to express this emancipation of individual disciplines into a fundamental unity. Such ideas are radically unacceptable to Loos's argument. For Loos, it is only on the foundation of specialized relations that one can construct languages endowed with meaning and hence usable and comprehensible. An interdisciplinary relation can be established based on the analytical recognition of the differences between languages and their concrete multiplicity. But this relation, in its turn, cannot be idealized as an overcoming of the division of labor: on the contrary, it corroborates these very differences and multiplicities, the specialization of languages. But the problem of the division of labor, in its structural sense, does not of course constitute Loos's central theme; yet it is essential to him, in his confrontations with his "mortal enemies," that he know how to speak *only* of specialization, and that he be well aware that specialization is not a condition of labor that can be overcome by going backwards.

"We need a civilization of carpenters. If the artists of the applied arts went back to painting canvases or swept the streets, we would have such a civilization."[19] But the Werkbund wants to teach the true "style" of sweeping the streets in the modern age. And the definition of this truth lies with the artist who determines and produces the "style." The "age" ineluctably summons forth the artist who determines its style: *Der Zeit ihre Kunst*. In this way a universal langue of quality comes to be disembodied from the diverse totality of this age: contradictions, divisions, and conflicts are flattened and reconciled; they are "for-their-own-death." The resulting synthesis automatically claims to be universally and eternally valid. The artist, intervening in the matter of the relations of production through a priori forms (through the form of his style), which are supposed to have value in themselves, immediately asserts the eternality of the quality of the use value that he has moulded. A teaspoon is seen sub specie aeternitatis, whereas in reality it is a *sub specie musei:* "the Guild wants to make things that are not in the style of our age; it wants to work for eternity."[20] In propagating itself, this notion of labor threatens to undermine the necessity and functionality of all specialized languages consciously and organically

Loos and His Contemporaries

limited by and to their specific materials. Ornament is only the most visible symptom of this contagion.

But the general ideological foundation of the concept of ornament resides in the concept of style. Loos's critique of style is part and parcel of his "logico-philosophical" critique of the Werkbund and the Werkstätte. Indeed, style is the fundamental schema through which the artistic idea leaves its mark on the object of use by transforming it into quality. The concept of style cannot exist except within the synthetico-historicist dimension that has by now been dismantled. The function that style serves is twofold: on the one hand, it establishes criteria of continuity and duration that overcome differences among the various epochs; on the other, it abstracts from each epoch its fundamental-essential expression. An evolutionistic conception of the history of art has no room for the concept of style, nor for the battle over applied art, synthetico-idealistic aesthetics, or musical drama.

Loos opposes style with his *Nihilismus*. He recalls with obvious satisfaction how the architects of his day called his Café Museum (fig. 2) "Café Nihilismus." [21] It was a question of the *immediate negative* versus the concepts of style, synthesis, duration. All anti-expressive, anti-synthetical, anti-natural composition is nihilistic.[22] Style is the writing of the interior *Stimmung* (disposition, humor): naturalism or naturalism of the soul.[23] Style is synthesis, linguistic confusion, ornamental non-sense. Style is "suspended tonality," a tending toward the abstract idea, toward number, and at the same time toward lived representation.[24] Nihilismus is the immediate negative set against all of the above: but only on this negative can one trace the great form, the composition, to come. The immediate negative means technique, discipline, reduction of necessary labor, and functionality: it means referring each element to the rules of this calculation, subjecting them to this test. The great form is founded on the analysis of the meaning of this language through the formalization of its limits. Composition does not imply a "total work of art," a reductio ad unum of the multiplicity of languages, but the acknowledgment, the explanation, and the comprehensible communication of contradictions. Style is *organic* language— composition is depth and historic contradictoriness, *primary*

Loosian Dialectics

plurality: among the elements exists an elective affinity, in the true Goethian sense.[25] Hence, when Loos speaks of Roman architecture, he refers not to styles, not to historically inferred continuities, but to this very concept of great form, of composition: technique-discipline, no new ornament, no nostalgia, no "recuperation." But the necessity of this measure, this calculation: this is great, *Roman* form.[26]

The Cafe Nihilismus and the Nihilismus house on the Michaelerplatz ("der neue Raum")[27] are necessarily situated in the Nihilismus city, the Metropolis where all the social circles of the Gemeinschaft have been shattered. City and style, as community organism or the nostalgia for such, are synonymous. The attempt to reconcile the form of the Metropolis and its specific ideologies with the spirit of community, is an integral part of the concept of style itself. Style is transformation of material, as though the latter were teleologically destined to gratify the interior, subjective Stimmung. In this way, to confer a style upon the city is to negate its metropolitan *being-there;* it is to conceive of it as an organism whose end, or whose Sollen, lies in the gratification of the ego. From being a simple schema between the artistic idea and handicraft quality in the industrial product, the concept of style has now come to represent the transcrescence between the communal value of city life and the relations of production and circulation of metropolitan life. But the place of the synthesis between art and handicraft, the real place of "applied art" and "musical drama," the place of the communal resolution of conflicts, is the city, not the Metropolis. In the Metropolis these past relations can reappear only as ornament. In the actual Metropolis, style is only ornament—and ornament as *tattoo.*

The entire work of Karl Kraus is marked by a similar fight against the "ornamental" image of the Metropolis. The house on the Michaelerplatz has the same effect as Kraus's essay in *Die Fackel* against the Vienna of the Secession. Ornament hides the true metropolitan relations, it falsifies. But Kraus's polemic assumes ornament to be a structural characteristic of these relations, and his criticism of it is always on the verge of sounding, illuministically, like a critique of metropolitan life *tout court.* Loos, on the other hand, isolates with great precision the re-

Loos and His Contemporaries

gressive implications of the communal ideologies that serve as a foundation for the concept of style. Style is not Metropolis, but *hangs over* its structure.[28] It appears as though the Metropolis were still inhabited by schools of artist-artisans who were constructing Renaissance palaces as though Florentine nobles inhabited them; as though these churches and public places were frequented by the people of the Gemeinschaft. For Loos, as well as for Kraus, this *tattooed* city (not masked—the mask is a "category of the spirit" that belongs, as we have seen, to Simmel's Venice) is decadent Vienna—where the coachman doesn't run over the passer-by because he knows him personally; where *Meinung* (opinion) has absorbed *Denken* (thought), and *die Phrase* has absorbed *die Sprache;* where the desperate quest, through language and through the order and measure inherent to the language of the Metropolis, to know all of its contradictions and conflicts, is overcome by fleeing backwards, into the utopia of style and ornament.

Style thus implies the will to work for the eternal—to disguise (to tattoo) with the eternal the concrete and immanent forms of the multiplicity of languages. Style is an act of synthesizing city and Metropolis, and therefore, it makes this Metropolis into a duration, an organism that has developed in time without solutions of continuity: that is, an organism whose substance is eternal. From the critique of the art-handicraft-industry synthesis, to the critique of the concept of style, to the critique of the historicist transcrescence between city and Metropolis, to the critique of the city à la Potemkin: Loos's progression represents a single framework, descending directly from the Nietzschean gay science.

But for architecture as well, strictly speaking, there exists a style, that is, a specific way of confusing its language, of reconciling it with others. In the world of style, the architect is the one who knows best how to design.[29] Design is that writing of the soul which forms the material of dwelling. But wherever the form is understood as implicit in the material—wherever a house must be constructed—wherever it is a question of giving order to its spaces, of making them usable in their varied multiplicity, and not of making them conform to an idea—the graphic talent becomes, in itself, mere ornament. No language

Loosian Dialectics

can be invented at the drafting table. No Esperanto can serve as the foundation for composition. Composition is grounded in the differences that make up dwelling, in the concrete languages that express dwelling, in the comprehensibility with which the functions of these differences must be communicated, and lastly in the analytical awareness of the materials that make construction possible. Just as the architect does not invent the spatial language, he also does not invent the language of the materials. He lets them appear. "Every material possesses a formal language of its own" that makes a specific repertory of forms possible.[30] The architect is "king" in the realm of materials not because he can transform them at will or reassemble them in any context (design them), but because he knows the language of each one perfectly, and thus knows the limits of each.[31] To let these spatial-material languages appear, to let their limits stand apparent: this is the architect's duty, his profession, his Beruf.

Around the same time Loos was writing the notes cited above, Schönberg was concluding his observations on Ferrucio Busoni's *Aesthetik der Tonkunst* (Toward a new musical aesthetics) with the following words:

> What craftsman is not delighted by a beautiful material, and what true musician is not proudly a good craftsman as well? The carpenter and the violin-maker rejoice at the sight of a good piece of wood, the shoemaker at the sight of a good piece of leather; the painter is delighted by his colors, his brush, his canvas, the sculptor by his marble. In these materials, they envision the future work—the work is as though standing before them. Each is well aware that this work does not of necessity result from these materials: it must be created. However, they already see its future in the material: at the sight of the material the spirit is reawakened.[32]

From this perspective, Schönberg criticized Busoni because he undervalued the role of the material. Later, in California in 1936, when Schönberg was thinking of the construction of a house for himself, he asked Kulka for explanations regarding the use of marble for the revetment of the walls. Loos was able to get slabs of 1 millimeter thick, but Neutra, to whom Schönberg had turned in this matter, did not know the "secret."[33] Loosian com-

Loos and His Contemporaries

position in general is made up of these secrets of the language of materials. Loos's Beruf has no universal missions to accomplish, no eternal spiritual substances to represent. The tone of *Das Andere* ("The other"), the name of Loos's review, implies precisely this: that is, the peremptory interdiction of images of the eternal. For Loos, this tone is "American", though it is definitely not a philistine faith in "progress". It is the same tone as that of his close friend Peter Altenberg.

But how does this radical Entwertung of the Werkbund and Wiener Werkstätte ideology, which goes right to their common source, affect the other side of the relations that we have analyzed and sorted out, a side that has thus far remained in the dark? *Das Andere* does not put forth any kind of program of aristocratic eccentricity. "The Other" is the difference, the systematic analysis that demolishes all linguistic synthesis. In this way, the artistic act itself must be other with respect to the Beruf of the architect, with respect to the work of the craftsman: no longer a romantic synthesis of contradictions and linguistic developments, the artistic act expresses one aspect of them—it constitutes one of their basic elements. The gamut of differences analyzed thus far cannot be fully understood unless it is extended to include the otherness represented by the artistic act in itself. Like Wittgenstein, Loos is not interested in any kind of "general aesthetic."[34] But, although all investigation of the "what" has been interdicted, there remains the inquiry into the "why" of this artistic act. It weighs heavily on the detachment from all symbolic universality, from all infinite and formally irresolvable expressive tension.[35] It could not be otherwise: the fight against all communal-city form is part and parcel of this detachment, this distance—this *Entsagung* (renunciation) and *Resignation* of which Simmel spoke in writing about Stefan George.[36] Only on this negative can the Nihilismus of the Café Museum and the Michaelerplatz house be based: this Baukunst is built on detachment—on the renunciation of all style, of all synthetical utopianism.

But for Loos, the form of Entsagung presents itself as absolute only in the "pure" artistic act. This is not aestheticism, as we shall see, but a testing of the argument thus far developed, an ability to "suffer" it through to the end. The "why"

Loosian Dialectics

of this language exists—but this language is not a synthesis of the others, it does not represent their destiny, nor their end, nor their Sollen. And yet this "why" lies in the absolute form of detachment—and hence in the purest manifestation of the otherness-multiplicity of the languages. In Loos's argument art represents what in the *Tractatus* is the "mystical": art is what remains after we throw away the stairs we have climbed during our analysis of the various forms of labor, their organization, their functions, and the Metropolis that defines their space. Art redeems this multiplicity when the craftsman or the architect could do the same: that is, for no reason. Not only does art not constitute a kind of ideal language capable of synthetically shaping the multiplicity of relations and languages, but its very "why" lies in demonstrating the radical otherness of its own signs, its own game. Art shows itself to be a manifestation of the ensemble of differences-conflicts that constitute the process of transformation, of composition. Its radically *utopian* character with respect to other languages therefore cannot serve to re-establish any new pan-aestheticism, and may even tend toward the negative. This utopian character is the ultimate verification of the reciprocal othernesses that make up these languages, as well as of the differences and "leaps" that are inherent to all languages. The particular organization of signs, the particular linguistic game that we call art, thus limited and defined, lies in the manifestation of the utopian form as a form and a condition of otherness and difference, in the manifestation of the utopian form as detachment-Entsagung (and only in its manifestation: there is no metalanguage thereof)—in freezing this form in this dimension. But all of this has meaning only in relation to other specific premises: without their inherent limit there could be no presence of "das Andere." And this limit is the condition of the form of otherness: it imposes suspension, pause, and prevents the return to "dominants," to "organic," natural form. The artistic act reveals an otherness, a conflict: But it does not resolve it, nor give consolation for it. On the contrary, it defines the space in which such conflict can emerge in all of its *tones*, in its most complex and at the same time most comprehensible forms, beyond all styles, as tragedy.

It is in this light that we must read Loos's discussion of "sepulcher and monument" as the only genres in which architecture can become an artistic act.[37] In them, one finds a total affirmation of the constitutive and integral presence of the negative, attained through the measure of Entsagung, the calculation of distance, and the analysis of the premises of meaning. The language of art is implicit in the dimension of the *Denkmal* (monument) and the *Grabmal* (sepulcher). Every one of its premises is penetrated by this dimension. The other that this dimension manifests is in its language like an "atomic fact" for which it is impossible to give further explanation. But Denkmal and Grabmal are also memory—but a memory grounded not in duration, but in consumption, in irreversibility. This memory, this dimension of memory, is implicit in the language of otherness-utopism that constitutes the artistic act. But sepulcher and monument, in as much as they represent the testing-limit of the meaning of architecture, must be part of every architecture endowed with meaning as its limit: a premise has meaning insofar as it acknowledges its own limits. In a most conscious and explicit way, the Grabmal is the interior of the Kärtner-Bar. Here all order, all form describes the effable and at the same time transposes it into the invisible, into memory—like the lyricism of the *Duino Elegies*. The order of the space of this "interior" has meaning because of its limit: the perfection of the effable implies the presence of the Other, of the ineffable. Hence the language acknowledges and manifests this new complexity: the utopian dimension of otherness, in the multiplicity of its forms, thus penetrates memory, Grabmal, and the mystical.

The dimension of the sepulcher also illuminates the earlier discussion of the interior and its radical difference from the "realm" of the architect: the wall and the materials. The interior, too, is other; it is a utopia in relation to the language of the walls and to the facade and the exterior. The interior is the space of lived experience, which cannot be predetermined. But lived experience is memory—it is both Denkmal and Grabmal. Dwelling assembles the objects and voices of memory in the space of the interior. They withdraw into the house. These movements of lived experience and memory, which withdraw into the interior just as things in Rilke withdraw into the names of the poet, are in opposition to the total calculation and standardization of the

Loosian Dialectics

exterior, and to the exterior as pure function, pure use value—as in the "rail-car" of the Stein house (1910) and the house at Northartgasse (1913). Art that expresses this process of de-mystification and fully manifests the conflictual nature of the measurement, the calculation, and the most pitiless game—the infinite conjectural and problematic charge that remains other with respect to every premise and is the other (the limit) of every premise—is, for Loos, revolutionary.[38] Not only does such art not ornament the production-circulation of merchandise, but its truth lies in the negative that is a condition for its existence—in the separation that is its foundation. The negative of this language, therefore, does not have an autonomous existence: the negative is inherent in its form, since this form is built upon its own limits and by means of its own contradictions.

However, having attained the summit of the tragic tension of its composition, Loos's argument begins to show a typical ideological warp which becomes more pronounced in the years after World War I. The initial logico-philosophical approach to the difference between interior and exterior, to the multiplicity of languages, to the reciprocal otherness-utopism of their constitutive forms and functions—themselves measurable crises that can be postulated—begins to take on the sense of a question of value. Value becomes the interior space of lived experience opposed to the reified measure of the exterior. Value becomes the potential "quality" of this space, insofar as it is the place of the emergence of the artistic act. But this emergence is not limited to underscoring a difference of language—it is transformed into a difference of value. When the preceding analysis is made teleologically functional to this moment—when composition is at the point of being transformed back into the end of the process thus far described—this same analysis and composition once again make room for style. The *negatives Denken* posited as a condition of the analysis of the multiplicity of languages is overturned and transformed into a stylistic condition aimed at the affirmation of its value—no longer a synthesis, of course, but in any case a "superiority" of interior over exterior, of the space of art over that of functions—a universality in the negative. And it is precisely in this manner that style reappears: this difference of value prevents both sides of the contradiction

Loos and His Contemporaries

from acknowledging the limit. The language of the exterior is no longer an inherent limit of the interior, but its simple, immediate otherness—and vice-versa. Therefore, in itself "absolute," the exterior can be formed as a style, it can assume a style—it can inherently be "pacified," regarded as autonomous. And the same thing happens in the interior cut off from its limit, from the limit that gave it meaning—the sequential measure of the exterior. Against this simple, immediate, "commonplace" otherness, the elements reappear as absolute, autonomous, and hence intrinsically synthetical, "organic." On the basis of this otherness one can then assert a value judgment totally foreign to the processes of the material—a language completely disembodied from writing—which determines a priori, abstractly, the hierarchy of its elements. And such a judgment places the emphasis on the artistic nature of the interior, at the same time, however, that it liberates the functionality-sequentiality of the exterior as having a meaning in itself. It is precisely this reversal, this "trap" of style present in Loos and increasingly visible in his work of the postwar years that forms the basis of the historical tradition that used his work as an example pure and simple of "rationalism."

Naturally, in light of the overall problematics of Loos that we have thus far analyzed, such a definition of his work is paradoxical. However, this definition finds its justification in an unresolved aspect of Loos's argument: the otherness existing between the area of architecture "as art" and the area of use values as the otherness of languages, and this very difference as a hierarchy of value—all of which undermines the very significance of the previous operation, the functional role of the limit expressed by this otherness. These two dimensions exist side by side in Loos. In this light, the reemergence of style becomes possible, and from both sides of the contradiction: in the sphere of the artistic act, and in that of the production and distribution of use values. Style exists, indeed—whether it is a *Siedlung* without lavatories, so that the fertilizers for the kitchen garden are not wasted, with the bath set up in the sink,[39]—or a plea in favor of art, "Der Staat und die Kunst," published in Vienna in 1919 in the collection edited by Loos himself, *Richtlinien für ein Kunstamt.*[40] Wittgenstein was shocked by this essay—as he was ten years later by the pomposity of the anti-metaphysical style of

Loosian Dialectics

the program of the Wiener Kreis.[41] He wrote to Engelmann: "A few days ago I paid a visit to Loos. I felt horror and disgust in his presence. He put on snobbish intellectual airs beyond comprehension! He gave me a short piece on a projected 'Office for Art,' in which he speaks of sin against the Holy Spirit. That is really too much!"[42]

We shall see how, about ten years later, Wittgenstein himself would seek to clarify these contradictions of Loos and overcome them in the house he designed for his sister Margarethe.[43] This house would be the most complete demonstration of the Aufklärung side of Loos—*one* side of Loos. This Aufklärung was not an overcoming of the negative, but *a positing of the negative in its own form:* a comprehension and communication of the negative. Aufklärung and nothing more: this is the reversal that Loos effects when he turns his argument into a value judgment. The task of going back to the conditions of this "nothing more," and of suffering it to the end, would fall to Wittgenstein's oikos.

8. The Contemporaries

Loos's critique of the Werkbund holds equally valid for the Wiener Werkstätte of Hoffmann. The problems and questions that Naumann put to the Werkbund in and of themselves raise its debate to the level of the form and socio-political significance of the processes of industrialization. In the Wiener Werkstätte

Loos and His Contemporaries

this debate does not in fact exist. The terms of the Werkbund and its very problematics are immediately translated into Viennese Gemeinschaft, into moderate Historicism. The communal-handicraft disguising of the Metropolis plays a much more explicit role in the Werkstätte than in the Werkbund. As a result, the quality aspect of the commodity becomes totally abstract—and it produces a spiritual reorganization not only of the economic relations of labor, but of social relations as well. At the Werkbund Exposition of 1914—in other words, at the time of its crisis—Hoffmann had the following words written on the bare wall of the large hall of the Wiener Werkstätte pavilion:

Nur wer von Sinn für Qualität durchdrungen ist, kann eine Ware erzeugen, die das Vertrauen rechtfertigt. Ein Unternehmen, das Vertrauensware herstellt, muss in jedem Mitarbeiter den Sinn für Qualität wecken und vertiefen. Dazu gehört, dasalles, was die Qualitätsarbeit umgibt, ihrer wurdig also gut und schön gestaltet sei. Im edler Umgebung gedeiht edle Arbeit.

(Only a person who is permeated by a feeling for quality can manufacture merchandise that merits trust. An enterprise that manufactures trustworthy merchandise must stimulate and deepen the feeling for quality in every co-worker. What contributes to this end is everything that encompasses quality work, everything that is worthy of it, that is, that which is well and beautifully made. Noble work thrives in noble surroundings.)[1]

But in the background of this avowed teleology still speak the unresolved tensions, the suspended tonalities, of the Secession: the problem of semantic relations here presents itself in much the same disunited manner as it did in that group. In this light, the philosophical approach of the Viennese is richer and more complex than that of the Werkbund, even if on the surface their argument appears to be exclusively concerned with a general ideological sphere. The problem of the early Secession (when even Loos was writing for *Ver Sacrum*),[2] the difficult transition from the tensions of mere *Nervenkunst* to a theoretical analysis of the means of expression of the medium itself, the possible order among the various elements of the language, and the

The Contemporaries

necessary functionality-comprehensibility of this order are still clearly visible in the Stoclet Palace, even though it is suffocated by the overall symbolic dimension that Hoffmannian "quality" tends to give the work. In this palace still live those who admire the tapestries of Olbrich and are unable to renounce decoration and ornament, even while listening to *Tristan*. This building, however, expresses only one tendency: the persistently sought continuum of the design, the order of the spaces, the very use of the materials, which are "revered" and hence transformed merely by being displayed, point to a univocal destiny, despite the traditional symmetrical layout of the plan and the Secession sculptures at the top of the tower.

Loos, in any case, was well aware of this "dialectic" between the Secession and the Wiener Werkstätte. In 1908, in the same way in which he attacks the Werkbund, Loos acknowledges that Hoffmann is progressively freeing himself from the Jugend-Secession decorative elements that had characterized its early stages, and that "as regards his constructions, [Hoffmann] has come close to what I myself do."[3] Loos here was thinking of the Purkersdorf Sanitorium, or the arrangement of certain exhibitions of the Wiener Werkstätte, set up by Moser, in which the "Japanese side" of the Secession found clear and concise expression, without any oriental exoticism (as happens in Olbrich), but as a rhythm, a prosody, a formal order—as one possible element of *Gestaltung*.[4] The historicist solution in "classical" terms that Hoffmann tended to give to this dialectic is also inherent in the overall problematics of the Secession—it is an exact parallel to Rilke's pilgrimage to Rodin, to Simmel's writings on Rodin. But it, too, appears to be a provisional solution, a problematical quality, only one possible order among many: Hoffmann never presents it sub specie aeternitatis—or, in any case, it cannot be understood in this way in the light of his life's work. The Austrian Pavilion at the International Art Exhibition of Rome (1911), the Austrian Pavilion at the Werkbund Exhibition at Cologne (1914), and even the Skywa House at Hietzing (1914), all broaden the use of linguistic materials, test different harmonies among them—and they cannot do otherwise. The use of intensely revisited classical elements functions towards order, not synthesis. And inasmuch as this function

Loos and His Contemporaries

permits a simplification-rationalization of the language of the exterior, it inevitably brings to maturity the interior's otherness, its negative. Indeed, this otherness will become radicalized into an otherness of functions: just as, on the one hand, in the garden and villa of Sonja Knips (who had already appeared in an 1898 Klimt painting immersed in the color of a garden—the glimmers of her dress being on the verge of dissolving into those of the garden—like a Monet girl in bloom), and on the other, in the working-class houses of the Stromstrasse and the Mottlstrasse (1924–1925).

Therefore, at the opposite end of the spectrum from Loos we find not Hoffmann, but Olbrich: the ideology of the freedom of poetic labor as a condition of the freedom of labor in general; the ideology of the synthesis between poetic *Ideen* and *Leben,* a synthesis ultimately capable of realizing living organisms, not just use value and merchandise; the indiscriminate application of neo-Kantian teleological judgment as a basis for the pan-artistic exaltation of the artistic vocation. All these are specific traits of Olbrich, and the majority predate the full emergence of the problematics of the Secession. Such ideas would find a sympathetic milieu not in Vienna, but in Darmstadt, at the court of the Grand Duke Ernst Ludwig von Hessen.

When the *Künstlerkolonie* was founded in 1899,[5] Olbrich already had many major works behind him: *Ideen,* dedicated to the Grand Duke, presented a synthesis and explanation of them.[6] This involved a rather mechanical reaffirmation of the poetics of the *Jugendstil:* the artist gives life to ideas; he invents a world that has never existed. But this invention has a *prophetic* import: the creation of a style serves as the prefiguration of a world to come.[7] The *Feinheit der Curve* (elegance of line)—a direct expression, a hieroglyph of the Nervenleben—and the real object of the Jugendstil, is the characteristic and necessary medium of this creation. This Feinheit cannot develop geometrically, inasmuch as it is Stimmung and Erlebnis—and inasmuch as every form must include-subsume in itself the life of the subject. Through this inclusion, all use value is transformed, emancipated. This inclusion is liberation. The poet "emancipates" all Handwerk from the stifling influence of industry and "frees" its demands from the mark of specific enterprises, from the domi-

The Contemporaries

nation of specific entrepreneurs.[8] The poet universalizes things, liberating them from the *principium individuationes*. But this task is required by the age, which perceives it as its own destiny. There is no doubt in the words inscribed on the fronton of the Palais-Secession: *Der Zeit ihre Kunst / Der Kunst ihre Freiheit* (Art for the times / Freedom for art).[9]

But the Feinheit der Curve and the Nervenleben of the Friedman Villa at Hinterbrähl (1898),[10] the Palais-Secession, or the buildings of the first Exhibition of the Kunstlerkolonie at Darmstadt (1901)—the coherence of Olbrich's original Jugendstil program—become confused in subsequent works, reaching a state of crisis in the final works of 1905–1908. The characteristics of this crisis were implicit in the original ideology. The synthetic-semantic import of the Jugendstil is intrinsically analogous to the position of Historismus: to resolve-sublimate lived experience in the work, and at the same time, to comprehend its languages, its "traditions"—to contemplate its history as though it were teleologically directed towards the present gratification that the modern work provides. But the Jugendstil ideology's recognition of its affinity with Historismus involves a resolution of its unresolved tensions: Historismus functions as a creator of order in the Jugendstil's development. In as much as synthetical ideology broadens the Jugendstil's powers, the experience of the negative implicit in the Jugendstil's original position must necessarily be cast aside. Never can the Jugendstil be pure organism, "naturally" resolved universality—only its transformation into an historicist phenomenon could permit such a total travesty. The "Romanesque" style of the Hochzeitsturm and the buildings for the Darmstadt Exhibition (1905–1908), where the influence of Behrens is also in evidence, is *Heimatkunst* ("regional art") on the one hand, and an already "organic architecture" on the other. The naturalism of the soul characteristic of the early Jugend is transformed into the organicity of the work, the full integration of the work into the natural surroundings: the Hochzeitsturm is above all an *Aussichtsturm* (belvedere). But earlier, Heimatkunst had already appeared with the facade of the Edmund Olbrich house at Troppau (1904)—and also with the affected rococo of the 1902 cottage in the woods for Princess Elizabeth von Hessen.

Loos and His Contemporaries

However, in Olbrich's most cryptic work, this Romanesque and this Heimatkunst coexist with still other languages, different "nostalgias"; in the Frauenrosenhof, built by Olbrich in 1905 for the 1906 Deutsche Kunstausstellung at Cologne, the diversity of languages is in plain view. The function of synthesis is no longer accorded to tensions or significations within these languages—but to the tone, to the overall atmosphere of the work, to the way in which the work must be experienced, to its Stimmung. This Stimmung keeps the different languages in a dimension of memory, as it were, in a lyrical dimension of detachment and renunciation, from which no privileged creator of order can emerge, and no general end can be attributed to the multiplicity of possible directions, harmonies, and sensations. There is the Heimatkunst of the portico of round brick arches, of the irregularly squared red stones; there is the richness and the oriental "luxury" of the interior hall, where the Secession ornamental motifs intermingle with recollections of the Alhambra; there is the well-defined profile, in the manner of a Chinese pavilion, of the west building, which resembles a Moser design, a Hoffmann interior; there are the basins of flowers in front of the building, the tones of the Klimtian plants. The "impressions" proceed from the peace of the entrance "cloister" to the light and Nervenleben of the hall, to the oriental "organicity" of the pavilions and the western terraces facing a small lake. It is the highest point of "suspended tonality" and of the awareness of such suspension ever achieved by Olbrich.[11]

In Olbrich's final works, the earlier Historismus, the organic elements and Heimatkunst elements—all of which had brought Jugend problematics to a point of crisis by developing their intrinsic aporiae—find a common inflection in the measure of a "precious" bourgeois language, in a prosody sustained by a conscious, detached decorum. As in the 1908 Kruska House at Cologne-Lindenthal, "Viennese," Hoffmannian elements reappear in this context, elements almost completely foreign to the original poetics of the Mathildenhöhe. The "classical" elements become essential creators of this new order: the building tends to enclose itself around them, around this value—dwelling "returns home". The accentuation of the classical elements—the Doric columns of the Feinhals House—together with the strict,

The Contemporaries

typically Wagnerian and Hoffmannian rhythm of the external surfaces, underscores the "quality" of dwelling, the building's artistocratic Stimmung. Indeed, one could say that the accentuation of the classical elements and rigor aims at expressing a transcendance of the bourgeois home and decorum in the form of the aristocratic life. Here finally reemerge the deep-seated motives of the original Secession ideology: the overcoming of the "bourgeois" existence of the home—the goal of expressing existence in a "classical" manner, sub specie aeternitatis— is a perfect complement to the redemption of labor in poetic activity, and to the redemption of use value in the "quality" produced by artistic form. The extreme classicism of Olbrich attempts to form, in a comprehensible manner, to clarify, and to communicate this distant argument.

The essential features of this argument resurface a generation later, in such "revolutionary" writings as Behne's *Von Kunst zur Gestaltung*.[12] The appearance, the revolutionary tattoo obtained by negating a totally mannered image of the artistic act (*Schmuck für Feiertage,* holiday decoration), makes it possible to ideologize the other aspect, the Gestaltung, in the same terms in which Olbrich exalted the poetic functions of the artist. The freedom that Gestaltung achieves (*der Kunst ihre Freiheit*) molds the entire community into its language and according to its principles (the world of the artist . . . *noch jemals sein wird.*) Gestaltung is an image of subjects working in freedom—a prefiguration of a totally de-alienated community. This image must be made real—to do so would no longer be *erklären,* to explain, (art has until now . . . explained the world), but *verändern,* to transform, (art, or rather Gestaltung, must now change it). In Behne, utopian traditions, *Kommunismus,* and the ideologies of *Planordnung* are all inextricably confused with the foundations of Olbrich's argument, with the radical origins of the Jugendstil ideology. Behne is still all ornament—that is, anti-Loosian.

Indeed, ornament here reveals another side of itself: that is, its inability to construct. Even Gestaltung is doomed to fail here. In the radical German circles of the postwar years, this failure is turned into a rejection of institutions, an anti-organizational argument.[13] Scheerbart's *Glasarchitektur* had already forseen this outcome. The supreme freedom of the "stellar house of crys-

Loos and His Contemporaries

tal," the exaltation of the "living, transparent, sensitive" man versus the "new institutions" that reify him are also characteristic of the Mathildenhöhe; indeed, it is at once its radical verification and its radical failure. In the pan-aesthetic exaltation of art, this fact is even more visible: "life aspires to absolute totality . . . to the science of sciences—philosophy . . . aspires to architecture, which is a threefold totality: it contains all the other arts within itself—painting, sculpture, the art of buildings, the art of gardens . . . It is the place of the totality of human life on earth." [14]

From this point of view, the very dissolution of Gestaltung is turned into a desperate reinterpretation of "l'art pour l'art": liberation from all interest, pure vision, utopia. What causes the despair is that these ideas now appear *post rem*. The happy prospect of their realization, which understood the ideas of the Secession, as well as those of the Werkbund and the Werkstätte, in a teleological manner, can now be seen only as dead: "Art wishes to be an image of death." [15] But this death is still "ornamented" with values—it appears as value—and thereby remains within the tradition it sought to destroy. The collapse of Gestaltung becomes a "cosmic" dissolution of forms; it is transformed into theater, into musical drama—it becomes *style*. [16] Here the utopian dimension is a negation of language, the opposite of what it is in Loos—the otherness and the presence of the limit constituting the very conditions for meaning. In Loos, the utopian dimension is inextricably immersed in the universe of language—and it is because of its presence that the Aufklärung of this universe is possible. On the other hand, the arguments of Behne and Taut, with their multiple concerns, define the limits and the traditions of an avant-garde, to which the "irrelevant considerations" of Loos remain totally foreign.

The work of Otto Wagner, by way of contrast, is primarily informed by an ultimate attempt at synthesis between the metropolitan perspective of these "considerations" and the transcendental functions of value and artistic form based on the presupposition of the freedom of artistic form, functions which tend to be realized as Planordnung, synthetical social organization. The interlacement of the two perspectives characterizes the aesthetics of *Moderne Architektur*. [17] Here, the concept of

The Contemporaries

style, presented in the exact terms of *Zeitstil* (style of the times), which Loos attacked harshly—style as the writing of the molding force of the Ego—is constantly and strictly controlled by the necessity of the material: it all boils down to the functions, the languages, and the real materials—in short, to the continually tested and acknowledged limits of the constructible.[18] The relation is no longer univocal; it is no longer presented in rigidly hierarchical terms of value. The transformation process moves from the material to the Zeitstil, and vice-versa. This dialectic is, for Wagner, construction itself: Baukunst, not Stilarchitektur. Although still teleologically described and dominated by historicist finalism (where all must appear as organism), the construction process, in its concrete substance, assumes the functions, the necessities, and the vision of the Metropolis.[19] Metropolitan ideology, even if not yet logicized, still unmoors the foundations of Gemeinschaft. Here we have historicism, but no Heimatkunst; organism, but no Gemüt. Historicist ideology is reinterpreted *functionally*. Hence, no pictoriality, no irrationality in the design of the Grosstadt, in the *Dekor* of its buildings. What comes first "ontologically" is the form of the whole: corresponding to this form is the totality of the metropolitan life. Historicism and synthetical ideology are valid only in so far as they appear functional to the economic organization of the urban space and to the communication of its signification, its values: this organization has, in fact, as one of its conditions, the artistic project— the Gestaltung derives from the artistic idea. But this project and this idea cannot impose any abstract language on the urban space: Gestaltung means the formation of the tendencies and the language of this metropolitan life—it implies giving them an order. Wagner's critique of the idea of the garden city is, in this light, really a critique of presentations of the city as an image of community (p. 21).

If the Metropolis is to become organism, this organism will no longer be, in any way, that of Gemeinschaft. The teleological judgment (which, to repeat, remains the basis of Wagner's argument) becomes a project of the further organization and rationalization of the Metropolis itself. On the other hand, this perspective cannot be implemented except through the disinterested and autonomous intervention of artistic action. Free rein

Loos and His Contemporaries

must be given to art in order to sweep away the lethal influence of the engineer. Again, we have a difference of value among the various languages. The language of the engineer in the processes of urban development is that of speculation; it represents "die Macht des Vampyrs Spekulation" (p. 17). Liberating the Metropolis from this vampire means re-creating it as an act of artistic language: as an image of organization, as disinterested community life. Wagner's Grossstadt in this way shows the profound influence of the Austrian neo-classical economic schools of the time, in their more socially committed versions: the struggle against the positions of revenue (theoretically confused with monopolistic profits), justice in distribution, the satisfaction of the consumer (in this case, the satisfaction of the subject that the Metropolis is supposed to "assimilate"). On the other hand, these versions of Austrian marginalism would also exert a decisive influence on the future urban policy of social democratic Vienna.[20] It is a question of the utopian reduction of the capitalistic market mechanism to the "pure" functioning of its "laws." The engineer twists these laws to fit the conditions of revenue. The artist reasserts their authenticity, and, on the basis of their tendencies, overcomes the fortuitousness of contemporary urban growth, outlining a rational plan for the development of the Metropolis.[21] Artistic *Gestaltung* becomes an organ-instrument of the realization of pure market values uncontaminated by the forces of speculation identified with the forces of chance, with nineteenth-century *Planlosigkeit,* and with economic Manchesterism. Artistic Gestaltung brings forth the values of Zivilisation-Rationalisierung inherent in the "laws" of capitalist development and the modern Metropolis— values that revenue and speculation obscure and stifle.

The idea that these "laws" do not exist except in a state of transformation was absent from the neo-classicals, as well as from the social democracy that Wagner "used." The awareness that the engineer and Spekulation are agents of these transformations, and present themselves as a historical problem central to modern urban development, is present in Wagner only in negative form. Whereas, that the total difference of value between Gestaltung and speculation can be reintegrated into the comprehensive ideology that we have seen interweaving itself

The Contemporaries

129

between Werkbund, Werkstätte, and Secession is demonstrated by the ambiguities of Wagner's own position regarding these movements, the Secession in particular. The absolute difference between Gestaltung and Spekulation reconfirms the transcendental, as it were, concept of quality as regards the production and circulation of merchandise. However, artistic Gestaltung, for Wagner, does not invent its own language, its own order, but derives it from the basic tendencies of metropolitan life. That these tendencies are understood in exclusively ideological terms should not permit us to forget the important divergence of this position from the previous ones that we have analyzed (and, in certain ways, its affinity with Loos's problematics). The Gestaltung can no longer in any way be understood as a sort of messianic proclamation directed at the Metropolis. Gestaltung expresses, through its formal laws, the development of this Metropolis, which is now "liberated" from the "distortions" that prevented its rationalization. That these "distortions" are in reality but the negative inherent in the language of the Metropolis—that there can be no language except in its "distortions," that is, as multiplicity and contradiction—was a decisive point reached by Loos, not Wagner.

The same unresolved dialectic of the Grossstadt is dominant in Wagner's constructions: from the "tattooed" house, the Majolikahaus of 1898–1899, to the building of the Neustiftgasse; from the autumnal, floral, almost Olbrichian interiors of the first Wagner villa, to the perfectly apparent, comprehensible space of the Postpaarkasse, where nothing alludes to anything and nothing is "hidden behind" anything else.[22] The same unresolved dialectic dominates these constructions and the Metropolis that surrounds them, or is supposed to surround them. Are these constructions a language of the development of the Metropolis itself? Symbols of an absolutely utopian metropolitan Planordnung? By whom are they inhabited? Are they, in spite of everything, still "furnished" by the Wiener Werkstätte? The multiplicity of these dimensions gets confused in Wagner. The philosophical import of this problematic would later be pointed out by Simmel (who treats it from within the same perspective of Kultur to which Wagner also belongs): to consider, as does Wagner, metropolitan life as a place where conflict

Loos and His Contemporaries

is "symmetrically" resolved in artistic Gestaltung, is a "spectral possibility."[23] But logically speaking, the answer to Wagner's dialectic—the meaning of the contradictions and conflicts of the architectural Kultur traced thus far—lies inextricably in the unicum of Wittgenstein, in the house designed for his sister: it constitutes, together with Loos, the other pole of this problematic. But despite the great distance between the two poles, they cannot be understood except in reciprocal relation with one another.

The Wittgenstein house was for his sister, Margarethe Stonborough. In a portrait of her by Klimt, from 1905, her figure, which passes through the space of the Klimtian mosaics and magic squares and into the total absence of atmosphere, epitomizes the somber Viennese apocalypse.[24]

9. The Oikos of Wittgenstein

The limit of the space of this house[1] is constructed inexorably from within—from the very substance of its own language. The negative is not an other, but comprises the very othernesses that make up this language. There are no means of escape or "withdrawal" into the "values" of the interior. And the exterior is not designed in a utopian way, taking off from the value of Gestaltung—nor is it possible to save in the interior values that the metropolitan context negates. The work recalls neither Hoffmann, nor Wagner—nor even Loos and his "suspended dialectics" of interior-exterior. The idea of a hierarchically defined conflict between two levels of value is totally absent here. The conflict is with "all that remains," which cannot be determined or transformed by the limits of this language; hence, it is a conflict with the Metropolis lying beyond this space, a conflict which in this space can only be silence. But, for this very reason, this space ultimately reveals a recognition of the Metropolis as now devoid of mystification or utopism, an acknowledgment of all its power.

In all this lies the truly classical dimension of the Wittgenstein house (fig. 4): the non-expressivity of the calculated space of the building is its essential substance.[2] The building's sole relation with what remains is the presence of the building itself. It cannot in any way determine or allude to the *apeiron* (infinite) surrounding it. Also classical is the calculation to which every passage is rigorously subjected, as well as the freezing of the linguistic media into radically anti-expressive orders, a phenomenon taken to the point of a manifest indifference toward the material (or rather, to the point of choosing indifference in the material, of choosing indifferent materials, materials without qualities)—but what is most classical here is the relation between the limited-whole of the house and the surrounding space.

The silence of the house, its impenetrability and anti-expressivity, is concretized in the ineffability of the surrounding space. So it is with the classical: classical architecture is a symbol (in the etymological sense) of the in-finite (a-peiron) that surrounds it. Its anti-expressivity is a symbol of the ineffability of the a-peiron. The abstract absoluteness of its order exalts the limit of the architectonic language; its non-power expresses the encompassing infinite. But at the same time, and as a result, this language constructs itself in the presence of this infinite, and cannot be understood except in light of this infinite. This presence of the classical in Wittgenstein represents one of the exceptional moments in which the development of modern ideology re-assumed the true problematics of the classical. Webern would conclude his life's work with this presence, linking himself with the first, lacerating modern perception of the classical—an anti-Weimarian, anti-historicist, tragic vision—: that of Hölderlin.[3] At this point the immeasurable distance separating Wittgenstein's classical from Olbrich's later works and from Hoffmann's constant tendency is clear. Olbrich's "classical" is a

Loos and His Contemporaries

transformation of the Secession mask into that of a reacquired order, a recuperated wholeness. Hoffmann's "classical" is an affirmation (or rather, an ever-contradicted, ever-disputed repetition) of the historicist dimension illuminated by a Weimarian nostalgia. But even Loos's notion of the Roman, as we have seen, is completely averse to any simple idea of recuperation or neo-classical refoundation, or even mere Gemeinschaft. And yet, not even a trace of this Roman element can be found in Wittgenstein's oikos.

The "Roman" is seen by Loos in terms of functionality and use. Its dimension is that of experience, of the temporal—and hence of *social existence*. Every project lives immersed in this general historical context: the light that brings it forth is that of time. In this way were the Romans able to adopt from the Greeks every order, every style: it was all the same to them. What was essential was the light that brought forth the building—and not just the building, but the life of the entire society. Their only problems were the great problems of planning. "Ever since humanity has understood the grandeur of classical antiquity, one single thought has united all great architects. They think: I shall build just as the ancient Romans would have built. . . . every time architecture strays from its model to go with the minor figures, the decorativists, there reappears the great architect who leads the art back to antiquity."[4] From the Romans, says Loos, we have derived the *technique* of thought, our power to transform it into a process of rationalization. We conceive of the world technically and temporally, just as it unfolds in the ribbon of Trajan's Column; we conceive of the Denkmal as a civil project—as architecture from the point of view of those who live it and reap its benefits.

This point of view, then, is the true a-peiron surrounding the Roman project. Its context is that of the *res publica*. It lives in time, in the flux of its own consumption. Wittgenstein's oikos is opposed to this Roman conception of the classical. Being inhabited, being seen is unimportant to the space of the oikos. It presents itself as apart from the existence of him who perceives it; for this reason, the movements of the subjects who benefit from it leave no trace. For it to present itself, all that is necessary is the postulation of its own limit and hence of the absolutely

The Oikos of Wittgenstein

ineffable a-peiron that illuminates it. "The house thinks of the present," says Loos; "the house is conservative," and its interior functions only towards the gratification of its inhabitants: "the house must please everyone."[5]

In stripping the house of all values, Wittgenstein by contrast abstracts it from all teleological considerations. His project is posited and resolved like a theorem. And a theorem is infinitely repeatable, infinitely extraneous to all value—but also infinitely unicum, not variable, not mobile, not subject to lived experience. The oikos is not there to please; the exterior is not supposed to allude to anyone "buried" there; it thinks neither of the present, nor of the future. It ex-sists in the present of the ineffable and its light. Its formal perfection is the sequentiality of the theorem; it is indifference towards style, material, ornament—it is the tragic perfection of its limit. This is classical dialectics. Nothing here could be farther from Loos's late-Roman vision of the classical.

Hence, it is clear why, in the regressive atmosphere of the post-war period in which he was elaborating his argument, Loos might want to realign himself with the classical-Greek as he understood it. For Loos, Greekness is preeminently the order of the monument, the Denkmal, the order of an artistry distinct in terms of value from the production-circulation of use values, and opposed to the life of the Metropolis. His project for a new office building of the Chicago *Tribune* (1922) bears witness to this anything but ironic reversal:

> As a paradoxical phantom of an ordering outside of time,
> Loos's column assumes gigantic proportions in an ultimate
> effort to communicate an appeal to the timelessness of values:
> but, just like Kandinsky's giants in *Das gelbe Klange*, the
> gigantic Loosian phantom succeeds in signifying only its own
> pathetic will to exist. Pathetic because declared in the face
> of the Metropolis, in the face of the very universe of change,
> of the eclipse of values, of the "decline of aura," that negates
> the actuality of this column and this will to communicate
> absolute significations.[6]

When he wants to exalt, in terms of value, his own difference from the Metropolis, Loos can only return to the pure Greek order—positing it as an overcoming, as a great end, as the architecture without qualities of the lower part, the base of the skyscraper. But this is precisely the opposite of the classical characteristic of Wittgenstein's oikos, which is a negation of all "universal aura," of all reactualization of values, of all declarations to the Metropolis. Which brings us back to its difference from Loos's "Roman" notion.

Loos's "Roman" can work, can exist in the concrete functions of architecture. Wittgenstein's oikos, precisely in its singularity, manifests an infinite distance from the source, and a total refusal to reactualize it. Wittgenstein's classical does not present itself as silence: it is totally uninhabited. The presence of the classical, the light of the a-peiron and the building that it encompasses and reveals, here reappear as silence, as absence. The Roman of Loos, on the other hand, functions as a possible direction that the project's discourse can take. No such indication emerges from Wittgenstein's oikos. Its radicality is totally negative— even with respect to the doctrine of the *Tractatus,* the semantic possibility described therein. What reappears here from this work, if anything, are the aporiae of its final pages. But this negative is the measure of the Loosian compromise, the real parameter of its "medianness," and at the same time exposes its interior mechanism, its hidden and, in many ways, removed side. In a certain sense, in spite of the profound difference between the two attitudes and the two projects, the Wittgenstein house is the "truth" of Loosian research. Once grasped, this truth cannot be repeated—such would be ornament, confusion—just as in Webern a sound cannot be repeated before the full exposition of the series.

But as we have seen, the concrete method of Loos's research remains in conflict, up to the end and in spite of everything, with the radicality of Wittgenstein's solution. Never will the "Roman" be a complete synthesis, a real, universal technique of thought, a real society. In this sense, Loos's utopia will always remain akin to the neo-positivistic utopia. And this utopia will always be expressed through its lacerating conflicts. Hence it is not the "Roman," the idea of the Roman, but these conflicts that constitute the ever-present problem and the true sense of Loosian composition.

The Oikos of Wittgenstein

135

Because of its problematic character—as well as its actual contents, which we have already examined—Loos's "Roman" can
be seen as closely connected to the research of the Viennese
school of art history, and to that of Franz Wickhoff and Alois
Riegl in particular.[7] This research was directed at confirming
that Roman art had little to do with the historicist-Weimarian
conception of the classical as universal; this conclusion was
based on the emphasis of the temporal dimension, of the lived
experience, in such art. This emphasis directly posed the problem of the subject as producer, and that of the specific forms
that this productivity assumed in overcoming the conception of
the classical as a totality of archetypal forms, as pure art. The
temporality of the "Roman" posed the problem of the specific
Zeitgeist of the artistic act, its process and the forms of its production and circulation-communication. The "social character"
of the Roman placed the focus on the artistic act's forms of existence. And these are the same factors on which Loos based his
own conception of the "Roman."

But the fundamental feature of Roman artistic form—or
rather, the reason for its modern-day re-emergence as a problematic—lies in the functional diversity of its constitutive elements and levels. This form is not the end-all and be-all of the
Weimarian neo-classical tradition, but the comprehensive representation of this problem, as it first arises, as it develops, as
one attempts to resolve it, and as it gives way to partial answers. The very temporal dimension to which this representation inevitably belongs leads to such a result: representation is
process, becoming, event; an analysis of it should shed light on
the plurality of aspects of which it is made up—as well as on
the inevitable *relativity* of all possible results, since they too are
subject to time, are themselves time. The relativity of the temporal process is itself the ephemerality of each result registered at
each moment. This dialectic appears in the composition itself:
indeed, it represents the meaning of composition. Nothing can
work for the eternal.

However, this combination of relations—the temporality and
relativity of the process, the ephemerality of the formal results,
and the representation—is not simply "resigned" to this state
of affairs, it is not at home in its immediate negative. It is con-

Loos and His Contemporaries

flictual, contradictory—and openly manifests these lacerations. The subject who lives and works in time wants nevertheless to achieve the perfect work, in spite of the fact that its representation must unfold through the temporality of the materials, the functions and the goals of the work. The subject shapes the materials in their becoming—but his will does not affect the immediate, a priori definable limits of the relativity and ephemerality of the result. From this basic perspective, the "Roman" represents not only the end of the classical utopia, the end of the nostalgia for the classical revelation of forms—but also the end of the very synthesis attainable between the subjective will and its various representations. The subject will never be "at home" in its representations—nor will it be so in its work, or in its art. This contemporary destiny of alienation was already present in the concept of the "Roman": its importance for Loos, and for the avant-garde movements in figurative art in the first decades of the century, cannot be understood without this essential fact.

The "Roman" appears when all historicist continuity is shattered; the ensemble of Loos's contradictions—functionality and art, relativity and value, the reaffirmation of value and the impossibility of representing it, the limit of representation and the will to surpass it—is "Roman." All composition is time, is subjectivity in time, and as such is ephemeral—but at the same time, beyond such representation, it is infinite necessity-to-be. The composition is therefore determined on the basis of the contradiction between this in-finite will (based in temporality, experience, and uprootedness) and the materials of time—all of the elements constituting both time and the representation itself. This is no longer "expressivity" in the manner of the Secession—unresolved tension, nostalgia, utopia—but *Expressionismus:* the demonstration of a laceration as irreversible as it is unbearable. This Expressionism is founded in and derived from the "Roman," as Riegl had synthesized it in the concept of *Kunstwollen* (artistic will). Art is the expression of a natural *Wollen:* this will is time, becoming. Its language is continually in an incomplete state; it is the ever-multiple language of the *creature*. Its products therefore cannot express any kind of all-inclusive understanding, nor any dominion over the process of

The Oikos of Wittgenstein

becoming—instead, they represent the interior products and moments of this Wollen.[8]

It is through the concept of Kunstwollen—the aporiae of the will in the process of artistic composition—that Riegl's "Roman" becomes profoundly connected with the crisis of the Secession ideology and the emergence of Expressionism. It is not philosophically possible to think of Expressionism outside of the context of Riegl's Kunstwollen and Loos's "Roman." Expressionism is no longer the suspension but the breakdown of classical tonal relations beyond all possibility of return. Kunstwollen asserts the insuperable temporality of the work—but this temporality is consumption, flux, conflict. The "Roman" is the breakdown of the classical utopia—but its very form appears as lacerated. Expressionism has its origins in the "Roman": on this foundation are based the "elective affinities" existing among the "great Viennese masters of language." In this light, one can understand, at the source, the profound relation linking Loos to Kokoschka—as well as Loos's break from all versions of Secessionist ideology, a break more analogous to the endeavors of Gerstl, Schiele, and Kokoschka, than to the "suspensions" and doubts of Klimt. And one can understand as well the connection between this research and that carried out contemporaneously by Schönberg—especially the need to paint that Schönberg felt in those decisive years.[9]

But the fundamental links tying Rieglian Kunstwollen to the very concept of Expressionism would not be fully elucidated until the appearance of Benjamin's essay on Trauerspiel.[10] And at this point our inquiry must come to a close. Benjamin's essay, which is in reality a comprehensive interpretation of the radical avant-garde, begins with the name of Riegl and concludes with a general outline of the aesthetics of Expressionism. Benjamin makes another connection as well—one which takes us back to the Viennese linguistics of the period that we have analyzed: with the Hofmannsthal of the dramas of creatures, of life and language as sign.[11] Hofmannsthal's figures were able to assume an aesthetico-philosophical importance because they were creatures of the time, ephemeral representations of the Kunstwollen, personae of the "Roman" drama.

Loos and His Contemporaries

Part III

Loos

and

His

Angel

10. Loos and His Angel

In attacking the fetish of the "creative life," Benjamin brings
Loos and Kraus together in his famous essay on Kraus.[1] "Could
there be anything more asocial than beauty, which is always
in front of a mirror?" wrote Kraus in 1915 in an essay-letter
addressed to Loos, perhaps the most important document of
their "elective affinity."[2] Could the *Unsittlichkeit des Lebens*
(immorality of life), the absolute absence of ethos, ever emerge
in a more tragic light than in that Secessionist brutalization of
taste,[3] which, by blurring the difference between an urn and a
chamber pot, nullifies the sphere of Kultur,[4] and against which
that *Rechtsgeher der Kultur* (cultural right-winger), one of the
few *Antiwiener*, Adolf Loos, had always fought?[5] The close
connection that Benjamin makes between Kraus's fight against
journalism and Loos's fight against ornamentation is a topos of
the *Fackel: "Die Phrase ist das Ornament des Geistes."*[6] The

Phrase puts the word into circulation and consumption, and ornamentation is its toilette. Journalist and aesthete alike are true *Realpolitiker.*[7]

But all this could too easily also be interpreted in terms of demystified rationalization. And indeed, this is how Loos is still understood, by and large.[8] With an exception: at the end of his piece on Kraus, Benjamin evokes the enigma of the figure of the New Angel. Kraus is an enigmatic messenger. In a way, his nature shows itself to be secretly satanic. Indeed, this side of himself emerges and displays itself with arrogance—with regard, precisely, to *right,* since the image of justice, which he reveres in the language, is superior to right. Benjamin grasped with extraordinary acuity the hubris of this process, which is celebrated in Kraus's tribunal: what stands accused (what the satanic side of the Angel intends to smite) is right (the "constructive ambiguities of right"), whose system of rules claims to be independent of the word and of justice, to which it owes its existence.[9] Right belongs to the world of the *Phrase* and of *Ornament* and constantly betrays the divine justice of the word—and for this reason, the word presents itself as *destructive* in its regard.

But even in Kraus, and especially in the lyrical Kraus (certainly the side most appreciated by Benjamin), the accusatory aspect of the Angel assumes a tone of lamentation. This is due to the double, indivisible meaning of *Klagen* (lament and accusatory discontent). Kraus's accusation covers a boundless *Leidland* (land of sorrow).[10] The clearer the voice of the lamentation in the whole of the *Klagelied,* the more profoundly one may then understand the other aspect of the figure of the Angel—the idea of redemption. This idea is a desperate one, in the literal sense of the word—without hope. The Angel, indeed, does not look towards the future.[11] He is free of the fascination of the future—he is pushed into it, but with his back turned. His hope is not part of the continuum of history; it is not promised by any law, by any causal chain.[12] The idea of redemption—of which the angel is also a figure—at the outermost limit of the Leidland, belongs to the dimension of the *Jetztzeit* (present day), to the moment that blasts apart the foundations of the "age of domi-

Loos and His Angel

nators." The dimension of the Jetztzeit is exactly like that of justice as the word that accuses-destroys "constructive" right.[13]

Like those of the Angel, the eyes of Kraus and Loos can see only the endless accumulation of ruins. They cannot dwell on the reconstruction of what is already shattered, which is above their task. The "sober language" that for Benjamin gives a lasting quality to Kraus's work is the language of this limitation. However excessive the hubris of the accusation might be, never is it confused with a claim to redemption. The idea of redemption flashes only in the "scattered fragments" of the messianic time that the present holds. Every second of this present might be the moment, the strait gate through which the Messiah will enter. But the Angel announces not the coming of this moment, but rather the *feeble* messianic strength that is granted us, "to which the past has a right." The Angel accuses the "brothel of historicism" and asserts this feeble strength. He cannot redeem—nor "does he sing hymns any longer."[14] He has forever lost his naive, immediate proximity to God's throne, and has fallen "for an unduly long period of time"[15] into the catastrophe of history—but he cannot extricate himself from this catastrophe (nor can he extricate his human partner) like a reborn figure of Hermes psychopomp. The storm that enraptures the Angel comes from Heaven; he *wants* happiness. But this is his only "message." He is eternally condemned on the path to his own origin. As are Kraus and Loos on the path to the word.

A feeble strength. The hymn was once able to revere the image of divine justice. The lamentation, the Klagelied, is infinitely remote from it. But only the ephemeral Angel, in his original state, could be transformed into the Angel of history. When his work comes to be "upset," he is thereby also released from his original destiny, that of dissolving into nothingness. His ephemeral nature is, so to speak, stalled. He lasts in the ephemeral. Before, his hymn lasted only an instant, but it sang the praises of the Immutable. Now his hymn is infinitely long and patient, but it has become a Klagendelied in the face of only chains of events and the shattered. The dimension of the moment itself is part of this structure of time. Its ephemerality has become *im-perfect*. If the Angel's origin, toward which he is supposedly driven, is the pure sound of the hymn that lasts only an instant before dissolving

Loos and His Angel

into nothingness, then the most hidden content of his message is the *perfect ephemeral*. This dialectic explains the enigma mentioned on the last page of Benjamin's essay on Kraus. There, Benjamin asserts on the one hand that the writings of Kraus establish their "dominance on permanence" and that they "have already begun to last"—and on the other, that his voice imitates that of the new Angel, which "quickly vanishes." His language lasts: it is now a conflict in the chain of events. But his language also imitates the perfect ephemerality of the hymn; "it has nothing to hope for along any path" that is not the one leading back to the word, the image of divine justice, pronounced in the moment. The moment is a figure of the original, perfect ephemeral. The patient wait is a figure of the imperfect ephemeral—of the ephemeral that lasts, that is forced to last, but that in this waiting is able to imitate the word of the hymn.

The mark of the relation between this duration, which is endurance, and the ephemeral in its duality as event and moment, hymn and Klagendelied, dominates the entire work of both Kraus and Loos. It is "spilled" into the ephemeral. Through 922 issues and thirty-seven years, *Die Fackel* endured in the ephemeral—earning its durability through this endurance. This dimension is even more evident in Loos's *Das Andere*. Their eyes are so focused on, so spasmodically attentive to the chain of events—which the Angel sees as "a single catastrophe"—that they are transformed into that chain, indistinguishable from it, and become its inextricable quotation. But the very patience with which they endure, a patience which "possesses claws and wings as sharp as blades," preserves "the glimmer of hope" and exhibits, in the present, the "scattered fragments" of the time of the Messiah.[16] They neither reconstruct nor reawaken the shattered, but know how to gather it together, to collect it. Under their gaze the shattered is collected—and reveals itself not as in the past tense, not dead. Necessarily powerless to compose, feeble in remembering and collecting, balanced in the present, they are nevertheless aware of the right that the ruins, which are endlessly accumulating at our feet, have over our present. The word that they seek, the search for the word, is the gesture that continually re-ignites the glimmer of hope in the past.

Loos and His Angel

It is hence the opposite of an enduring in the ephemeral simply for the sake of computing-rationalizing it. This ephemeral constantly seeks the imitation of the moment, the happiness that would come from a return to the perfect ephemerality of the hymn, to the direct praise of divine justice. The ephemeral is not the event in whose chain we take up our place—it is rather the multiple events, the catastrophe that the Angel sees and seeks to drag behind him "into the future whence it came." After all, he seeks happiness, not simply the eternal return of the event. He does not announce, against the homogeneous and empty time of historicism, the cyclical time of the eternal return, but rather the moment that exceeds all duration, and that every second may carry within itself. If this tension were to vanish from Kraus's work, all that would remain is the face of the accuser, of "right," and not that of hope, of "justice." Just as in Loos, all that one would be able to see is the simplicity of the constructive, the progressive, the empty and homogeneous image of duration. Of course, it is only in rare, happy moments that Kraus goes so far as lamenting his own too feeble strength in collecting the shattered and entering with it into a *sympathy* deeper than all critique, than all judgment—but for Kraus as well as for Loos, the past still continues to suffer and hope, scheming secret understandings with us, waiting for us. But though their eyes be turned to the past, never do they seek therein an "eternal image," or a model with which to oppose the ephemeral present. There is no respite in the past that they see, just as there is no flight toward the future: their backs are turned to it. The past is transformed into the vision and hearing of a living, incessant questioning—into a problem par excellence. It is in this relation, which develops through detours of the longest sort, through the longest waits, that we are pulled away towards the future. Indeed, what we call the future occurs in this dialogue. The very language of Kraus and Loos is this dialogue: it is the relation—which is all the more indestructible as it is less nostalgic—not with tradition *tout court,* but with tradition that has preserved in language the "search for a lost image of the primordial," [17] which has not blurred the difference between moment and hope, between hymn, lamentation, and accusation.

Loos and His Angel

For this reason, it is impossible for the language of this relation to be contained in that of criticism. In criticism, the moment of listening is only a moment of passage on the way to the pronouncement of judgment; it is an eternal "once upon a time." Judgment is the application of well-established rules. Criticism always exhibits a positive right. Only the object captured in its perspective is ephemeral—but this perspective wants to be true, to be *right*, to overcome the ephemeral. The language of the Angel, on the other hand, is, in its entirety, included in the ephemeral—between the perfect ephemeral, which is origin and end, and the imperfect ephemeral of its Klagenlelied. Judging is no more its task than redeeming: if it could interpret and fully explain the shattered, it could reconstruct it. Its infinite patience symbolizes the unattainability of a "center" from which the fragment might be judged.

The form that this patience takes is perhaps that of the *commentary*. It differs not only from the perspective of criticism, but also from that of the essay, which in its revolving around the text circumscribes and dominates it, even while collapsing its center. The commentary has nothing to do with a Text (the "eternal image"), but rather with mutable landscapes whose contours are unpredictable. The "text" of the commentary is that chain of events that extends without end, accumulating without respite. The object of the commentary flies away, together with the gaze of the Angel. But in this "together" there is no *Einfühlung,* no mutual identification in the wavering light of simple sentiment. The difference is insurmountable. The commentary devotes itself to listening to *these* fragments, which in forming and unforming themselves stir up the scene of the past. Equally ephemeral, since at every moment it changes its position and point of view, the commentary is, however, always in front of them. It lasts not only in the ephemeral, but also in this difference. The "secret life of the commentary," which Scholem so pointedly grasped in Benjamin's language, derives from this insuppressible presence of fragments, "texts," presuppositions, which no critical alchemy can dissolve or subsume. The commentary form is as lacking in creative freedom as were the ancient commentaries

Loos and His Angel

"of archaic texts imbued with authority."[18] The commentary does not "wallow in creativity," it does not look at itself in the mirror, it does not irrupt as judgment.[19] It gives life to labyrinths, interlacements, dialogues with the past, and thus does its future occur. It never sets itself up as a new fetish of autonomy and freedom. And only in its saturnine light is the hope of redemption preserved, a hope about which *nothing can be said.*

But therein lies the paradox of the commentary: it no longer stands before the text to which Scholem refers. Its "text" is the ephemeral. To treat the ephemeral and its movement, its accumulations of questions and expectations as though it were still a text, as though it still had authority, means embracing the ephemeral with a profound, desperate seriousness. This is the quintessential message of *Die Fackel.* Within the limits of this "as though" falls the work of Loos. But this vision of the ephemeral is made possible by the fact that at any moment, as we have seen, it might witness the unpredictable moment, the happy chance that breaks up the chain of events and redeems the past itself. The commentary form is necessary to him who wants not only to put an end to constructive ("creative") right, but also to grasp and prove, in the ephemeral, the existence of that "glimmer of hope." Loos is obsessed with renouncing language that claims to be liberated from all presuppositions and to serve as Text in itself. He sees in it the diabolical gesture of those who abandon the past, who do not recognize the right that it has over us, and hence persist in desiring its overthrow. The "freedom" of the avant-garde and the hubris of its criticism shatter the delicate balance of the figure of the Angel and dissipate the feeble messianic strength that it announces to us. On the one hand, the avant-garde decrees the "once upon a time," and reduces things to "eternal images"—on the other, it turns its gaze to the future and, like a fortune-teller, looks for "what lies hidden in its womb." For the Angel, on the other hand, the ephemeral of the present *senses* that of the past, and its future lies in the moment, which is origin. And in any case, how could the Angel destroy all presuppositions, if the very happiness for which he yearns is itself presupposed?

Loos and His Angel

11. Being Loyal

In many places Loos asserts his work to be a commentary on tradition. The house on the Michaelerplatz is a problem of Viennese architecture: it must be able to be understood against this background, to carry on a dialogue with the Hofburg, and to resolve compositional questions "in terms of our old Viennese masters."[1] In his important essay of 1910, "Architecture," to which we shall return at the end of this chapter, Loos reconfirms in even more general terms the fact that he belongs to the history of language, the only ground in which thought can grow.[2] Here the critique of the fetish of the "creative life" becomes radical: he opposes the solipsism of its beauty in front of the mirror with the meaning of tradition and belonging. And he opposes "invented" architecture, the lie that walks beside us, with "the truth, though it be centuries old."[3]

It is necessary to dwell upon the philosophy of these assertions, which logically emerges from Loos's commentary. Their accent does not fall on the nostalgia for patriarchal handicraft-culture; their polemical target is the architect as dominator—the dominance of one meaning, of one direction, of one organization over the combination of materials and languages that produce the work. In the impatience for the new that is expressed in the architect's "artistic creation," Loos sees a pretense to erecting a work as text, or to erecting a work to serve as a central language, around which the other languages degenerate into

Loos and His Angel

means or instruments, and those of the past become an "eternal image." Loos's conception seems to come strikingly close to Wittgenstein's critique of the "single language" capable of "representing" the world.[4] Here the world is "represented" by multiple games, constitutive forms of opening onto the world, forms of life. No game is comprehensible by itself and in itself. They all confront each other, argue amongst each other, and exist in a dimension of openness and discourse that does not accept a single solution. Loos's relationship with the craftsman is a constant questioning of the single language, a continual problematicization of language as a combination of linguistic games, a repetition of the assertion that to speak of one language (or of one game) is mere abstraction. Language is tradition, use, praxis, comprehension, and the contradiction existing among the various openings onto the world: it is the accumulation of events—which do not demand contemplation, but rather the fleeting gaze of the Angel, who remembers and collects, symbol of the "discourse that we are."[5]

In this light, Loos's critique of architecture's "degeneration" to the level of graphic art assumes particular importance. "All of the new architecture is invented at the drawing table, and only later do the resulting drawings find their graphic realization, like paintings at a wax museum."[6] It is significant that it should have been Schönberg who, in the Festschrift for Loos's sixtieth birthday,[7] underscored this spatial, three-dimensional character of his work. In Loos, it is a question not only of indicating the specificity of a language—in this case, the language of architecture—but also of demonstrating the impossibility of reducing any language or linguistic game to *writing*, the impossibility of explaining and resolving the openness of a linguistic game in the unidimensionality of its written notation. The "dominating" architect dominates through pencil and book: the instrument of writing and the result of writing. The work follows the project. The project directs the praxis of handicraft labor. The conception of language expressed by this dialectic grounds the centrality of the *planning* intellectual and his *writings* in the linguistic praxis where intentions, uses, and forms of life are interwoven. Loosian language is a praxis that makes the various games of which it is made up relative to each other—it

Being Loyal

questions them, establishes difficult discourses among them. It is the language of the old masters, the language of material, the tradition of the craftsman. In Loos, there is no project that synthesizes these games, or that can restrict them to one language—but rather a process of trials, errors, suggestions, and gestures, in which only the possible is represented, the openness to the transformation of the rules that have been in play until now.

The craftsman, in Loos, is the very image of belonging. He is proof that the dimension of the game excludes all aesthetico-philosophical solipsism. Participation in a game is the fruit of learning and custom. One cannot play except by belonging, by habituating oneself to the rules that have shaped the game. In this "habit" new combinations, new possibilities emerge. The deeper one's participation in a game, the more these openings issue from practice itself, from habit. The truly present has deep roots—it needs the games of the old masters, the languages of posthumousness. This tradition therefore does not unfold from book to book, drawing to drawing, line to line, but follows the long detours, the waits, the labyrinths of the games among the languages, among linguistic *practices*.

But here emerges the problem, a central one for Wittgenstein as well, of the relation between this dimension of belonging, and choice, decision, innovative intention—without which the transformation of the game would be inconceivable, or would be reduced to a natural, biological change. "Following rules, giving messages, giving orders, playing chess are *habits* (uses, institutions)."[8] A language is a technique that we master only through habit, by belonging to it—that is, by practicing it. But Wittgenstein seems to posit habit and choice as in clear contradiction with one another: "When I follow the rule I do not choose. I follow the rule *blindly*" (p. 114). Following the rule seems to preclude all possibility of transgression, intent to decide (to decide is to break the rule). In Loos, too, we find indications that lead one to assume on his part a "blind" conception of belonging to the game, to tradition. "The blows of the axe resound cheerfully. He [the carpenter] is building the roof. What kind of roof? A beautiful or an ugly roof? He does not know. The roof." In building his house, the peasant "follows his instinct. Is the house beautiful? Yes, it is beautiful as the roses, the thistle,

Loos and His Angel

the horse, and the cow are beautiful."[9] Does the peasant therefore "blindly" follow the rules of the game played up until now?
Does the master saddler, about whom a memorable passage
of *Das Andere* tells us, oppose the inventions of the Secession
because he "does not know" *what kind* of saddles he is producing? Do training and habit create nearly automatic practices
that contradict in toto the possibility of decision, a possibility
which for this reason belongs to a totally different genre, that
of art as a kind of absolute linguistic practice? As we can see,
an interpretation of this sort leads to insurmountable aporiae.
If art must also be defined as a combination of linguistic games,
its dimension cannot transcend the problems of belonging and
habit that are connected to the structure of the game. A different
conception of art would necessarily lead to that *Unsittlichkeit
des Lebens* which has its symbol in Kraus's image of beauty before the mirror. The difference between the "family" of artistic
games and that of the practice of handicrafts not only must be
at every moment reexamined as problematical, but also, in a
general sense, it cannot be based on a distinction between habit-
custom on the one hand, and exception and innovation on the
other. It seems to me that the entire Loosian aesthetic, in spite
of the obvious critical strains of the spirit of his commentary,
moves in this direction: that is, it endlessly attempts to define the
perpetually mutable limits of the space in which the practices
of art and handicrafts harmonize and contrast with each other,
becoming relative to one another without ever claiming to give
way to a single language representative of everything.

What Loos's craftsman is in reality unaware of is the fact that
he is modern. His purpose, his vision, is not focused on the
present, much less on the future. But he does have a purpose:
that of commentary. His gaze is fixed on the tradition that he
follows, on the language that dominates him, but within which
his thought can grow. To follow tradition, hence, is to let this
thought develop—in essence, to choose this path of patient
growth full of winding roads and wrong turns. All behavior
guided by rules is not simply conditioned, but implies a comprehension.[10] The desire to follow a rule is a purpose in itself. The
desire to preserve this rule is not "instinct," but, as Loos explains
in the "Master Saddler," a decision that breaks all "alliance"

Being Loyal

with the fetish of the artist's imagination. The master saddler returns consciously to his saddles; he knows what kind of saddles he produces. Yet this still does not explain the Loosian problematics of art, as such, which we will confront later; it explains instead through what conditions one might determine the interrelations, the close affinities, existing between the dimension of art and that of handicraft. The craftsman's strict participation in the game should not be seen in any way as a blind following, but rather as the renewal of a sought-for and cherished habit. It is a relation devoid of emphasis, almost silent—like that of old Veillich with his chairs.

But these very pages, which are among Loos's most beautiful, explain how the terms we have used thus far—habit, learning, praxis—should be understood in regard to the "vanished masters." Such an understanding should also bring us to the background of the Wittgensteinian thought so readily exposed, in the pages mentioned, to the blind Anglo-Saxon analyses that have appropriated it. Habit is not repetition, it is not the automatic recurrence of forms and actions—it is ethos. In the Anglo-Saxon notion of habit-custom the sense of ethos is completely lost, just as in the "modern" interpretations of Loos, his "Romanness," his classical Roman aspect, is lost.[11] Habit is the conscious belonging to a tradition—the more it is conscious and endured, the more it is recognized as a game, and its language becomes relative to this fact. Belonging to the ephemeral—here, today, the sense of the commentary comes back, in full view. Loos tells us with what patience and endless care Veillich worked at his furniture. In his work, following the rules is a right totally subject to the justice, however ephemeral and uncertain, that lies in the preserving of tradition, in devoting care to one's own language as though it might still serve as text—a right subject to the justice of this ethos, which is not only far from, but also opposed to, any kind of morality. But habit is also *loyalty*. It is the loyalty that binds Loos to Veillich, and that binds both of them to what lasts: the beauty of the material, the happy forms of tradition. In this way, Veillich, who creates perhaps the most ephemeral of things, furniture, lives in that which lasts. In this way, Loos, in writing *Das Andere,* shows that he knows how to last. Loyalty cannot be mere conditioning, blind following. Loy-

Loos and His Angel

alty is lasting in that which is known to be ephemeral—since there can be no loyalty where one stands on the solid rock of language, of the solution. One may speak of an ethos of loyalty only where things die.

And when Veillich dies so do his chairs. Loos writes the proper, most fitting obituary for his friend. Although the ethos of loyalty reveals the essential reason why the praxis of the craftsman, in Loos, is opposed to all blind following, this ethos is not an eternal and necessary structure of the linguistic game that can somehow be broken down into an abstract logic. This ethos dies with Veillich. It belongs to history—to that chain of events which for the Angel is a single catastrophe. From this perspective, the translation of the Loosian loyalty to tradition into custom-habit is inevitable, however frightful it might seem to Wittgenstein. Of course, everything is lost in this translation. But in reality, everything comes to be lost anyway: "thus do things die." [12] There is no consolation in knowing that all behavior guided by rules implies an understanding, that every tradition is renewed in the purpose that assumes it—since this only shifts the problem to the history of this understanding, this purpose. The ethos of loyalty implies a loyal subject; it is not passed on hereditarily. It implies a decision, a choice whose secret only Veillich knew, and "why should I unveil the secrets of a shop that no longer exists?" [13]

Rilke seems to speak of this same secret in the *Duino Elegies*. The *gedeutete Welt* (interpreted world)—of which Kraus, too, in the above-cited essay addressed to Loos, presents a desperate image—is perhaps resisted by "a tree on the slope, that we may see again each day/yesterday's street still remains/and the jaded loyalty of a habit/that felt good with us and so stayed and never left." [14] *Treusein,* the ethos of loyalty, becomes a habit, is bent and twisted—becoming almost devoid of purpose, of any new opening. Here *Gewohnheit* seems to translate as habit-custom—it seems to have become a blind following. But in Treusein still resounds the Loosian loyalty to tradition. Rilke's verse contains a history, the final stage of "decay": that decay that makes Treusein "jaded" to the point where it becomes mere Gewohnheit. In Treusein, the commentary finds its quintessence, as long as it still recognizes its origin: *mens, comminisci*—a

Being Loyal

positing of the mind so intense as to transform itself into *Imaginatio*. But habit inevitably becomes separated from Treusein, like Veillich from his planer and Loos from Veillich.

The *Duino Elegies* admonish us to show the Angel the simple, *das Einfache,* that which from generation to generation is shaped and reshaped, and for this reason is loyal to each. We should show him things, not the inexpressible, because in this we are but novices. And yet these things are dead.

12. The Other

A loyalty to the search for the justice of the word is implicit in the struggle against right; the simplicity of Treusein resists the rules of right. This basic theme undergoes many variations in the pages of *Das Andere,* the review that published only two issues, in 1903, as a supplement to *Kunst,* a publication edited by Peter Altenberg. The model for *Das Andere* is clearly Kraus's *Die Fackel,* and yet, in certain ways, the style of its writings, especially those by Loos, is closer to Altenberg.[1] Its rhythm resembles more the melancholy rhythm of a stroll than the insistent tempo of a critique. Loos moves about the various sites of his loved-hated Vienna, studying its customs and colors and lingering in front of store windows. He judges and teaches while he is strolling. But he does so without teacher's desk or pulpit— and this throws an ironic light on the "demon" of judgment. The form of the critique here "spills over" into the ephemeral: it posits the ephemeral—as we have seen—with extreme seriousness, but posits it as ephemeral, without pretending in any

Loos and His Angel

way to overcome or sublimate it. And the critique itself ends up exhibiting the features, the tone, of the ephemeral. Loos teaches by "strolling," by indicating, by hinting. And his thought is most penetrating when it attains the simplicity and clarity of the brief aphorism, the illuminating anecdote. The commentary is very close to this mode of discourse, which takes upon itself the risks of equivocation and misunderstanding that are part of the dimension of the ephemeral into which it has now ventured. The more the commentary approaches the living word, the more it becomes true discourse, dialogue, forever balanced between understanding and equivocation.

Wie ich es sehe is the title of Altenberg's first collection of sketches: "as I *see* it"—not as I think or judge it. Thought grows within sight, within the language of sight. This is the essential addition that Altenberg makes to Kraus's "torch" (*Fackel*): language opens onto the world with the same richness as sight—language *sees* the world. And sight has nothing of the pure cogito—it is connected to a body that lives, moves, suffers, seeks happiness, feels nostalgia, and linked to a name that is a symbol of this nostalgia (Peter Altenberg: the nickname given him by his first sweetheart and also the name of the town on the Danube where she lived). What does not fall, from the start, within sight, will never be found in judgment either. Thought is not a going beyond sight, but its maximum aperture: a sight that in its language rediscovers the richness of its own traditions and that in preserving them produces the new. *Das Andere* trains us to see. Loos educates us while accompanying us on his stroll.

The term "impressionism" has been misused in regard to Altenberg. If this term is meant to indicate, as it would seem, an immediacy of sight, then it cannot be applied to Altenberg, and even less to Loos. Altenberghian sight is a form of vision and language, of vision and thought. The "telegraphic style of the soul" means not a supposed elementary sharpness of vision, but a work of abbreviation, decantation, purification. The describing of "a man in one sentence, an experience of the soul on one single page, a landscape in one word" [2] is not characteristic of any mythical primary, original sight, but of this sight that grows with language and thought, that exposes their root in the body proper of the henceforth troubled, contradictory, analyzed

The Other

dimension of the "I." Hence this sight is not dissipated in the ephemeral, but flows into it in order to last.

From this perspective, it is easy to recognize how "Western civilization (Kultur)"—whose introduction in Austria is sought by *Das Andere*—is in reality a Kultur of sight. This further explains the reasoning behind the notions of behavior, habit, and tradition discussed in the preceding chapter. The Loosian ideal is that this Kultur should become habit, behavior. There are absolutely no models given in *Das Andere,* no paradigms representative of "Western civilization." Loos seeks to train us even before educating us, to train us in modes of behavior, habits, reactions. Western Kultur must become a way of see-ing, "wie ich es sehe." One can teach systems, models, strict paradigms, but not *this* Kultur, whose thought becomes be-havior and perception, and whose natural reactions are con-stantly in the process of becoming awareness and thought. Read-ing *Das Andere*—as well as Altenberg's *Die Kunst* and often *Die Fackel*—requires not only an "intellectual" effort, but also readiness, agility, open-mindedness, and an ability to partici-pate in a game whose prevalent aspects require an agnostic athleticism: problems of etiquette and fashion, cabaret-like pro-grams, questions of furnishing and handicrafts, impious anec-dotes, politico-moral interventions. An exceptionally serious spirit of frivolity embraces and imbues each subject. In these pages, Western Kultur means "to be in good form" in every subject—and, once again, to last in the ephemeral.

Inasmuch as the modern artist and his style strive to become the only form of this sight, or else dissipate this sight in an equivocal, confused immediacy, according to the polarity characteristic of the avant-garde, they represent the necessary polemical target of *Das Andere*. Loos opposes the artists who seek to "capture" art between the walls of their house—and who go so far as to *apply* it to the ring of the doorbell[3]—with the modernity that the craftsman achieves by himself, whose forms arise from his praxis and from the search for function.[4] But Loos distinguishes among his contemporaries. He not only "lowers his sails" be-fore the genius of Otto Wagner,[5] but also shows a discriminating sense of judgment in his commentaries on Hoffmann. In *Das Andere* and elsewhere, the real enemies are Olbrich and Van

Loos and His Angel

de Velde. Their works are an "insult" to the life that is supposed to take place in the home, an attempt to contain it, to make it unchangeable. The ornamental superabundance of the Jugendstil reduces life to a single dimension and creates suffocating interlacements of lines. Loos, the master of *dwelling,* sees in the Jugendstil an essential moment of the decay of the home. Although his interpretation of ornamentation and, more generally, of the various secessionist movements of the time may appear at times reductive, it must be remembered that the target of his criticism is not these movements in themselves, nor their representative members, but the overall process of the uprooting of the home and of dwelling. We shall discuss this central theme in greater detail below, but even at this point it is clear that it explains the emphasis with which Loos juxtaposes the design of an Olbrich room and the sacred scene that he imagines happening in this room: the suicide of a young woman and the farewell letter on a table beside her. What room, what bed, what table could suffer this scene without insulting it? For Loos, this is the question we must ask ourselves before embarking on any project. And such a question should immediately nullify any pretense to drafting a project. These interiors cannot be reduced to design, to the design of the "modern artist," to asylums of applied art or true art, asylums now "without roofs."[6] Here too, Loos does not present himself as teacher, but as *trainer.* He trains us in the quick glance, in the correct reaction, in the "natural" disdain of all ornament—just as no civilized man goes around "naturally" tatooed, "whoever wants to fence must take the foil in hand." No game is learned merely by watching others play.

The pages of *Das Andere* devoted to the "serious things in life" are more directly influenced by Kraus than by Altenberg. The hypocrisy of society, the morality of the majority, epitomize the principle of ornamentation. The journalistic *Phrase* embodies, at bottom, the indecency of moralism, against which the naked facts of life rise up in contradiction. Hence there is no shifting "to another genre" when Loos confronts the disasters of political morality, but only the necessary "explanation" of the struggle against the dragon of ornamentation. When, in the column "How the State Provides for Us," Loos looks at "this family from up close," where father, mother, children, and even occa-

The Other

sional guests live together in a single room, and juxtaposes this family with the gossip of the current morality, his tone is the same as that of *Morality and Criminality:* "There are no dangers of the street. It is protected by the community. *There is only the danger of the family.*" Not to mention, together with Wedekind and Kraus, his *Spring reawakening,* "a tragedy of childhood." This emphasis on childhood is, moreover, shared with Kraus and Altenberg. The melancholy of Altenberg's young characters derives precisely from the impossible promise of a free life emanating from them. The tragedy of childhood becomes blurred with the insurmountable "primacy" of the family and its morality. The death of these figures mars springtimes and reawakenings, as though these things arose from lacerating conflicts and rotten organisms. In Kraus, Altenberg, and Wedekind the "conscripts of life" meet their end in ornamentation, the moralistic *Phrase,* renunciation, and desperate quests. It is perhaps in the destruction of these "rights" and in the rediscovery of the relation between childhood and the word that the deeper purpose of their work lies: the moment where "origin and destruction meet face to face" marks the end of the demon and perhaps the uncertain beginning of the new Angel.[7]

In this unlikely realm where the eye for clothing, furniture, and objects meets and converses with the problem of dwelling, good manners with the great tradition, and cabaret criticism with criticism of morality—Loos and *his* Vienna are the guides. They want to introduce to Western Kultur anyone who is alien to it: *Fremdenführer für Kulturfremde* (Tour guide for the culture tourist). But this Kultur has nothing in common with the stereotypical image of the West; it is, rather, a critique of this image. Loos wants to introduce one to a culture which, in commenting on tradition, frees itself from all philistine separation of thought from sight, of morality from the "joy of living." The West, for Loos, is the incessant, endless quest to liberate games from language, to love and preserve their difference, to comment. The words of Alberto Savinio could easily be applied to this task: "The intelligence of Europe has a unique function: it divides and separates. . . . The European spirit hates the cluster. . . . To disunite is not to destroy. Disunifying action is healthy. . . . Europe, when it is truly 'European,' understands that no idea

Loos and His Angel

comes 'before' the rest, that no idea merits being central." The only "requisite for health" is the maintenance of this differentiating power, and the continuous fight against that "phantom God" (this god is no longer but a phantom) in whose name it is taught that "to unite is good and to divide is evil." Even in his harshest and most unjust polemics, Kraus remains loyal to this spirit, to the Western Kultur Loos wants to introduce, and for which division, disunification, and differentiation are necessary in the face of every "social cluster" and every totalitarian idea.[8]

But this West is the other—*Das Andere*—the other West: difficult to preserve, always in danger, it is mortal, like Veillich's objects. As would seem to be the case in the later writings of both Kraus and Altenberg, it has perhaps already withdrawn into the word.

13. Tabula Rasa

Hevesi's designation of the Café Museum as "Café Nihilismus" must have seemed even more applicable to the Michaelerplatz building.[1] But, as should by now be clear, this definition is inexact. If what appears to be nihilistic is Loos's position with regard to ornament and the impatience of the new, the reasons behind this position are essentially constructive. The quest to insinuate tradition, as well as the compositional solutions of the work, into the urban fabric and into language, is for the sake of *permanence*. The building with three fronts dominates the main intersection of the city's center, between the Kohlmarkt, the Herrengasse, and the Michaelerplatz. Revetted with very fine, variegated marble, the building's lower part, comprising ground

Tabula Rasa

floor and mezzanine, solidly anchors the austere rhythm of the whole. This absolutely anti-ornamental effect is underscored by the main entrance's four columns, between each of which, in the original design, there was not to have been any glass. But we cannot get an adequate idea of this rhythm by limiting ourselves to the design. The design may even appear nihilistic or "without qualities"; but to assert, like Otto Stoessl, that every part of this building, "every wall, window, surface, and angle is connected in a clear and precise way to the beneficent sobriety and clarity of a specific signification, in a manner not unlike that of a good wardrobe," is to emphasize only the external characteristics of the design, rather than the actual complexity of the spatial solutions.[2] Loos's struggle against ornamentation does not take place on the facades; rather, it concerns the (already mentioned) principle of the tridimensionality of architectonic thought. This applies to both public buildings as well as private homes, even if in the latter the Loosian spatial rhythm deals with other problems—such as the general problem of dwelling. The simplicity and comprehensibility of the building's design should not make one shrink from entering into it and discovering the multiplicity and complexity of the solutions resulting from research in the various problems of the use of the space (the large salesroom on the ground floor and its staircase; the apartments; the rooms for experiments; the workplaces for apprentices, and so on).

Kraus called Loos the architect of the tabula rasa, and the surface of the Michaelerplatz house is truly *rasa,* being without superstructures or jutting elements, save the sharp line of the cornice that delimits-encloses and underscores the compositional value of the building. But Loos makes no "clean sweeps" of "our old Viennese masters," nor does he reduce the spatial qualities, the tridimensional movement of the interior. Making a clean sweep of the superflousness of modern architecture coincides with rediscovering the necessity of the constructive-spatial effort of architectonic thought. Elsewhere, Kraus himself shows his understanding of this real justification for the struggle against ornamentation (ornamentation, by its very nature, is anti-constructive, anti-spatial) when, in his polemical piece on the Michaelerplatz building, he asserts that Loos, with this building, has built a thought. And he reaffirms

Loos and His Angel

this idea in his beautiful eulogy at Loos's grave, August 25, 1933: "A *Baumeister* [*not* Architekt!] you were, in the space of an existence through which the house, inside and out, vanished in a flourish. *What you built was what you thought*" (emphasis added). *Bauen* and *Denken* belong to each other in a single space.[3]

But how should we understand this notion, *to build a thought?* Loos is forever in search of that which might render a thought architectonic. This problem broadens the dimension of the game and the multiplicity of games. Indeed, one could even speak of a multiplicity of linguistic games and still see them as revetments of a single thought or of a shared plane of ideas, as different ways of expressing a single ideal dimension. But in this very notion lies the true essence of ornament. It lies not in the impressionistic nullification of that ideal dimension, but in the separation of this dimension from the specificity of the games—in making the game a revetment. In Loos, on the other hand, different ways of speaking *are* different forms of thinking. In Loos, one does not find just *one* form of thought: one finds musical-thoughts, pictorial-thoughts, philosophical-thoughts—and architectonic-thoughts. The multiplicity of the linguistic games is the multiplicity of the forms of thinking with which we open onto the world. The essence of the principle of ornament lies in making the game simply a game, alluding to an idea or claiming its nullification. To play is instead to think—as Kraus wrote, "In making you set down the rules"[4]: in the practice of building you discovered the permanences, the affinities, the principles of composition, that which lasts—in making you were thinking. But this "making" is precisely that of the Baumeister, and it is characterized by that specific form of space. To build a thought means: to define the specific form of thinking that is the game of architecture; to define it with maximum precision with respect to the other forms, and not to confuse it, blend it or attempt impossible, nostalgic harmonies. Ornament is that which does not reveal its own game as thought, as making-in-thinking, as having its own rules and conditions of use and changeability.

Ornament is the dissolution of the tectonic and the Denken (the search for permanence, rules) connected to it. Indeed, it is the furthermost point in a process of "assault against architec-

Tabula Rasa

ture," to quote Sedlmayr, a process of the sublimation-reduction of the Baumeister to Architekt. But Loos's place in this historical framework itself shows how Sedlmayr's schemas must be seriously re-examined. In Loos, there is a purposeful absence of any "pictorial characteristics"; also absent is the tendency to make the wall an abstract surface of delimitation, "from which derives the ideal of a shell made exclusively of glass." In Loos there is a total lack of animistic-vitalistic influence, and yet for him, too, there is no such thing as dead material. In Loos the architecture is perfectly autonomous, in the sense that it (its thought) is freed from "extraneous mixtures"; and yet, this is not why his buildings seem "without country or land," "cosmopolitan," uprooted:[5] his whole argument regarding tradition proves exactly the contrary. Loos continually resorts to pure "revolutionary" geometric forms ("pure" figures),[6] but their use always corresponds to functional-constructive, tectonic demands, to the exigencies of the organization-composition of the space. In the light of experiences such as those of Loos, Sedlmayr's casuistry and its like lose all meaning. The tectonic lies not in striking roots in mythical "land," but in striking roots in the process of the thought-game of which one is part, in operating with it, relating to the material and its body as to an organism that can never be reduced to a mere instrument of construction, seeing in the material a compositional factor, and defining, in this same operation, one's own rules, *seeking* to define them. For Loos, the specific tectonics of architecture lie in all of the above, and not in extrinsic elements (for example, the specific geometric figure used, the nature of the terrain, and so on). Their very autonomy must not be taken in an abstract sense, but, as we have already explained, in a historico-relative sense: neither the boundary, nor the relations between the games are definable a priori; rather, these relations come into being only when each language-thought seeks to define itself, to *think itself*.

Sedlmayr fixes, rigidifies the meaning of the tectonic dimension of architecture, which in Loos is formed and driven by the relations established between tradition and modernity, practice and thought, form and material. The tectonic dimension of architecture in Loos has nothing in common with a communal-organic

Loos and His Angel

traditionalism. This sort of traditionalism is as much part of the principle of ornament as are the free lines of the Jugendstil. It reduces things to one language and conceives of the compositional endeavour in a reductivist manner, abstracting it from its history. The tectonic makes a "clean sweep" of ornament, but it is not itself tabula rasa. In the Loosian tectonic, one does not lose that discourse between ephemerality and permanence, that precarious equilibrium of the game "pulled away" toward the future, which cannot be penetrated by any project." In the Loosian tectonic there is no assertion of a new nostalgia for the foundation; what is asserted, if anything, is the struggle against the masks of the foundation, its ideologies—which are very like those "free-form dances" limited to repeating its death.

In the term tectonic resounds the *tekné* of the carpenter, the joiner, the craftsman, the Baumeister.[7] Loos's notion of *handicraft* is tectonic. This handicraft, to which the Baumeister belongs, *covers* the dwelling. The tectonic is *tékton* (tego): to cover the house, to build its roof (*tetto*). To build the roof is to *complete* the house, to define it. The Baumeister is he who gets as far as the roof—he who forms the work. But the tekné of the craftsman is praxis, habit, behavior; comprehension and thought grow together with this element, Treusein. The craftsman has his gaze fixed on the past, but in Loos, he moves at the same time toward the future—toward a future that is formed in his making, that is included in this making, but is never foreseeable, never the simple product of a project. In Loos's tectonics resounds another element as well: not only tekné as dominance, as total mastery, but also the unpredictable game of the transformation of the rules in the very use of the tekné, in the very use of the inherited norms. In Loos's tékton also resounds the *tyche*—the chance that eludes dominance, the moment of exception to the norm. The loyalty to recognized tradition is constantly open to the chance that reforms it, the processes that transform it. Tekné, in Loos, is not only the form of the total master of tradition, but also the happy moment that is the origin of new combinations, that gives life to new forms. The tectonic in Loos is not the eternal return of the norm, but its understanding and openness to the moment that surpasses it, to the

Tabula Rasa

propitious tyche that renews it. An infinity of possibilities resounds in Loos's tectonic. This tectonic must define, give form
to, and *cover* that which remains ephemeral.

14. The New Space

But what space in Loos's work poses a problem? What space is
a problem for the Baumeister's tekné, which we have just outlined? The questions posed by Heidegger on the subject of plas-
tic art can be seen to assume a certain relevance in this context.[1]
For the Baumeister, is it a question of taking possession (*Besitzergreifung*) of dominating (*Beherrschung*) the space? Do the
tectonics of architecture correspond to the technico-scientific
conquest (*Eroberung*) of space? But the space that is the object
of this conquest is pure uniform expanse without characteristics of its own and equal in all its parts, a simple correlate of
the subject-ego that subjugates it. Does this dimension exhaust
the characteristic of the space? Is the space reduced to planned
space (in other words, the correlate of the ego's project)? This is
the case with the "rationalist" Architekt. But is it also true for
the Loosian Baumeister?

A space arises when, through deforesting and plowing, *das
Freie* and *das Offene* (the free and the open) are produced for
man's settlement and dwelling. The space is linked up with the
dimension of dwelling. Making-space is *Freigabe von Orten,*

Loos and His Angel

giving places, opening-freeing places where man recognizes himself, negatively or positively, in his destiny as dweller; in such places he is able to live in the happy possession of a homeland, in the presence of a God, or else in the *Heimatlosigkeit* (homelessness) from whence the gods have fled—in one home or another, he inhabits places that are part of his destiny as a dweller. Making-space means establishing such places, making-place for the destiny of dwelling.

"But in the making of space, a happening (*Geschehen*) speaks and hides simultaneously." It is the arranging and harmonizing of things, among themselves and in relation to dwelling. In the place (*der Ort*) given by the making of space, things are collected in their mutual belonging. The characteristic of the place is this "collection." If we can say that in the term "space" resounds the making-space that establishes places, we can say that in the term "place" speaks the arranging-harmonizing of things. These things do not belong to a place, but are themselves the place. Hence, the space is no longer the pure uniform expanse of the technical-scientific project, but a game of a combination of places. Each of these places is a collection of things, a cluster of events. A place is a home for things and a dwelling for man amidst them.

The conquest of space by the project implies its rendering as omni-measurable, its subdivision, and hence its conception as quantitatively calculable and manipulable. The conquest of space is the liquidation of the place as a collection of things, as a mutual belonging of things and dwelling. The conquest of space is the plundering of places: it conceives of space as a void to fill, a pure absence, a lack. Space is mere potentiality at the disposal of the technico-scientific project. To the Architekt belongs precisely this conception of space: space is pure void to be measured-delimited, void in which to pro-duce his new forms. It is hence necessary, for this pro-ducing, to *empty* space of places—a radical Ent-ortung of space. Making-space here becomes liquidating-nullifying, making-void, "displacing", rather than giving-places. For this producing, the void is nothingness. But in this same notion of the void (*die Leere*) we do not hear nothingness, but rather *das Lesen*, the collec-

The New Space

tion, "in the original sense of the collection that dominates the place." To empty is, then, to prepare a place, to grant a place, to collect in a place.

In these pages of Heidegger, which should be read together with his other work on dwelling and thinking, there comes to light a counterposition essential to an understanding of the philosophy of modern architecture. This counterposition concerns the very substance of the architectural endeavor as what Loos calls a "thinking in space." What are the specifics of this space? Is this making-space an endeavor that establishes places? And are these places a "collection", a mutual belonging of things and dwelling? Or is this making-space an Ent-ortung, an annihiliation of the places, an arranging of the land as an empty and uniform space at the disposal of the new project? This radical choice remains unquestioned as long as one limits oneself to emphasizing the specifics of architecture as being thinking in space.

For Sedlmayr, the historical course of modern architecture coincides with the process of Ent-ortung. That which he often banalizes as a "release from the bond of the land" actually finds its real meaning in Heidegger's framework. Modern architecture tends to become autonomous from the earth, to free itself from all earthly roots, inasmuch as it is an annihilation of place. The Earth is an equivocal reference. Place is, instead, a specific term. Architecture does not establish places, but pro-duces Ent-ortung, it defines-measures-calculates in an empty and uniform space. Even the house least "raised" from the earth can for this reason be part of the Ent-ortung. The lifting of the bodies, the overcoming of the foundations, of the bond with the earth— in sum, the dominant project of the entire architectural avant-garde (up to and including the ultimate, stellar freedoms, the metaphysical transparences of Glasarchitektur)—can be taken as a tragic symbol of the rupture of the bond between space and place, a symbol of the metaphysical affirmation of space as abstract, uniform and equal in all its parts, as foreign to all establishment of places and destructive in regard to all possible "collection." And this process is seen to be a manifestation of freedom. Freedom here coincides with the successful release, separation, with the happy success of that *ars-tekne* which aims

Loos and His Angel

at a total liberation from all places. We no longer belong to places where things have a home together with us; we are *pars,* that which results from *arpazein,* seizure, rape, plunder; we are products of the very plunder of space by the places that we bring about.[2] By freedom we mean the absolute loss of place.

Even the loss of spatial delimitation that one encounters in the history of the city is also, in reality, a loss of place. Indeed, the calculating power, the ability to define-measure, develops without encountering any apparent resistance. But these delimitations establish themselves over an empty space and, because they are all equal, can be repeated ad infinitum. The city becomes completely profane only when the time of production and circulation, whatever direction it takes, encounters no more places—only when the establishment of places becomes impossible, inconceivable. The cities then become, in exact accordance with their present image, a total *Besitzergreifung des Raumes,* an occupation-plundering of space. It is the triumph of the *urbs*—the city that cannot be defined, cannot be collected in one place; the city that reaches out, by way of roads "carefully and permanently marked, paved and kept visibly distinguishable from the voracity of the grass, mud and woods," in all directions; the city which is "raised" from place to world, and "liberated" for the "urbanization of the planet," for the overcoming of the countryside, for the worldwide affirmation of the *ars* of the man who subdues all things.[4]

Is this the only "new space" possible? Is this the space produced by radical Ent-ortung? And how can one conceivably combat it without making the Angel's gaze toward the past a mere act of nostalgia and consolation? Carl Schmitt devoted perhaps his most conceptually rich and committed research to the problem of Ent-ortung;[5] without his assistance it would be difficult to bring out the essence of our references to Heidegger and Sedlmayr. In the Ent-ortung it is the destiny of the West itself that runs from the rooting of the *Nomos* in the *justissima tellus,* through the discovery and occupation of the new spaces of the Americas ("free" spaces, that is, considered totally available for conquest, totally profanable: devoid of places), up to the universalism of the world market: *"eine totale Mobilmachung*

The New Space

intensiver Art, eine allgemeine Entortung (a total mobilization of an intensive kind, a universal displacement)"—the definitive crisis of all rooting of the Nomos, of all positiveness of the law linked to territorially defined states (p. 210). The State, which had made the city's boundaries explode, is assaulted by the same process: the urbanization of the planet is its crisis as well. The State is the last form, the final *universum* to be swallowed up by the *Pluriversum* of the "world market" (p. 216ff.)

This Mobilmachung, a term characteristic of the *Aktivismus* of the early twentieth-century avant-gardes, thus finds its definition in its own historical dimension: as a reduction of the entire planet to "free space", it is part of the destiny of Entortung. The nature of this Entortung is *utopian* in the fullest sense. The Entortung plans utopias. This process is the overcoming of all places on which once rested the ancient Nomos tied to the earth (p. 146ff.) The utopia, which is the key-sign of a negative-nihilistic relation with the tópos—and which is able to imagine happy topoi (eu-topia) only through the negation of all relation with the topos (ou-topia)—is in this sense an exact reversal of the Angel's gaze. And the utopia, the utopian goal, accompanies the planning ego throughout its course—up to the total Mobilmachung of the avant-gardes.

Just as the history of the European *jus publicum*, so masterfully traced by Schmitt, comes to an end in this Entortung of the Nomos—for which reason the destiny of right is this Entortung—in the same way, it can be asserted, according to Benjamin's reading of Kraus, that the idea of justice resides in the idea of place, or cannot exist except in a place, in a making-space that is freely given by places. When Heidegger begins his inquiry on the proper meaning of space by jeopardizing the hearing of language (*"Wir versuchen auf die Sprache zu hören,"*) he singles out this justice in the language; that is, he singles out the place where this justice is preserved. Only by questioning language can we grasp a sense of making-space that is not swept away in the destiny of the Eroberung of space. The place belongs to language. The dimension hereby opened up is utterly Rilkean. The operation that establishes places occurs in language, jeopardizing its hearing. The establishing of places has withdrawn into

Loos and His Angel

language, into the poetic search for the living word through the hearing of language. But does this not therefore mean that it is no longer possible to build any place in the current of the appropriation of space, of the urbanization of the planet? And what non-nostalgic, non-consoling signification can we then assign to the Baumeister and to his regard for tradition?

In Loos, the dimension of Entortung gains predominance the more he questions it—the more this dimension becomes problematic in his work, the more it becomes manifest and seems to assert itself. The dramatic singularity of Loos's experience lies in the exploration of this irresolvable relation, in the effort to combat it head-on, poised as though in infinite transition. The motifs that establish the relation of his experience with handicraft Treusein, and that in themselves exclude that utopian hubris of language that is the foundation of the Entortung, recur everywhere in his work, even in the most minute compositional details. If the exteriors of the Steiner house (1910), the coach house on the Nothartgasse, and those of the Strasser house (1919) bring to mind that "mobilization" (Mobilmachung) of the building that renders the building "interchangeable" with the modern machine, with the haste with which its forms appear and disappear while reproducing themselves, the finished, classical presence of the Rufer house (1922) emphasized by the eurhythmy of the arrangement and the forms of the windows, although strictly connected to the interior rooms, seems to negate the very principle of Entortung. Loos himself underscores, in one place, the roots of certain works of his (Villa Khuner, Villa Karma), and elsewhere, the need to assume contemporary furnishing as a compositional model: the cabin of the ocean liner, the railroad coach, and so on. Loos's compositional intelligence springs from this polarity: it is in constant tension, never resolved. And this is the case not only with regard to the problem of the interior-exterior relation, to which I shall return shortly, but also with regard to the very dialectic of the interior. It is clear that this dialectic cannot be reduced to the process that distinguishes and articulates the space in terms of its use. The transparencies between the living room and dining room of the Rufer house, between the dining room and music room

The New Space

of the Strasser house, the variations of level—real variations on the base-text, the search for unexpected "solos" that animate these spaces and release them from simple "multipurpose" concerns—all reveal Loos's search for *place*. Loos's making-space in the interior always tends to give places—even in the common spaces, which can be more easily "enslaved" to the principle of the machine, and not only in those places for retiring (the bedroom, the study, the library)—where this search is in any case emphasized. The importance of the furnishing and the care for the material (care in the sense of a profound sympathy) are part of this search for place, this commentary on the idea of place.

I say "commentary" and "search" precisely because there can be no "pure" place in the destiny of Entortung. To attempt to create a pure language of place would be sheer nostalgia in the age of radical Entortung. The idea of place flashes between interior and exterior, between "multipurpose" functionality and handicraft Treusein, between the sequentiality of compositional rhythms and the beauty of the material. The place endures in and because of these contradictions—unforeseen seductions of the Entortung. Like his exteriors, Loos confronts the absence of place *head-on:* to attempt to reverse its destiny would be to turn the idea of place into a utopia, and, paradoxically, to reconfirm the very principle of Entortung he is attempting to investigate and put into question. In the Entortung every "pure" language of place is a utopia and hence part of the same destiny of uprootedness or displacement that accompanies the *ars aedificandi* of the West. For this reason, Loos's architecture does not seek the rationalization of "pure" places, but is aimed at showing the endless contradiction between the thought-out space of calculation, the equivalence of the exteriors, and the possibility of place, the hope of a place. The Loosian house preserves this hope, just as the gaze of Benjamin's Angel preserves the "glimmers" of the past. That which can be shown is not the "redemption" of place, but the dissonance existing between the equivalence of technico-scientific space and the characteristic of space as a game of a combination of places, where things are gathered and dwell with man. This dissonance must be composed: even the extreme dissonances must be the object of composition.

Loos and His Angel

But the Loosian exterior cannot therefore be reduced to a simple fiction supposedly hiding the truth-justice of the place. Its right is more subtle than this and programmatically so in certain works, such as the villas and the Rufer house (1922). The place can no longer appear in total unconcealedness, in truth. The exterior, therefore, cannot be conceived of as a concealment of the truth of the interior, since this truth, as such, does not exist. The place henceforth can be shown only in relation to the space of the exterior; but this means that this space is now truly necessary to the showing of the place. The house is not inhabited by an imprisoned truth. The fiction of the exterior is truly *necessary* to the "truth," precisely because it does not let it appear. The "truth" of the place is served by being kept concealed. To pretend to make it manifest would be the same as to liquidate it as a utopia. Hence, the exterior is neither a mirror image of the "truth" contained in the interior (the modern exterior that reveals the structure), nor a mere fiction or veil that hides a place otherwise analyzable, "a word not feigned, a meaning that does not deceive."[6] The exterior does not allude allegorically-metaphorically to lost places, nor is it treated merely as a simple obstacle to the transparence of a place that supposedly really exists in the interior. A demystified exterior reflects the space of the Entortung, but only inasmuch as the existence of "pure" place has become impossible. A continuous search for, an unending comment on the place lives in the interior; but to the extent that this interior is not an analyzable psyche, it is not a truth that ends up dictating "the fictional element of its manifestation."[7] The idea of place, in Loos—which makes it fundamentally impossible to assimilate him into the currents of progressive rationalism, in architecture and elsewhere—lies in the same difference, the same dissonance that prevents the place from becoming a utopia at the same time that it questions the frozen repetitiveness and equivalence of technico-scientific space.

Since our eyes are *"wie umgekehrt,"* as though reversed, our making-space does not lead to das Offene, to das Freie, which Heidegger spoke of as the place for man's settlement and dwelling. Das Offene disappears with the urbanization of the planet—or as Schmitt would say, with the *globale Zeit* that

The New Space

poses the problem of a planetary right uprooted from any specific relationship with the earth. The "umgekehrt" gaze produces the "gedeutet Welt," the world reversed in thought, the world of interpretation, mere correlate of the ego. Our existence is a *"gegenüber"* existence, always facing something—we are turned toward everything but never toward the open.

> Who has so turned us around, that
> whatever we do, it is always as though
> we were about to leave? Like
> he, who on the last hill, which shows him
> its whole valley one last time, turns, stops, lingers—
> thus we live, forever taking leave. (*Die acte Elegie*, w.
> 70–75.)

However, as we already know, the Angel's gaze, too, is as though turned around; he, too, in his flight, acts as though forever taking leave. But it is the discourse between his gaze and the event that preserves the hope of the moment, the feeble messianic strength granted us. We know that we belong to the gedeutete Welt, to the world where place has been lost, since our gaze is reversed—and yet, *"Werbung nicht mehr . . ."* (no more plead for mercy) (*Die siebente Elegie*, v. 1); we do not seek consolation, since we are given *"das atmende Klarsein"* (breathing clarity, v. 24), the clarity of the word that preserves, the interior where endless acts, memories and things occur and elapse, and

> where each has always
> an hour, perhaps not even
> a whole hour, something barely measurable with the meter
> of time
> something between two moments—that was an existence
> Completely. Veins filled with existence. (vv. 42–45)

This is the Benjaminian moment that shatters the duration. In the Loosian interior we have not the utopia of this moment but the *care* of its potential.

Loos and His Angel

15. The House

The Loosian house is the problem of these exterior-interior relations: neither exterior so powerful as to spatialize every place—nor interior place that *utopistically* eludes space (thereby negating itself). Entortung and *Freigabe von Orten* (liberation of place) meet and clash in the Loosian house—and it is only through this dialogue-struggle that they exist.

In the -*kei,* to lie, of oikos, Severino hears not the ars of building, of deciding (evading the tyche), but the *place,* as always given and immutable. In the oikos man obtains his destined seat (Italian: *sede*); he is *sedatus.* The rooted, "earthly" Nomos of the *vorglobale Zeit* is that of the oikos; it forces man into a *sedes.* This original relation still echoes in the term "economy." But already in the Latin *domus*—as in many other examples of passage between Greek and Latin—the house as a place in which "the mortal is both dominated and protected" disappears in the house as space at the disposal of the dominus that governs and administers to it, at the disposal of its ars.[1] The houses of Mycenae appear "sedated," dominated by an invincible Nomos, almost as though calling for protection. The houses of the *civitas romana* are, on the other hand, planned by the ars, dominated by the tekné of mortals. Entortung originates in Rome.

Loos is a *Roman* Baumeister, as he explicitly declares whenever he can, but he is by now at the apex of the Entortung. He can turn around to watch its chain of events—its single catastrophe. The gedeutete Welt, Roman in origin, becomes in him

The House

175

a self-reflective, self-recognizing process. That is, it returns to being a problem—it ceases to appear a normal development. Its structure opens up: it is no longer "sedatable." It recognizes its own historicity and hence its necessary opening up to the possible. What it was originally—place, oikos—may return at the end. In the face of this questioning, technico-scientific space's claim to totalization becomes incessantly problematic. Loosian composition could be defined as a tireless questioning of the Roman domus.

This same questioning of space has a central place in the *Duino Elegies*. In the Seventh Elegy, (1922) the world as "interior" world is opposed by life's *Verwandlung* (transformation), its transmutation into ever more wretched forms:

> Where once there was a durable house [*ein dauerndes Haus,*
> a rooted, "sedate" house, safe from *Verwandlung*] /
> now appears a fantastic image, all askew, belonging only
> / to the conceivable, as though it still stood whole in the mind.

The house is prey to Entortung, it is "reversed" in the world of thought; it is no longer in the open, but in the closed brain of the gedeutete Welt. The spirit of the times "knows Temples no longer"; it no longer knows a thing *gebetes, gedientes, geknietes* —a thing once for prayer, devotion, and kneeling. *Gestaltlos*— formless—are the "vast storehouses of power" that the spirit of the times makes: the measured-calculated space of the will to power replaces the places where things are collected.

When the Angel is shown Gestalt, form, "rescued at last", rebuilt *inner-lich,* in the interior, in the "terribly vast" place, truly our own, of the word, it is, paradoxically, precisely the sense of the *tectonic* that is affirmed. The form that once stood, "great as Chartres," "like a thing that is," and that now displays itself prodigiously in the invisible of the word, in the utterable, yearns for the tectonic. This is what we must say to the Angel: "house, bridge, well, gate, jug, fruit tree, window— / at most, column, tower." The house is *ein dauerndes Haus,* but now "sedated" only innerlich, in the most intimate place of the word. The bridge is the quintessence of road, the road that spans waters, that nullifies the greatest obstacle, the greatest separation, that succeeds in making a path over the current, over the very principle of

Loos and His Angel

movement.[2] The column, the tower indicate the symbol of the tectonic, monument of its constructive power. The gate serves as a prodigious hinge between the interior place and the space of the remaining world—separation that overcomes separation, limit that at all times also presents to man the possibility to fling himself beyond into the open. The window demands that one look outside, into this open; it is "a road for the gaze"[3] towards the well, the tree, the fruit—a road that unites the things collected inside with those clustered in the surrounding places. Endlessly, the interior empties itself outward and the exterior inward: the jar.

In Rilke, all this lies in the utterable. The oikos is preserved in the utterable. The place, today, is utterable only. Loos's entire life's work is a rage against this totally acknowledged limit— if, in the face of the assertion that decrees, "this is unutterable," one must counter with "try to utter it," in the same way, in the face of the invisible, Loos repeats: try to show it. Every happy immediacy becomes a lie, at this point. What it is already possible to show is the trying itself—how it has its origin in the destiny of Entortung, how it questions this Entortung, how it makes the Entortung's figures problematic and exalts its differences. Just as the attempt to utter does not signify a return to the living word, in the same way the attempt to show the characteristic power of the tectonic does not signify a rebuilding of the Temple, the end of the diaspora, but rather the ephemeral composition of places, the paradoxical composition-reconciliation of place and ephemerality—where the place preserves the hope of the Temple and the ephemeral unfolds in relation (dialogue-difference) to the metropolitan Gestaltlosigkeit. Thus, this composition eludes the "virile" logic of the decree; it neither limits itself to a falsely disenchanted acceptance of Entortung (which would imply an embracing of the "freedom" promised by such), nor idolatrously contemplates things lost.

In the more significant passages that Emmanuel Lévinas devotes to the theme of the house in *Totalité et infini*,[4] these Loosian presences are only partially noticeable. Yet if we are to give a true interpretation (Erörterung) of Loos we cannot ignore Lévinas's fundamental point about the "privileged" position occupied by the house in the "system of ends" in which

The House

human life is situated. The house constitutes a "primary intimacy": all "consideration of objects", all contemplation proceeds from the house, has the house as its premise. No theory is ab-solute, independent of the house. The idealism that asserts the ego as perfectly dis-placed corresponds to the idealism of the Architekt who would like to build the house *ex novo,* who understands the house as a free product of his transcendental purpose. In this respect, Loos's life work is a programmatic indictment of all architectural idealism. What metaphysically distinguishes Baumeister from Architekt lies precisely in the fact that the productive aim of the Baumeister grows out of the house and the language handed down to it; this aim is, a priori, "dwelling", while that of the Architekt imagines itself and strives to be "free", and does not apply to itself the right of the past—it plans idealistically.

But the notion of the house in Lévinas ends up assuming, too directly and naively, the stamp of the oikos. Here man collects himself and receives his things. Here all possession has a place and is not dissolved in the figure of money. Here the relation with the thing is continually updated, it is not dissipated in immediate enjoyment. But this house also has a door and a window: the house actually unfolds, opens up to the Other; it possesses a language that transcends its physical delimitation. Through the door we can go out into the open and receive the guest—the house gives place to the guest (*Freigabe von Orten!*) and joins him to the intimacy of its dwellers.[5] But the time of this notion of the house, a "pure" time uncontaminated by that of the Metropolis, becomes once again utopian. To what world does the house open up? and with what language? Of the term "economy," Levinas analyzes only the first root, oikos. But how can there be oikos outside of Nomos, where Nomos is totally uprooted? Would not the idea of house be, in this case, comparable to Entortung? And how, given this similarity, can the idea of house be naively preserved within the original stamp of the oikos? Would not this stamp become problematic? Would it not become a dissonant composition of place and space, dwelling and Metropolis? What other quest for house can there be, when the door is now conceived in order to be closed to all transcendence, the window is confused with the wall that divides,

Loos and His Angel

and this wall makes visible every discrete reception, every intimacy of the interior, thus nullifying the window? And yet, in this space, we are there to try to utter and to show.

16. Lou's Buttons

The meditative "stroll" that Lou Andreas-Salomé sets out upon in *Zum Typus Weib* begins with a remembrance of buttons.[1] They represent the epitome of that which "is never given away but is instead collected"—they represent the inalienable, the non-equivalent. In this sense, the button is the opposite of money: it opposes division, circulation, and exchange with the principle of the secret and the hidden. Money exists in a dimension exclusively external and public; the button, on the other hand, is the unattainable maternal relic, preserved in the most interior part of a virgin mountain (the association with the Jungfrau that Andreas-Salomé makes). Money is collected as equivalent in order to be spent, and its being-spent brings about an acquisition, a possession; the button is put away as unicum, as treasure. Money is intrinsically productive; it does not reside "out in the open," but "makes things open" in the sense that it brings all things into the space of the purely acquirable, sees and makes one see every thing as possession. The button jealously guards its own unproductivity, flees the visible, and hides itself, as long as it can, in the "box of wonders." It is easy to see how Andreas-Salomé would associate the productivity of money with the univocal aggressivity of masculinity, the unhappiness of "man's hurried step," whereas that characteristic slowness of the woman close to the primary communion of mind and sensibility (however much this image may seem obscured by the very progress of the spiritual, of the Geist felt to be in opposition to the Seele) seems to recede into the marginal, apparently abandoned, and insignificant figure of the button. The button represents the remains of the productive, that which has remained and resists its typically constructive language. Reduction to the margins of insignificance is the form here assumed by the resistance to the universe of equi-valences.

But how does one collect buttons? and where does one collect them? Is there still the possibility of a space of the "collected," a space opposed to the market of things visible? This space is an interior, but not every interior can be the place of the collection of that which resists in unproductivity. The difficulty of defining such a space derives from the fact that it must correspond to the unhappiness of the productive and the sacrifice that this implies. If this dimension were to be ignored or eliminated, the figure of the button would have to be relegated to merely a chronological past, to a time absolutely lost—about which it would be false to attempt to speak. If the childhood of the button exists and operates, it must appear here and now, in connection with the space of money, of the market that divides and exchanges it, and the route that it takes in being circulated and spent. The space of the collected must in short exist within the productivity of the Metropolis. But how is this possible?

Andreas-Salomé does not fully grasp this problem, since the details of her button's childhood are vague. She seems to believe that the box of marvels can preserve childhood as such. But if the button does not become the margin and remains of the Metropolis, it is transformed into a fetishistically guarded treasure, and ceases to exist as true childhood. It becomes again a possession, though an unproductive one. Unproductivity is not enough to "surpass" the language of the Metropolis—childhood must find its own interior within the relations of the Metropolis.

Not every interior is a place of the "collected." For example,

Loos and His Angel

the bad poetry or Heimatkunst that sees the home as a protection from the Metropolis constitutes the exact opposite of such a place. This house wants to be seen as a box of wonders, but in this very desire exposes its own interior and makes it visible. And that which is pro-duced into the visible by the claim to being a place of non-equi-valence is a farce of money, not its opposite. On the other hand, the totally metropolitan house (the building) rightly criticizes the false childhood of the box of wonders, but unknowingly represents its exact reversal—in the space of *Modernität,* however. In fact, even in that box there was nothing obscure or secret: it aimed at the same pure visibility of the metropolitan building. Thus the box of wonders is nothing but a travesty of the Metropolis, and its very presence in the metropolitan fabric makes evident the intrinsic tendency of the latter to liquidate any possible place of the collected.

The interior that preserves buttons can exist only in the Metropolis, and only as absolutely different from its exterior. The exterior must not betray that which is collected in the interior; the exterior must follow money's course and remain in its dimension. Indeed, it must have the value of pure money—it must function within the universe of circulation and exchange. This universe must not be embellished, but made to function. If within this universe there should be an authentic place of the collected, it could only be found within such a language, the unpredictable reverse of its pure money. But this in no way implies that the exterior should be treated as a kind of obstacle or physical impediment to the Seele. On the contrary, it is precisely the reified purity of the exterior that permits the existence of an authentic interior. If the exterior were treated in allusive forms, or were metaphorically forced to indicate that which it conceals, or were still taken as an obstacle, as non-I—if, in short, were to fall back into this wretched late Romantic ideology of the reasons for building, not only would we necessarily fall back into ornamentation (which in the dialectics of allusion has its own a priori condition), but we would conceive the interior as imperfect until the moment of its expression, the moment in which it becomes language—that is, it would be impossible to conceive of any interior as childhood. There can be an interior

Lou's Buttons

only where the exterior is purely and entirely felt—and where it is studied, analyzed, calculated and realized, with the greatest vigor, in its specific rhythm and in relation to the rhythm of the Metropolis. Only where the exterior is also revered as Kraus reveres language can there be a dimension other than it, a dimension inalienable as unproductive and because unproductive, an internal childhood of language. For this reason, the place of the collected is neither, strictly speaking, the "poetic whole" of interior and exterior (the box of wonders), nor can it be found in the harmony of exterior and external surroundings, or simply in the interior in and for itself. The place of the collected is this very difference between interior and exterior—this impalpable utopia that separates them metaphysically at the same time it renders them indivisible.

So difficult is it to understand these processes that Loos can still be made to pass for a pioneer and prophet of the modern, whereas his calculated perfection of the exterior is actually a Krausian *pietas* for language, stripped of that totalizing and patriarchal ethic of the *Fackel* and entirely devoted to reducing things to the transparence of the linguistic order. The exterior of the possible place of the collected is pure language, charged with its history, with its nearly intractable articulations, and with its inertias that can only be moved with obstinate patience—but it is not transparence. Of course, nothing on the outside asserts (like a store sign) that this language has an interior. But neither does anything have to assert that it does not have an interior, as is instead the case with the boxes of wonders, with allusive ornament, and with the "virile decrees" of happily metropolitan buildings. This exterior does not express, does not produce, does not have transparences—and for this very reason it may (perhaps) enclose an interior, an authentic place of the collected. It leaves open, so to speak, the possibility of an interior.

This leaving-open the possibility of a place for the collected within the conditions of the Metropolis, which are here acknowledged without illusions, and the care shown for such a possibility without involving nostalgia for the impossible nullification of the exterior, could be termed facets of Loos's profoundly "feminine" side. In the interior of his residence (now

Loos and His Angel

"visible," alas, only at the Museum of the City of Vienna), this emerges quite clearly, even formally speaking. But this is not the essential point here. What is essential is the vast difference between exterior and interior, not the formal solutions revealed by the composition of one or the other. This expanse is the secret of the Loosian house: the measure of this difference is the measure of Loos's care for Lou's buttons, that they should have a place that is not a box of wonders.

In a beautiful passage from *Partage des femmes,* Eugénie Lemoine-Luccioni speaks of "the intimate bond that ties a woman to her objects." [2] Without her objects, the woman seems lost. But her objects inhabit an interior, they cannot be transformed into money. The house in which they are collected must be *inhabitable,* not visible from without. The act of seeing a house is in principle different from that of inhabiting it. Defining the possibility of inhabiting through this difference, and not abstractly in itself, as though it were a question of style or furnishing, is, I would say, the greatest accomplishment of Loos's feminine aspect. His concern is for a place where the thing is secure in its intimate link to our experience, and where those *Extrakte des Lebens* (extracts of life) that have formed our experience are collected in the thing (since the thing is collected). To continue Altenberg's explication, this thing cannot validly go outside and produce, but it is not for this reason a literary protest against Metropolis, technology and civilization. On the contrary, its very withdrawal into the interior is perhaps meant to signify that the world is henceforth "simply full of things" (in the indefinite plural) (p. 185), or, in other words, that the thing is henceforth only that which is totally manipulable-alienable, stripped of all substance and separated from being. These things only exist, they are seen and spoken. The thing of which Andreas-Salomé speaks, on the other hand, refers instead to a forgotten dimension of dwelling and of the experience connected to dwelling. The Loosian difference between seeing and inhabiting, interior and exterior, seeks to preserve yet another place where this dimension might be collected. This difference is the utmost interior.

The soul of Andreas-Salomé's things seems to be metaphysi-

Lou's Buttons

cally opposed by the soul of Rilke's dolls.[3] Impenetrable, carefree, self-satisfied, impure, "privy to the first unutterable experiences of their owners," and yet mindless of those very first trembling solitudes, they yield to every tenderness and show neither remembrance nor gratitude for a single one. If now we should pull out a doll "from a pile of more participant things," we are almost revolted by its "gross obliviousness," its boundless lack of imagination; we are disturbed by the sight of this "ghastly alien body, into which we have thrust our most genuine warmth." Nothing could bring back that useless, heavy and stupid material, much "like a peasant Danae ignorant of everything except that incessant golden rain of our inventions." Lou's buttons bear more resemblance to those "participant things"— not only to the smile of oft-worn gems, but also to home looms, to the devotion of a violin, to the very simple things that strike their roots in the human, to the "simple and consenting" soul of the ball, to the inexhaustible soul of the picture book, to the "deaf funnel-soul of the excellent tin trumpet." These are the things that seek the difference of the interior, that make an interior necessary. The doll inhabits places of oblivion, remote hiding places, and when by chance she emerges from them, then does our hatred for her erupt, a hatred unconsciously bred during the long hours when we sat before her and vainly expected something in return.

And yet, the unresponsive doll does not pass away in vain. This is so, not only and not so much because "we needed to possess such things, which offered no resistance to anything," when "even the simplest exchange of love exceeded our understanding," but because the doll taught us silence, "that silence larger than life, which forever returned breathing to us from out of space whenever we reached a place at the limits of our existence," *unseres Daseins*. The doll teaches us to recognize our soul's inclination, which no childhood exhausts, toward that which is impracticable and not to be hoped for. The doll's absolute lack of imagination points to the silence that surrounds us. And in this respect, Lou's buttons resemble them. The objects without which the woman seems lost are at once dolls and participant things: Lou's button responds to the overflowing af-

Loos and His Angel

fection of its keeper and evokes a dwelling, but at the same time it points to the silence that this dwelling encompasses and to the soul's unstoppable inclination toward its abyss. In this way does the repository of Lou's buttons resemble that hidden and forgotten place of the dolls. In Lou's button, the quintessence, as it were, of the doll is preserved.

At the crossroads where the silence of the doll becomes an acknowledged dimension of the "participant thing" and its language—where the participant thing not only reciprocates our affection, but reveals its metaphysical inclination to silence—the soul of the marionette begins to take shape. "The doll is as inferior to the thing as the marionette is superior to it": "a poet might fall captive to the sway of a marionette, since the marionette has nothing if not imagination." But the imagination of a marionette is not simply the quintessence of the participant thing; it also leads us to direct our inclination "there where it has no hope." The marionette is not a simple and direct negation of the doll, no more than Lou's buttons were. This "not to be hoped for" had already been suggested by Kleist: it is the rediscovery of the "most radiant and imperious grace" after having traversed the infinite of knowledge and reflection. The totally unconscious grace of the marionette seemed to Kreis a symbol of the utopian grace that we may rediscover only after having tasted anew the tree of knowledge. It is towards this non-place that the marionette pulls us. The string that animates it is like the staircase by which the gods descended from the heavens to meet with men. The bridge, which for us has collapsed mysteriously, endures for the marionette. Kleist's nostalgia for the marionette is a nostalgia for the man still interwoven with the cosmos, of which Plato spoke in the *Laws,* an ensemble of cords and interior strings by means of which the gods lead and guide this man. In the marionette is preserved the memory of the golden chain that once united the universe with indissoluble links.[4] In the doll, this memory has completely vanished—indeed, the doll is characterized precisely by a state of dejection, limpness, radical historicity. But since today the marionette is a utopia, one can rediscover its image only by filling with nostalgia the absolute void of the doll's silence. If such a void had not formed

Lou's Buttons

185

itself within us from childhood, the unhoped for quality of the marionette could not have appeared.

The work of Paul Klee is interwoven with these same, nearly evanescent relations among money, participant things, buttons, dolls, and marionettes, relations that express unlikely sympathies, paradoxical theophanies, and ephemeral orders of movements and flights. The figure of the Angel seems to reassume them and preserve them in himself. His gaze is focused on them: he must reconcile and arrange them in order to save them from apparent fragmentariness and contradiction. The Angel of things perceives the necessity of the process that leads from the merely conversant soul of the participant thing to the naming of the doll's empty silence, and from here to the divine image of the marionette. The Angel prevents the marionette from going limp, just as in Hofmannsthal's experience that evening in December of 1918, as recounted by Burckhardt, he prevents the marionette from withdrawing into an unutterable past. Klee's figures, wrote Benjamin, "are, so to speak, planned at the drawing table, and just as a good car, even in its styling, obeys the needs of the motor above all, so these in the expression of their features obey their own 'interior.'"[5] These figures are, therefore, in essence, marionettes. The Angel is the prince of marionettes. The Loosian interior would seem to have been conceived for such figures. Its compositional clarity, its care for the materials, and all other effects obtained through the most laborious practices must be made to appear necessary, natural. At the end of the road that has taken us from money to marionette, we must try to cast into image the gesture of this latter, as though we had discovered him by some lucky chance.

Loos and His Angel

17. The Chain of Glass

At the beginning of his *Infanzia e storia* (childhood and history), which many of my above observations have echoed, Giorgio Agamben analyzes the brilliant short essay by Benjamin from 1933, "Experience and poverty."[1] The degeneration of experience, or its present poverty (of which, as Agamben explains, the various philosophies of life are a confirmation and not a refutation), finds its exemplum, in this essay, in the developments of the modern movement in architecture. The functional architecture of glass and steel represents the systematic liquidation of the very premises of experience. Its explicit purpose lies in making it impossible to "leave traces," to pro-duce any kind of secret place, and in making totally visible the house as a simple building—not only its individual physical structures, but its relation with the entire organization of the city. In this pure visibilist operation, glass is the preeminent material, the prince of materials. Glass, indeed, embodies the very principle of transparence. As Scheerbart said in a passage quoted by Benjamin, "we can very well speak of a *Glaskultur*. This new glass environment will completely transform man. The only thing we must hope for is that the new civilization of glass will not have too many opponents."[2]

But glass is not only the enemy of all aura, as Benjamin seems to believe. It attacks the very idea of interior. For this reason, Loos cannot in any way be seen as part of Scheerbartian Glaskultur.

The Chain of Glass

Only indirectly is glass opposed to possession. The fundamental reason behind its Kultur lies in opposing the existence of a place in which the thing (the collected) might be for the individual an inalienable experience. Hence glass does not oppose possession per se, but the idea of an inalienable possession. By showing, producing, manifesting all possession, glass would have it exist only as money, on the market. Glaskultur's critique of possession is conducted exclusively from the perspective of circulation and exchange. In the uninterrupted flow of stimuli-perceptions made possible by the city of steel and glass, in the continual enrichment of the life of the spirit, what is desecrated is not so much the ancient auras, but the very possibility of experience—what is pro-duced is the poverty of experience. In universal transparence every thing is assumed to be of equal value, equivalent. The transparence of glass lays bare and betrays-delivers every interior to the equivalence of the passer-by, whose lamentable attire was sung of by Baudelaire. Hence the names without history of Scheerbart's novels, his "totally new" (Benjamin) creatures, their radical lack of interior. They live in the open— but like Hofmannsthal's *Namenlosen* (nameless), they are prisoners of the disenchantment *of Olivier.*

We know that Loos's interior is a far cry from those plush furnishings to which even Benjamin likens it. The Loosian interior expresses a principle opposed to nostalgic lingerings at the threshold of that "virile" acceptance of the times that characterizes all of its "best minds". On the other hand, it is true that by starting precisely with the Loosian interior, it is possible to render transparent the aura still predominant in Glaskultur and in its rhetoric on the modern. Glaskultur decrees that experience is already dead, and declares itself its only heir. Its glass reflects the present poverty. In spite of its avant-garde pose, which rejects the paternal language and opposes its presumed organicity with the arbitrary and the freely constructive, Glaskultur belongs to a perfectly logocentric civilization. Its will to render transparent, to lay bare, to demystify, expresses a utopia that fully and progressively identifies the human with the linguistic: every secret must be spoken aloud, every interior made manifest, every childhood pro-duced. Language, and its power,

Loos and His Angel

are here absolute. It is precisely its new, free constructiveness that enables it to seize the staff of command of the subject-ego. Finally liberated from even the *intentio* of the subject, the language speaks, grows, is transformed in itself and by itself. Man is the animal that language possesses—but this language is the language of transparence and production, the language of technique. Which means bringing to fulfillment the very metaphysics of the ego that says: I think. Glaskultur is just one of the forms in which this fulfillment is refracted.

Criticizing the limits of this power does not express a powerlessness to suffer it, but a desire to thwart it and to show its organic link to the present poverty. The very fact of its being a cause of the present poverty is precisely what Glaskultur tends to obscure. Take, for example, an author as profoundly influenced by Scheerbart as Bruno Taut. In explaining his own *Glashaus,* a model or Platonic Idea of the house of glass exhibited at Cologne in 1914, Taut speaks of a kaleidoscopically rich, fascinating, multiform architecture. The principle of glass here is embellished and adorned with every word that he speaks. Not even the link, so prominent in Simmel, between the intensity of the stimuli of metropolitan life and the poverty of experience, is remembered here. Every effort is aimed at harmonizing the overbearing emergence of Glaskultur with the nostalgia of the soul and Erlebnis. The loss of experience is cosmogonically exalted in an exceptionally naive metaphor of the alchemical experiment, Taut's drawings of *Der Weltbaumeister* (1920) dedicated to the spirit of Scheerbart, in which, through a series of operations of *separatio* and *coniunctio,* there arises into the light of the summer sun, and to the song of children, the perfect crystal of the House, *das leuchtende Kristallhaus,* and the stone opens wide to show its wonders. Here the principle of glass, far from being treated, as Benjamin thought, without any illusions whatsoever, actually claims to open up to the quintessence of an interior. But the glass has no interior to manifest and hence none to negate as such in the total control of the language. And indeed, the interior that its word seems magically to produce is nothing if not still *blitzendes Glas:* the glass sterilely reproduces itself— it reflects reflection. All panic-cosmic *cupio dissolvi* of the indi-

The Chain of Glass

vidual and finite form is a poor substitute for lost experience; this is but an indirect path back to the same beginning: the chain of glass.

We must add that glass has an entirely different value in the work of Mies van der Rohe—and that it is to Mies that Benjamin should have turned, not to Scheerbart. Transparence in Mies is absolute because it is born out of the precise and truly desperate awareness that there is nothing left to "collect" and hence, to make transparent. In this sense, the glass no longer violates the interior, but appears henceforth as that meaning of the thing that it has helped to destroy. But does this decree, which in Mies is finally given strict definition, also apply to the problem grasped by Loos? When glass plays a fundamental compositional role, as for example in the American bar, it reflects and multiplies an interior, it does not "communicate". It is no more transparent than a polished and precious slab of marble (Loos's search for ever thinner slabs of marble clearly points to his aim of finding a substitute to the glass principle). The glass does not say that experiences take place in this interior, it does not emphasize the space that it encompasses as though this space were a "box of wonders". But neither does the glass pro-duce it in the language—rather, it holds back its development, its possible development in this direction. The glass dilates the interior in a long pause, in a suffered delay. In this delay, the interior reflects itself in its difference, and makes one reflect on a possible place of experience, on a possible "not yet." It may be ridiculous to pursue backwards what in experience is no longer, but it is also ridiculous to decree that henceforth everything shall be glass and steel. The possible does not proclaim itself, does not shout its presence, nor does it liberate; but it gives, perhaps, a meaning to the silence and collects while waiting.

Loos and His Angel

18. Of Progress and Pioneers

A conspicuous example of how all of the themes of the Loosian commentary thus far singled out can be systematically ignored, is the Festschrift for the sixtieth birthday of the Viennese Baumeister,[1] in which a great majority of the contributions do not touch upon these topics. On the other hand, many of the themes that would later reemerge regarding Loos's lifework are anticipated in this volume, by Kulka[2] and Münz, among others. For this reason, the historical importance of this volume cannot be underestimated.

The search for the characteristic of Loos's oeuvre is supplanted by the predominant theme of anticipation. It is not what constitutes Loos's singularity, but his supposed modernist "banality" that interests such minds as Eisler, von Ficker, Oud, Polgar, and Bruno Taut. It is Loos who prefigures the present koiné—who anticipates its features with the sole apparent purpose of having them fulfill his prophecy to perfection.[3] The importance of Loos is thereby reduced to having created, "a generation in advance," that which was already destined to triumph. In this way, his fight against the "superfluous" becomes but a precursory image of the utopia (in the sense explained above) of the contemporary architectural rationalism. The Loosian dialectic is flattened to

Of Progress and Pioneers

the abstract measure of a metropolitan exterior, and his *Klarheit* (clarity) to the repetitive simplicity of his space. "Sound human reason and practical living": in the name of this binomial is supposedly celebrated the final triumph of Loos's ideas.

In other entries in this volume, the unqualified insertion of Loos into the history of the contemporary architecture is more fully conscious, if not more refined. Markalous, for example, correctly underscores the anti-pathos of Loos's oeuvre and its spatial, constructive, anti-pictorial value—he hints at the Benjaminian theme of the fight against the fetish of the "creative life"—only to precipitate the whole into a moralistic-demagogic saraband, to the tune of "to serve the public, the people, the State (sic!)" The difficult paths by which the critique of the "creative life" leads back to the language of tradition and by which language is connected to the theme of place—the great distance separating Loos's West from a simple Entortung naively apologized for—cannot possibly be touched upon by someone who limits himself to seeing this operation as *angewandte Ethik,* as applied ethics (Polgar). This applied ethics is a subspecies of applied art. What is instead truly ethical in Loos's work are its overall problematics; in them, there is no ideal truth that is applied, that stoops to writing.

All of these observations on the part of his contemporaries hardly assert the abstract exceptionality of Loos's experience with respect to contemporary architecture. In Loos, there is a programmatic refusal to embrace naively the "philosophy" of this architecture. In the polyphonic dissonances of Loosian composition, the compact utopian-progressive design of Zivilisation (and its critique of the "creative life") explodes in a kind of suspended composition that is just as total as that found in the pages of Schönberg of the same period. Loos's modernity is not a paradigm that emerged in anticipation, and that can hence be later fulfilled; the modernity sought by Loos is the perfect *actuality* of the work, in the mutual belonging of language and thought, corresponding to the forms of living. The typically avant-garde theme of anticipation necessarily shatters this correspondence, favoring the architectural idealism of the project, which seeks to construe dwelling as a correlate to its

Loos and His Angel

transcendental purpose. But a truly *actual,* present modern will never again be present. At the very moment of our flight into the future, with our gaze "reversed" to the past, which we are, we are *gegenüber* (facing) new landscapes, new questions, new tasks. We know that the perfect actuality (presentness) of this idea of the modern is destined to appear a perfect inactuality (non-presentness). This modern is the opposite of the contemporary, which is project, anticipation, Entortung, utopia of the all-foreseeable, reduction of Western Kultur to directly embraced metropolitan Zivilisation. What constitutes the essential actuality of the Loosian modern also constitutes its inactuality with respect to the contemporary. What else could Loos have meant when he said his were "words in the void"? It is pathetic how the overwhelming majority of the contributors to the Festschrift fail to understand this decisive statement. It is assumed as a sign of a vague pessimism that his later success should have erased, as evidence of a no longer "present" disappointment in the reception of his work. In the void Loos speaks, instead, of Veillich and his death, of the possible place and its time, which is barely perceptible in the external configuration of space. In the void Loos speaks of the difference between art and architecture, a point on which we shall conclude our commentary. Perfectly inactual with respect to the contemporary, perfect actuality is void. But the void also points to a place disposed to receiving, a making-space that can be given.

There are those who, in the Festschrift, do lend an ear to these words in the void. Else Lasker-Schüler describes her residence by speaking of Loos—of the "lotus soul" of the interior, which flashes from the interior, whose gaze strikes "from another thought, from another, unknown, mutable land." The order that Loos brings "into the world which the man who does not want to be himself leaves in the hands of the architect," originates in this interior, in this gaze "withdrawn behind thoughts as though behind thousands of bars." Richard Schaukal, translator of the French Symbolists and author, in 1906, of a book central to early twentieth century Vienna, *The life and opinions of Sir Andreas von Balthesser, dandy and dilettante,* also seeks this "withdrawal" of Loos's thoughts. His references are essential to

Of Progress and Pioneers

his attempt to define Loos's Kultur: from the Kleistian theater of marionettes (which had a great influence on numerous authors, from Hofmannsthal to Rilke), through the discovery of a compositional innocence opposed to the gedeutete Welt, up to the theme of irony. Schaukal grasps with intelligence the centrality of these motifs in Loos. The interweaving of themes in the permanence of their differences marks the ironic experience, in its most fundamental Romantic sense. This irony has, moreover, lost its all-dissolving emphasis, and reemerges, each time, as clarity of gaze, necessary detachment, serene and mature renunciation. The reference to Grillparzer, a very subtle Biedermeier, in whom every laceration is as though repressed in the modesty of the word, preserved in its internal face—this reference, for such a Viennese master as Loos, is invaluable, illuminating. To the remains "of a submerged world" cared for by Loos, along with the correct use of the language of material and handicraft tekné, must be added Kleist's marionette and Grillparzer's irony. As we have seen, the critique of the project (of the Architekt's claim to "transfer into the space at his disposal" his "book of models") is enriched and illuminated by being related to those pages of Kleist; but it would be impossible, except in the Viennese literary tradition that has in Grillparzer a kind of symbol, to understand in this manner such writings as the farewell to Altenberg or to Veillich, where the irony becomes, as in Kraus's best work, a weapon, a school of resistance against uprootedness, utopia, and the freedom of ornamentation. "The witticism is truth in a form that renders it tolerable," says Robert Scheu in his portrait of Loos. Today, irony alone is capable of "opening up the abysses" in all their nudity. And, as one might say, paraphrasing Tristan Tzara in the Festschrift, irony is not *photogenic*, it excludes illusory beauties, and can only attain perfections that are rich in all the contradictions, the edges, the *impurities* of life.

Loos and His Angel

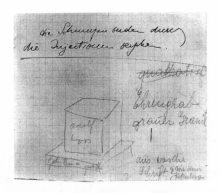

19. On Loos's Tomb

Only over the course of his life's work does Loos hint at what is meant by "speaking in the void." What is really pronounced in the void is Loos's art, or rather, the problem of its difference from tradition and from tradition's notion of "building". This difference lies at Loos's end, and it can be said that his entire oeuvre exists for the sake of this end.

The usual way of understanding the dimension of art in Loos is to conceive of it as a kind of space-beyond, of abstract Other, attainable through illumination. Artistic illumination in Loos is instead strictly profane. Far from being the simple negative of the language that grows with thought and of the decision and innovation that grow out of the loyalty to tradition, the very idea of this art is comprehensible only in this context and because of it. This art is the unutterable of this language; it is part of its structure and reveals itself in its word. The radical manner in which Loos at certain moments separates art and architecture as unconnected realms—architecture being a slave to ends, art being abstractly free—should not let us forget the overall logic of his argument, which we have followed thus far. No architecture, however complex its composition, can in itself explain-exhaust the problem of art. No art can derive from or be explained on the basis of the architectonic-constructive-handicraft *operari*. But neither can the language of art claim to be "extraterritorial";[1] we are able to try to utter it because its place is not utopian. It is a place of language, a place of the crisis of language—a place that emphasizes above all the tensions, the

On Loos's Tomb

195

revolutionary power, the imaginative capacity, of language. It has its roots here, and it renews its roots here. It is the prospect of the maximum judgment-innovation of language over language—but also of the deepest comprehension-sympathy over its "original" living words. It is a very risky game with all of the resources of the "mother tongue," risky to the point of its own rupture, to the point of its own Entortung—but it takes risks precisely in order to oppose this uprooting. It is this dimension accompanying every premise, a possibility preserved in language, which as exception explodes from language, and does not come crashing down upon it.

The problem of art concludes Loos's critique of all linguistic confusion-commingling. Art is not a right to be used in every space, according to the most arbitrary combinations. It marks "exceptionality", the paradox of that moment in which the language of tradition becomes new thought and new form, and in which the space of the functional and the measurable is "surpassed" not by "rendering sublime", but by the illumination of a place, of a word that was preserved in this place, and was also necessary in its silence. Unlike the "captors" of art, those who make it a purely habitual be-all and end-all in the everyday practice of construction, Loos remains loyal to this listening to this place, which is like the interior of language, unforeseeable, "unprojectable" from the exterior, and which nevertheless has a necessary relation with this exterior, as is precisely the case with Loos's house. Loos opposes the position that liquidates art in mechanical reproduction—as well as the totally complementary position that separates art from the reproducible and thus reduces its language to ornament—with the entire behavior-comprehension dialectic that dominates his figures of the craftsman and the Baumeister, to the point where this dialectic explodes in the revolutionary prospect of the work of art. And what reemerges here is precisely the theme of the moment— and *its* unutterable, which is so fundamentally linked to every process, to every catastrophe. Just as this moment is not given, in the same way, the work of art can occur only to him who with endless patience takes care of his own language and has remained loyal to it, in its essence.

Just as for Benjamin every second can reveal the "little gate" of

Loos and His Angel

redemption, in the same way, for Loos only a "very tiny part" of architecture can be opened to art.[2] The exception lies at the margins, exposed to the open like no other stamp of language, and yet it remains distant, elusive to hurried glances: it is at once maximum nudity and maximum intimacy.

One can therefore say that in Loos, art is the "coffer" in which unutterable values are preserved, where only facts have the right to speak[3]—but provided that this unutterable is not taken to be a realm (the Unutterable) exempt from all limits and games. One can gain a true understanding of the game only by acknowledging the indissoluble, mutual belonging of right and justice, space and place, tradition, custom and art, norm and exception—only by manifesting the silence that accompanies each word and resounds in it. But this mutual belonging is not a mutual "domestication." The predominant problem in Loos's writings on art, as in much of his contemporary culture, is the sense of the unstoppable self-exhaustion of place, of exception—the sight of complacent understandings and reassuring phrases that, good only for today, claim to be art. The artist, says Kraus, brings forth that which has no use; he discovers the new. But toward this discovery he must beat his head against the wall of language and withdraw all bloodied, and still try once again.[4] Such a notion fundamentally contradicts all contemporaneity: not only because it opposes all consolation, but also, and much more importantly, because it implies a spanning of the whole language, an intimate participation in its catastrophe.

The statement that art, in architecture, can exist only in sepulchers and monuments, must not, however, be taken in a simplistic thematic sense. This assertion indicates, in the blunt manner of one who provokes and "conspires" ("the conspiracy that is art," says Kraus), that only very narrow gates, nearly spectral possibilities, can "blow up" the process of language in art. And that these gates will open only for those who do not confuse facts and values, who do not "apply" art nor "render sublime" the "conservative" functionality of the builder—only for those who can bear to analyze, distinguish, divide, and in this way reject every "beautiful whole" and every consoling nostalgia for its forms. If sepulcher and monument were to be understood thematically, they would not in any way escape the universe of

On Loos's Tomb

functions. What Loos means to assert is that art takes place where it is the idea of sepulcher and monument, the idea of a place of exception that life has led up to, but that transcends or reopens life's functions. But the fact that it is the sepulcher that indicates all this is demonstrated by this art in its apparently total hopelessness. With the collapse of Veillich's "bridges" and things, art now combats the general Entortung only in the field of hopelessness. Its interior is that of the sepulcher, and there it is preserved—but this is also the place that language continues to put into thought and against which life is continually shipwrecked.

If, in this age, the possibility of the exception lies in the sepulcher, one can also say that existence has always been "collected" there. It is also true that the sepulcher does not denote an eternal image of the past. Only there can we still find hope that is not consolation or flight, not ornament or illusory harmony. No decree of silence, hence no metaphysics of renouncement. The refusal to feign exceptions, the demystification of the dominance of the premises of fact, is the other side of the waiting and listening for the moment. The power of this waiting emerges only at the height of danger, at the culmination of hopelessness. And only where the listening is focused on the sepulcher can we hope to reach this height.

Loos and His Angel

Epilogue:
On the Architecture
of Nihilism

To paraphrase Kraus's "school of resistance," which Canetti described,[1] we can speak of Adolf Loos's notion of *dwelling* as an *act of resistance*. In philosophical terms, the problem that presents itself in Loos is that of the possibility and meaning of dwelling in the age of Nietzschean *nihilism fulfilled*.[2] Although the reconstruction of the historical development of modern architecture through the macroschemas of the Modern Movement, Rationalism, and so on, has become legend, it is still absurd to claim an understanding of the meaning of this architecture without having a grasp of the problem, the unique drama, that provokes the various positions and responses to it.

This drama is the emergence, over the course of the past century, of an architecture of *nihilism fulfilled* as this architecture comes to pervade the image of the Metropolis: it is the very figure of pro-ducing, of leading-beyond, of continuous and undefinable *overcoming*. The obsession with overcoming is embodied in the work of "radical uprooting" carried out by this architecture: an uprooting from the limits of the *urbs*, from the social circles dominant in it, from its *form*—an uprooting from the place (as a place of dwelling) connected to dwelling. The city "departs" along the streets and axes that intersect with its struc-

Epilogue

ture. The exact opposite of Heidegger's *Holzwege,* they lead to no place. It is as though the city were transformed into a chance of the road, a context of routes, a labyrinth without center, an absurd labyrinth. The great urban sociologies of the early century perfectly understood the uprooting significance of this explosive radiating of the city. In these sociologies, the Metropolis appears as the great metaphor of the calculating intellect devoid of all ends, whose *Nervenleben* (life of the nerves) is immersed in the succession of equi-valent cases. The architecture "without qualities" of the Metropolis—a conscious image of fulfilled nihilism—excludes the characteristic of the place; in its project, every place is equi-valent in universal circulation, in exchange. Space and time are a-rithmetically measurable, detachable, and reconstructible.[3]

The crux, then, is the project-limit of the architecture of fulfilled nihilism; within it, the multiplicity of vernaculars is set in order. The naive apologia for processivity, transformability, and infinite convertibility, which continues well beyond the early twentieth-century epigones of nineteenth century progressivism and is echoed quite emphatically in the many marriages of art and industry, is consummated in the absurdity of wanting to make a culture out of fulfilled nihilism.[4] This is the case with the impotent pathos of the nostalgic attempts to charge the products of universal uprootedness with quality, propriety, and values—to combine the equivalence of exchange with the pretended authenticity of use. The developments of modern architecture are marked by these vain efforts at peaceful "transcrescence", these combinatorial-consoling hypotheses. Different from this, or at least much more complex, is the quest of one who imagines in symbol the general *Mobilmachung* (mobilization) of the epoch: the elimination of the place is here transformed into the *imago* of the whole Earth made place. The disappearance of the "brick" that preserves and separates is not experienced as a simple desanctification but as a kind of extreme, paradoxical, and often ironically self-destructive *templificatio*[5] of the whole cosmos. *Entortung* is seen, on the one hand, as a condition—peculiar to this epoch—for the affirmation of a renewed Metaphysics of Light, but on the other hand, the paradoxicality of the attempts to make this affirmation be-

Epilogue

comes transparent, since no metaphysics of light is conceivable in the deflagration of forms. In the works of Bruno Taut from his "expressionist" phase, as well as in the writings of Scheerbart, the imago is for this reason always on the verge of degenerating into a mere game of fantasy. This sort of research is opposed by the nihilism of the total loss of semantic aura, allusiveness, and allegorical mobility: the dream of an order of fully transparent function, of an immanent and forever alert criticism of ideology. The order must be given synchronically; the theory embraces it in the totality of its parts. No place can withstand this work of unconcealing; every place is required to be visible function. In the organization of this project contradiction vanishes, or it represents only a contingency that has been overcome. Once contradiction has been reclaimed, the asceticism of the sign without qualities reveals the new *ratio,* the eminently productive ratio of technique and its power of control, manipulation, and foresight. This ratio renders its own future past. And in all this lies precisely the *utopia* characteristic of the project of fulfilled nihilism: to present its own *novitas* (the exceptionality of the order that it wants to make valid) as a perfect idea of the state—and to manifest itself, at the same time, as a maximally uprooted process so fully engendering order as to "abolish" the unforeseeable, or to render marginal the contingency of the system.[6]

Loos's resistance to this project, which is so diversified in its internal articulations, is difficult to analyze. Some of the elements of this resistance seem to recognize the figure of this project as the perfect type of fulfilled nihilism. Is not Loos's harsh critique of the concept of ornament, of the very idea of applied art, and of the nostalgia for the autonomous self-manifestation of use value, perhaps above all directed at the pathos of the resistance to nihilism? The origin of and reasons behind Loos's resistance come from the opposite end of the spectrum. His resistance is born out of the ground of the most disenchanted nihilism. It works with sober means; it holds in horror all that adorns the defects of the planning intellect. Loos's resistance is born out of a radical questioning of the project of fulfilled nihilism and its architecture.

At the center of this questioning lies the very concept of *project*

Epilogue

201

and its paradoxical constitution: the project is the assertion of a
novitas torn away from all tradition and presuppositions, and at
the same time, a will to state, a perfect utopia of state, or Utopia
tout court. Therefore, at the center of Loos's critique we have
not only the irreducible logocentrism of the project, but also irresolvable contradictions of what is thought within this project:
the maximum opening up-to and the maximum closing off-of
coming into being, at the same time. For this reason Loos's most
characteristic trait, the one which most clearly distinguishes him
from the other masters of contemporary architecture, is the total
absence of utopian elements in his language. The design of Loos
the *Baumeister* develops through differences (often imperceptible ones, so as to preclude all pathos), composes contradictions as such, and gives form—a possible form—to their dissonance. Traditional elements, craftsmanship, and the creative
word are all interwoven according to complex forms of life—
they are never merely reproducible, never merely relatable to
the project's utopia of resolution.[7] It is a game—but inexorable
in its irresolvibility—between interior and exterior, wherein the
exterior cannot "unconceal" the interior, and the interior, in its
turn, is not an ultimate "box of wonders," but rather an element of this relation, a function of this whole, a conflict of its
being there.

It is in accordance with this *rhythm* that Loos composes, not
in accordance with the measure of the number of *a-rythmos*, the
uniform measure of absolute space-time. *Ab-solutus:* that is,
uprooted from all place, from the "propriety" of this place or
this event, and hence able to be "freely" cut up, dismounted and
re-composed, totally at the disposal of the project. There is no
nostalgia in this Loosian critique; on the contrary, it lays bare
the mortal aporia of the nihilism of the project: that if the dimension of space-time is in itself absolute, this absoluteness can
only be a product of the project itself. According to this logic,
the project becomes the new subject, the substance of this uprooting power. The power that negates all place claims in this
way to be the sole characteristic, the true foundation-subject.
The assertion of an absolute space-time introduces, in the end,
as root or foundation, the power and action that, by absolutizing, uproot. Resisting such an aporia therefore implies recog-

Epilogue

nizing non-absolutizable presences and places, moving according to relations, functions, and recurrences through the rhythms attempted by difficult compositions. Loos's resistance finds its raison d'être in the following notion: that the architecture of fulfilled nihilism is also its completion. The insatiable builders, slaves of Hephaestus,[8] who have torn all place away from space and all time away from indifferent duration, have completed their work. The great project shall now be replaced by the sober means of the *grammatologies,*[9] the Benjaminian time of "poverty"—and this project's Time shall be replaced by the multiplicity of times that must be recognized, analyzed, and composed, times connected to the various places which in the program must be questioned: tradition, custom, environment, function, exterior and interior, number and rhythm. And it is precisely because no absolute may resound in this space-time that interior, rhythm, tradition, and the very furniture of master Veillich can resist it, without this resistance becoming sentimental pathos, regressive nostalgia, or new utopia. It is, rather, a sober and demystified expression of nihilism's fulfillment, whatever its duration may be.

But what exactly is fulfilled, what is brought to an end, in the architecture of nihilism fulfilled? And how should this be understood? This question is of utmost importance to a full understanding of Loos's critique, that decisive move by which the perspective of nihilism fulfilled is turned back on itself to the point where it discovers its own fulfillment. In ignoring this question, the various schools of history overlap almost without distinction: according to them, the rift between the metropolitan project and the symbolic, religious, and cultural rootedness of dwelling[10] supposedly has an ab-solutizing effect. Whether this situation is coolly acknowledged or condemned in the name of the shattered values (or idols?), never is the critical attention centered around the novitas the project claims as its characteristic. An approach such as this inevitably ends up nullifying the term *architecture of nihilism* in the era of universal Mobilmachung and the interminable productivity of the Metropolis (the excess of which Nietzsche also spoke);[11] it understands the language of this era as invention ab-solved from all problems pertaining to the dimension of tradition. This approach is a

Epilogue

direct, naive vision of the process of secularization, or better yet, it is the apologetic self-interpretation that this process has often provided of itself. Within its own language, its originality, the architecture of nihilism, in short, believes every root, form, and traditional symbolic measure to be totally exhausted. What is asserted as fulfilled in this architecture is the process of the secularization of this root, or else the process of liberation from it. What is fulfilled is the process of the ab-solutization of the project. The project can finally emerge auto-nomous.

The deconstruction of this dialectic—which coincides with that of the modern term *project*—is not immediately evident. It must unfold through two fundamental moments that correspond to the two terms the self-assertion of the project would like to synthesize (ab-solutization and overcoming). In the project, indeed, in the project proper to nihilism fulfilled, one does not stop with positing the complete ab-solutization of the technico-productive power of the Metropolis, but views this as an overcoming of the previous forms of *religio*. Between ab-soluteness and overcoming, there is a perpetual short circuit: what is fulfilled, inasmuch as it is a completion of the preceding process, overcomes for this very reason every form constituting this process. But the term "ab-solute" echoes only the dissolution of the preceding condition and not its overcoming; the power of a radical separation and not that of a "higher" understanding; the emergence of a fully "enfutured" novitas, and not the "destiny" of the previous languages. In the synthesis of the two terms one encounters an insuperable absurdity: if we radically assert the ab-solutizing power of nihilism, this power can no longer have any relation to the preceding process; though its language may be completely free or invented, it is powerless to serve in any way as completion. If, on the other hand, we insist that nihilism has been fulfilled, is complete, there can be no question as to its ab-solute position, since it is, in the end, but the extreme product of a process that fully comprehends it as neither free nor "invented."

Loos's criticism and work, like Mies van der Rohe's asceticism in other respects, can be appreciated only in the context of the problem of the logical untenability of the architecture of fulfilled nihilism—above all, the untenability of its ab-solutizing

Epilogue

will. In Loos and Mies, we reconsider the secularization process in light of the structural permanence, within it, of instances and elements that allegorically refer to traditional religious dimensions. The very constitutive aporiae of this process render this reference structural, as we shall see. After considering the assertion of the negation or overcoming of these elements, we then study the transformation that their presence undergoes, the "translation-betrayal" to which it is subject. In the end, this analysis makes a logic of overcoming inconceivable: it arrives at the difference between the various languages, which is not hierarchically ordered, either in historicist terms or in terms of value. The analysis perceives the irreducible specificity of the difference together with the combination or context of its transformations, its interlacements, and its references. Difference is not a new uni-verse. This approach is a critique of any vision that sees transformation as some form of overcoming, realization, or negation—of any vision that rearranges the space made up of the places of difference into a new hierarchical order. In transformation, this approach is attentive to the specificity of that which is handed down—translated-betrayed. There is no ab-solute difference, but neither is there any overcoming of this difference in transformation. There is neither fixed "original" tradition in itself, nor is there any realization of such in the process that translates it, as appears to be the case when teleologico-symbolic factors reappear in the ambit of the architecture of nihilism fulfilled. The recognition of the structural function of these surviving elements (unlike the way in which they are considered from the ab-solutizing perspective of nihilism) must coincide with the detailed analyses of the difference existing between their present function and their previous significations—a difference that cannot be reduced to hierarchical orders. This fact is evident in Loos's harsh critique of all borrowing of symbol that is immediately integrated into the modern project and at the same time into its *pietas* for the pregnant symbolism of the work of art. In Mies, the notion of difference presents itself in a similar manner: the abstention from all symbolic value is not a nihilistic assertion of the fulfillment-overcoming of the symbol, of the project ab-solved from symbol because it is a "higher" understanding of it; it is, rather, a true

Epilogue

205

preserving of the symbol in the invisible. It is not correct to assert, in speaking of Mies, the simple otherness existing between symbol and project, since the idea of otherness reintroduces that of the ab-solute. In reality, there is in Mies dialogue, reference, transformation—but analysis arrives at this point only as its final result: the transformation of the symbol into the invisible. But without the ability to perceive this invisible, without an eye for its manifestness, one will reduce even Mies to the code of all too actual rationalism, to the equi-valent space of its order. The verification of these connections would require a groundwork of research too vast and difficult to be even summarily attempted here.[12] We shall limit ourselves to outlining several courses of interpretation, focusing exclusively on the further clarification of the perspective of the fulfillment of nihilism fulfilled and its architecture, in the light of the general schema presented above.

It was Robert Klein who more than anyone else, underscored the systematic solidarity, rather than affinity, existing between architecture and utopia.[13] His analysis focuses on the ideal urban forms of the Renaissance; however, the theme of the voluntary city, the city capable of eliminating from its design all chance, risk, and unpredictability, certainly cannot be reduced to the rational order of the "Cartesian" city, nor can it be thought of as merely its antecedent. Before becoming an immanent lawmaker of the urban form, the ordering Logos was a symbol of the cosmic dike. Before serving as the calculation overcoming the inextricable *vanitas* of the cases that make up the anarchic city of man, the architect was a meteorologist, mirror of an immutable order according to whose rhythm the polis stood. There is of course an eral discontinuity between the two "types", but there is also a profound problematic connection, and indeed the city perfectly resolved on the rational voluntary plane must now appear as utopia, precisely because the polis-dike symbol has been shattered. This symbol is the place where the city once "dwelled"; once this place is used up, the struggle against devouring time, which is the purpose of the lawmaker-architect, is inexorably consigned to the process of becoming. It becomes one of the forms of becoming—precisely that form through which, in the process of becoming, the symbolic purpose is represented as utopia. This approach is the exact opposite of that of the pro-

Epilogue

gressive demystification of this purpose. Inasmuch as the project is the will to power over all place and the "overcoming" of all place, it is also the secularization of this purpose; it must measure itself against this purpose and must somehow reactualize it—as utopia. The will to power of the rational autonomous project in fact contradicts its own purely temporal nature, its pro-ductive and uprooting structure, and cannot respond to this contradiction except in utopian form. This seems to hold true down to the most instrumental and conventional articulations of the project. The solidarity between architecture and utopia therefore includes, upstream, an unrelinquishable symbolical purpose, and, downstream, the aporia inherent to the structure of the project between the maximum openness to the irreversibility of time and the modalities of time's stopping in the order of a reason that progressively relinquishes all firm rooting. This aporia points the destiny of the project toward a form that is nothing but conventional-artificial—but it is now clear that the possibility of this form to have value and power, to *stand,* must be represented utopistically. And the utopia necessarily ends up re-integrating a dimension of symbolic religio, which was previously presumed to be definitively demystified. In this way, in the microcosm of the ideal city of the Renaissance, these connections are already visible in all their problematical force: on the one hand, this city's design is a lucid project of the pure geometrization of space; on the other hand, the overwhelming presence of astrological, hermetic, and magical motifs is anything but ornamental or nostalgic—rather, it points to the aporia necessarily encountered by any project of the geometrization of space that wants to serve at once as a project of the polis and as a putting into state of becoming. For this reason, the symbolic purpose fulfills a structuring function in the overall design of the ideal city—it is this city's harmony, its con-sonance with the transparent order of technico-scientific reason, an accord that can exist only in utopia.[14]

The architecture of fulfilled nihilism bases its own criticism precisely in the lacerating contradictoriness of these connections. The nihilism of the project of geometricization is torn away from those motifs that tended to harmonize its product with symbolico-religious traditions. It renounces the utopia of

Epilogue

such a harmony, and through this renunciation acquires a maximum productive power. This is a fundamental, inexorable moment that marks the entire development of modern architecture: in it, the dilemma of the Renaissance utopia is recognized as intrinsically irresolvable, the subsequent turn toward convention-artifice as destiny, and all attempts to reintegrate symbolic significations into the process of the annihilation of place carried out by the project, as nostalgic *confusio*. It is from this base that the idea of a completion of the architecture of fulfilled nihilism arises—a completion that signifies neither a rejection of its history, nor a going beyond it, but the possibility of questioning it in the entirety and complexity of its elements and its intentions, as they go into effect.

This questioning leads to conclusions similar to those that have been drawn from the work of Loos. Fulfilled nihilism absolutizes the linear time of the project. However, within the limits of the language of nihilism, this very absolutization once again acquires a utopian resonance. Nothing within these limits makes it possible to exclude the survival or return of other times. The absolute conception of time characteristic of fulfilled nihilism disregards only one of the aspects of the Renaissance utopian "knot", and for this reason nihilism's claim to being a radical rupture from and of this knot seems unfounded. The time of fulfilled nihilism is but one time of the Renaissance drama: to absolutize it as a unique time contradicts the very idea of the project as a solution of the symbolic purpose. For this reason, within the limits of fulfilled nihilism, this solution is in fact impossible.

Looking at the fulfillment of nihilism fulfilled—at this other side of its *Vollendung*—implies looking at the end of all pretense to overcoming and resolution, of all decrees of *consummatum est*. It is not therefore a looking beyond, since it cannot but reconsider, in different ways and in different compositions, the very forms and times that nihilism sought to include within itself, to complete in itself. What is brought to an end in this consideration is the very idea of solution. Fulfilled nihilism cannot do without this idea, in as much as it is will-to-the-absolutization of its own time, which is perfectly quantifiable by the time of rhythm, and will to the absolutization of its own

Epilogue

space, which is quantifiable by that which is "collected" in the place. As nihilism cannot do without solution, not being able to "resolve" its own resolutory purpose, the project animating it is forced to remanifest itself, surreptitiously, in a mythical key: to mythify its own immanent will to power. The tectonic exaltation of its own productivity, visible everywhere in the architecture of fulfilled nihilism, exemplifies this aporia. The building (*edificio*), or rather, the power of building (*edificare*), a traditional metaphor for the stability of the soul, for the unshakable foundation of its values, is transformed into a metaphor for the interminable productivity of technique. But the language of technique is by its very essence a reduction of value to valuation, a reduction which as such stands in the way of every *solidissima petra*. Hence, it is the absolutization of this language that makes inevitable the absurdity, the *á-topon*, of the recuperation, in this context, of the religious metaphor of the *aedificium*. [15]

A necessary part of the fulfillment lies instead in grasping the intrinsic, mutual irreducibility of these times. This fulfillment implies the task of effecting their numerous possible reconciliations, not their single synthesis. In this fulfillment, in its difference, may therefore live either the "spiritual" time of the edifice, which is not manipulated by the absolutizing purpose of technique, not being a simple function of its utopia; or the time of the microcosm-city in its specific symbolic root, which is not directed toward the geometric transparence of the project. Fulfillment implies neither the task of effecting solution nor that of effecting the end of all solution, but the idea of composition as a listening to the differences, as an acknowledgment of their characteristic and as the comprehensible communication of this characteristic. Along this line is situated Loos's resistance—the possibility of understanding the architecture of fulfilled nihilism as complete and concluded. What is nostalgic, then, is not the listening to those "characteristics" that the project sought to overcome, but on the contrary the very persistence in that hierarchicizing language of overcoming proper to the project. It is in this language that is preserved, and absurdly so, an absolutizing will, which continuously reproduces romantic mixtures with mythico-symbolic dimensions always claimed to be illuminated.

Epilogue

The time of nihilism is akin to that of the historicist continuum. It, too, declares the last victor to be the rightful one. The time of the fulfillment, on the other hand, reflects the dis-continuity of the process. The shattered here is never realized by the position that shatters it. The shattered also is individuum, and its form, as such, endures in its propriety. That which in fulfilled nihilism seems forced to return, deformed and unrecognizable because of the violence of the absolutizing and auto-nomous claim of nihilism itself, does not return here, but may be listened to and understood. Restorative nostalgia is as foreign to the spirit of the fulfillment as it is akin to the spirit of fulfilled nihilism: this latter, in fact, needs to preserve the once upon a time, to show it as its base—perfectly preserved ruins, perfectly restored shatterings. The spirit of fulfillment knows that the shattered cannot ever again be relived; for this reason, it does not overcome it or subsume it but rather listens to it in its specific being-there, seeks it out in the invisibility of its being-for-death. It is the chain of single catastrophes that unfolds before the eyes of Benjamin's angel. The time of the fulfillment is the context, the composition of these singularities, which no dominant time may declare dead, and which no dike may assign to anything other than themselves. And unlike nihilism fulfilled, which claims precisely to constitute the liquidation-realization of the "once upon a time"—which claims to possess its true name—the gaze of the *Vollendung* perceives the absence of origin of its own composition; it knows that the listening to the individuality of the shattered is precisely its own listening, and never an original in-itself of its own. Indeed, it recognizes that the form of the shattered was once, in its time, composition and listening. . . .

In this way, from the perspective of the fulfillment, the religious metaphor of the aedificium does not in any way become the tectonic power of the architecture of fulfilled nihilism—and not becoming this, neither is it lost nor can it be said to be exhausted. Similarly, the harmony of plenitude and multiplicity that resounds in the term polis and the harmony of stable residence that resounds in *civitas* [16] do not return in the a-rythmos geometric order of the metropolitan *ratio,* nor is this order the

natural heir to Renaissance symmetry.[17] No nostalgia can re-
store the symbol of the *imago Templi*[18] conceived by the science
of this symmetry. But it can indeed be saved—by imagining it
freed from the continuum, not pre-disposed to synthesis, and
not dialectically "educated."

Epilogue

Notes

Introduction

1. Enrico Berlinguer, "La politica che il paese esige dopo la caduta del governo Andreotti-Malagodi (comizio al Festival Nazionale dell'Unità a Venezia, 24 giugno 1973)," *La questione comunista, 1969–1975,* a cura di Antonio Tato, vol. II (Rome, 1975), p. 584. My translation. Translations from all French texts and from Italian texts aside from Stephen Sartarelli's translation of Cacciari are mine, unless otherwise indicated.

2. Massimo Cacciari, *Metropolis: Saggi sulla grande città di Sombart, Endell, Scheffler e Simmel* (Rome, 1973). This essay, whose title was taken from Fritz Lang's film *Metropolis,* was the rewriting and the expansion of Cacciari's article "Note sulla dialettica del negativo nell'epoca della metropoli (saggio su Georg Simmel)," *Angelus Novus* 21 (1971), pp. 1–54. Cacciari was coeditor of this mainly literary review. *Metropolis* was the introduction to selected texts by the German sociologists and the German architect (August Endell) mentioned in the Italian title.

3. See Antonio Negri, "La teoria capitalistica dello stato nel '29: John M. Keynes," *Contropiano* 1 (1968), pp. 3–40; and Mario Tronti, "Estremismo e riformismo," pp. 41–58. Works by Antonio Negri published in English include *The Savage Anomaly: The Power of Spinoza's Metaphysics and Politics,* trans. Michael Hardt (Minneapolis, 1991); *The Politics of Subversion: A Manifesto for the Twenty-first Century,* trans. James Newell (Cambridge, England, and Cambridge, Mass., 1989); *Marx beyond Marx: Lessons on the Grundrisse,* trans. by Harry Cleaver, Michael Ryan, and Maurizio Viano (South Hadley, Mass., 1984).

4. Alberto Asor Rosa, one of the editors of two essential journals in the early 1960s, *Quaderni rossi* and *Classe operaia,* is a professor of Italian literature at the University of Rome, "La Sapienza." Among his most important works: *Intellettuali e classe operaia: Saggi sulle forme di uno*

storico conflitto e di una possibile alleanza (Florence, 1973); *La lirica del Seicento* (Bari, 1975); *Storia della letteratura italiana* (Florence, 1985). Since 1982, Asor Rosa has been directing the series *Letteratura italiana,* published by Einaudi. In 1989–90 he directed the Communist weekly *Rinascita.*

5. On the question of the economic development of the Veneto region see Silvio Lanaro, ed., *Storia d'Italia: Le regioni dall'unità a oggi: Veneto* (Turin, 1984), and especially: Silvio Lanaro, "Genealogia di un modello," pp. 5–96, which pinpoints the explosion of Mestre as a factory-city, where by 1972 half the population worked in the factories; Wladimiro Dorigo, "Venezia e il Veneto," pp. 1039–1065; Giorgio Roverato, "La terza regione industriale," pp. 165–231; Mario Isenghi and Silvio Lanaro, "Un modello stanco," pp. 1069–1085. Cacciari insisted in several articles on the overwhelming presence of the chemical industry (in the 1960s the textile factories lost twenty thousand workers), noting the end of the distinction between "general" and "professional" workers. See Massimo Cacciari, "Problemi e prospettive dello sviluppo industriale: Le proposte del PCI per un nuovo tipo di sviluppo economico," *Atti della Conferenza economica regionale del PCI, Quaderni di "Politica ed economia"* 6 (1972), p. 95; see also Cacciari, "Struttura e crisi del modello economico sociale veneto," *Classe VII,* 1975, pp. 3–19.

6. See Massimo Cacciari, *Ciclo capitalistico e lotte operaie: Montedison Pirelli Fiat 1968* (Padua, 1969), pp. 21–22.

7. Massimo Cacciari, "La Comune di maggio," *Contropiano* 2 (1968), p. 462. Cacciari wrote extensively on political and economic questions. See Massimo Cacciari, "Forza lavoro e/o classe operaia nel revisionismo italiano," *Contropiano* 2 (1968), pp. 447–455; "Sviluppo capitalistico e ciclo delle lotte: La Montecatini-Edison di Porto Marghera. Parte prima: 1950–1966," *Contropiano* 3 (1968), pp. 579–628; "Sviluppo capitalistico e ciclo delle lotte: La Montecatini-Edison di porto Marghera. Parte seconda: 1966–1969," *Contropiano* 2 (1969), pp. 397–447. Massimo Cacciari and Giannina Longobardi, "Sindacato e classe nel maggio," *Contropiano* 1 (1969), pp. 239–259; "Teoria e organizzazione in Francia dopo il maggio," *Contropiano* 2 (1969), pp. 451–473. Massimo Cacciari and Paolo Forcellini, "Stato e capitale nelle lotte contrattuali," *Contropiano* 3 (1969), pp. 579–616; Massimo Cacciari and Antonio Manotti, "Linea delle lotte alla Châtillon di Porto Marghera," *Contropiano* 1 (1970), pp. 91–128; Massimo Cacciari and Stefania Potenza, "Ciclo chimico e lotte operaie, *Contropiano* 2 (1971), pp. 343–398. See also Cacciari, *Ciclo capitalistico e lotte operaie* and Massimo Cacciari, ed., *Che fare. Il '69–'70: Classe operaia e capitale di fronte ai contratti* (Padua, 1969).

8. Berlinguer addressed women, young people, and a large section of the "productive middle classes" as possible allies of the traditional basis of the PCI, peasants and workers. See Enrico Berlinguer, "Le masse fem-

minili, forza di rinnovamento della società," *La Questione Comunista,* vol. 1, p. 301.

9. Alberto Asor Rosa, "Rivoluzione e letteratura," *Contropiano* 1 (1968), pp. 235–236.

10. See Aldo Rossi, *Teatro del mondo* (Venice, 1982), p. 104.

11. Charles Baudelaire, *Les Fleurs du Mal, Oeuvres complètes,* vol. 1 (Paris, 1975), p. 86.

12. Alberto Asor Rosa and Massimo Cacciari, "Editorial," *Contropiano* 2 (1968), p. 238.

13. Ibid., pp. 239, 243.

14. In 1988 Alberto Asor Rosa wrote a preface to a new edition of the 1964 volume *Scrittori e popolo*—a controversial book that was seminal for an entire generation in Italy. He alluded to the weight of time and the changes in politics and expectations: "Twenty years have gone by since that time [the publication of his book]: but they seem many more. Something of enormous importance happened in the meantime: at that time we thought that the factory working class would take power; today we think that, in the social displacements that took place in these twenty years, *no* class is able to take and control power: for the good reason that there *is no longer* a class that would be capable of taking power" (Alberto Asor Rosa, "Vent'anni dopo," *Scrittori e popolo* [Turin, 1988], p. vii.)

15. Massimo Cacciari, "La Montecatini-Edison di Porto Marghera" (1968), pp. 579–627 and (1969), pp. 397–447; "Sulla genesi del pensiero negativo," *Contropiano* 1 (1969), pp. 131–200.

16. See Alberto Asor Rosa, "Il giovane Lukács, teorico dell'arte borghese," *Contropiano* 1 (1968), pp. 59–104; "Mann o dell'ambiguità borghese," *Contropiano* 2 (1968), pp. 319–376, and 3 (1968), pp. 527–578; "Dalla rivoluzione culturale alla lotta di classe," *Contropiano* 3 (1968), pp. 467–504; "Sindacato e partito dopo i contratti," *Contropiano* 1 (1970); "Composizione di classe e movimento operaio," *Contropiano* 3 (1970), pp. 423–464; "Lavoro intellettuale, coscienza di classe, partito," *Contropiano* 3 (1971), pp. 443–490. Mario Tronti, "Estremismo e riformismo," *Contropiano* 1 (1968); "Classe operaia e sviluppo," *Contropiano* 3 (1970), pp. 465–477. Manfredo Tafuri, "Austro-marxismo e città: Das rote Wien," *Contropiano* 2 (1971), pp. 254–311.

17. Asor Rosa, *Scrittori e popolo,* 2d ed., p. 9.

18. See Massimo Cacciari, *Krisis* (Milan, 1976); *Icone della legge* (Milan, 1985); *L'Angelo necessario* (Milan, 1986); *Dell'Inizio* (Milan, 1990). On *Dell'Inizio,* see Vincenzo Vitiello, "L'impossibile: Discutendo con Massimo Cacciari," *Aut-Aut* 245 (September–October 1991); and, in *Iride* 7 (July–December 1991), Sergio Giovine, "Fra necessità e libertà," pp. 232–235, and Franco Volpe, " 'Fare' senza radici," pp. 235–243. I would consider *Dallo Steinhof,* the first of his books published at Adelphi (1982), as a work of passage between the early and the middle

Cacciari. It is interesting to note, in the context of the Italian publishing industry, the left-wing politics of the publisher Feltrinelli in Milan in the seventies, where Cacciari published another politico-economic study in 1975 (Massimo Cacciari and Paolo Perulli, *Piano economico e composizione di classe*), or Marsilio at that time in Padua, where Cacciari published his first studies, like his preface to Georg Lukács' *Kommunismus* (1972), his preface "Negative Thought and Rationalization" for Eugene Fink's *Nietzsche* (1973), and when Marsilio moved to Venice, *Pensiero negativo e razionalizzazione* (1977).

19. See Walter Banjamin, "On some Motifs in Baudelaire," *Illuminations* (New York, 1989), p. 175.

20. Cacciari, "Sulla genesi del pensiero negativo," *Contropiano* 1, 1969 p. 138.

21. Ibid., p. 138.

22. Ibid., p. 138.

23. Ibid., p. 139.

24. Negri, "La teoria capitalista dello stato nel '29: John M. Keynes," p. 7.

25. "The 'irrationalism' of the romantic period here analyzed is only apparent" (Cacciari, "Sulla genesi del pensiero negativo," p. 133).

26. A few years later, Cacciari criticized Gilles Deleuze's position on the unconditional religion of desire. See Massimo Cacciari "Il problema del politico in Deleuze e Foucault," in Franco Rella and Georges Teyssot, eds., *Il dispositivo Foucault* (Venice, 1977), pp. 39–71. Tafuri constantly warns against the dangers of "l'imagination au pouvoir," which he called one of the most ambiguous mottoes of 1968 in France. Asor Rosa stressed his distance from Herbert Marcuse's position, which he labeled "political romanticism." See Asor Rosa, "Dalla rivoluzione culturale alla lotta di classe," *Contropiano* 3, 1968 pp. 472–474.

27. Massimo Cacciari, "Eupalinos or Architecture," *Oppositions* 21 (1980), p. 107. Stephen Sartarelli translated this article.

28. See Pierre Bourdieu, "Intellectual Field and Creative Project," *Social Sciences Information,* vol. 8, 1969, pp. 89–119; and Fritz Ringer, "The Intellectual Field, Intellectual History, and the Sociology of Knowledge," *Theory and Society* 19 (1990).

29. Baudelaire, *Les Fleurs du Mal,* p. 86.

30. A Nietzschean analysis of the persistence of a redemptive ideology in the conception of art is offered by Leo Bersani in *The Culture of Redemption* (Cambridge, Mass., 1990).

31. In an early essay, Cacciari wrote on the question of alienation as the fundamental form on which is constructed the radical concept of the State during the Enlightenment: "All the constitutional model is, with Rousseau, based on a complex process of alienation. The radical state of the Englightenment is the State of completely dominating alienation—or better the product of an alienation process that pervades all elements of the historical process: on the level of Right with Rousseau, and with Smith on the level of economics" (Massimo Cacciari, "Entsagung," *Contropiano* 2 [1971], p. 411). This reading of the Enlightenment alien-

ation culminates with a brilliant analysis of Mozart's *Don Giovanni* as representing the defeat of the utopia of the individual alone against the political principle of society. This article is a review of the work of the historian of German literature Ladislao Mittner, who taught at Ca' Foscari University in Venice.

32. See Benjamin, "On Some Motifs in Baudelaire," pp. 155–200; and "Paris, Capital of the Nineteenth Century," in *Reflections* (New York, 1989), pp. 146–162.

33. The reference to Benjamin was crucial for Tafuri's seminal book *Theories and History of Architecture*, first published in Italy in 1968. Tafuri's reading of some of the most important features of the modern movement —and its concept of architecture as an *ambiguous object*, as shown in Loos's project for the *Chicago Tribune*—is accompanied by Benjamin's realization of "the new values resulting from the crisis of introducing reproduction in the processes of architecture and the visual arts" (*Theories and History of Architecture* [New York, 1980], p. 85).

The quickness with which many Italian intellectuals grasped the importance of Benjamin—well before the French, for example—is in part due to Italian publishers' interest in foreign productions, which also expresses a resistance against a national, centralized Italian identity. This resistance, already multicultural in its impetus, is typical of an Italian tradition dating to the Renaissance that rejected the Italian language and displayed an exorbitant production in various dialects that always ran parallel to the one in Italian, disfiguring, deforming, challenging it with the explosion of vernaculars (but wasn't already vernacular the first inaugural language of Dante's *Divine Comedy?*). This other Italian tradition took various forms in the twentieth century, from the snobbish internationalism of avant-gardes like the Futurists, whose manifesto was first published in French, to the great novel and poetry in various dialects (such as the literary production of Pier Paolo Pasolini, or the experimentalism of Carlo Emilio Gadda, whose novels reached the plurilinguistic inventiveness of James Joyce, playing with various languages and Italian dialects). The interplay of the local and the international has been typical as well of several twentieth-century architectural productions, such the work of Giuseppe Terragni and the Gruppo Sette. The projects of Aldo Rossi can also be read as being at the confluence of the modern movement's international style and local memories. It would be enough to think of his famous Gallaratese (Carlo Aymonino and Aldo Rossi, 1969–74), where the imprint of the Milanese working-class houses with balconies dwells in the geometrical purism of his basic forms; or of San Cataldo cemetery (1971), where the shape of the nineteenth-century cemetery by Costa persists in Rossi's blocks and galleries.

The bibliography on Benjamin is immense. I would just recall two of the first to study Benjamin in Italy: T. Perlini's "Critica del progresso: Temi del pensiero negativo in Benjamin e Adorno," *Comunità* 156 (1969), and "Benjamin e la scuola di Francoforte," *Comunità* 159–

160 (1969); and E. Facchinelli, "Nota a Benjamin," *Quaderni Piacentini* 38 (1969), and "Quando Benjamin non ebbe più nulla da dire," *Quaderni Piacentini* 1 (1981). Facchinelli reads the interest for Benjamin coming from the German students' movement and links Benjamin's thought to 1968 and some of its problems. See the bibliographical note by Edoardo Grebbo in *Aut Aut* 189–190 (May–August 1982), pp. 269–272. The entire issue is devoted to Benjamin, with essays by Derrida and Szondi, among others. Cacciari's essay, "Necessità dell'Angelo," pp. 203–214, influenced by his reading of G. Scholem, is concentrated on the problem of representation constituted by Benjamin's image of the Angel.

34. "Along with the commercialization of the very medium in which he was working [printing], the other inescapable phenomenon facing the writers of Balzac's era was, not yet so much industrialization—this was only beginning to make its impact in continental Europe in 1830—but urbanization" (Peter Brooks, "The Text of the City," *Oppositions* 8 [Spring 1977], p. 7.)

35. *Cantata di Strapaese* is the title of a satirical poem by the Toscan Mino Maccari, who edited the review symptomatically titled *Il selvaggio* from 1934 until 1943. "Selvaggismo" is the trend of some Italian twentieth-century literature (Papini, Soffici, and Malaparte) completely focused on a rural, anti-urban ideology. On the Italian attachement to a rural tradition, see Asor Rosa's exhaustive *Storia d'Italia: Dall'unità a oggi,* vol. 4, t. 2 (Turin, 1975).

36. Antonio Gramsci, *Letteratura e vita nazionale,* quoted by Asor Rosa, *Scrittori e popolo,* p. 177. The debate on the conservative and progressive forms of Italian populism is extremely complicated and offers some crucial questions in cultural analysis, such as national identity, canon, popular culture. Asor Rosa often suggests venturing "in a very delicate but tantalizing area of experimentation." He proposes, instead of the Gramscian ideology tout court, to reexamine "the Gramscian thought itself, with its internal articulations and contradictions" and to read them "as a network of various problems from which we can learn much, exactly at the condition of not integrating them in the unity of the [Gramscian] system" (Asor Rosa, "La teoria marxista e le altre," *Le due società: Ipotesi sulla crisi italiana* [Turin, 1977], p. 88.)

37. The Italian film critic Roberto Escobar wrote that in *Ultrà,* Tognazzi "looked for the story of an Italy that has never been loved by cinema: that metropolitan and violent Italy—so hard that ideology and good feelings cannot tame it. Then he developed that story privileging elliptical narration and montage technique" (*Il sole 24ore,* March 31, 1991). Any Italian radical enterprise cannot but oppose the myth of origins, roots, countryside, nature. It must reject the motif of the organic, wherever it comes from, even the leftist thought of Gramsci, whose most simplistic slogan is that the intellectual must be organic.

38. Frederic Jameson, "Architecture and the Critique of Ideology," *The Ide-*

ologies of Theory: Essays 1971–1986, vol. 2, *Syntax of History* (Minneapolis, 1988), p. 48.

39. Ibid., p. 49.

40. See Lewis Mumford, *The Culture of Cities* (New York, 1938), and *The City in History: Its Origins, Its Transformations and Its Prospects* (New York, 1961).

41. See Raymond Williams, *The City and the Country* (New York, 1973).

42. Stuart Hall points out that the whole emergence of cultural studies is connected to a crisis in the humanities, their social role and definition in a moment of great cultural and social transformation in Britain due to mass media and advanced technology. Cultural studies at Birmingham launched its project of popular culture, of reading and understanding its manifestations and social meanings against Oxford and Cambridge, against the humanistic persistence of a tradition of good authors signifying nothing to the people. The popular content is indispensable to grasp the British experience of this new left who wanted to displace the sturdy, nineteenth-century Marxian definition of the working class and dismantle the class (aristocratic) vision of culture transmitted through the British system of higher education at least since the nineteenth century. See Stuart Hall, "The Emergence of Cultural Studies and the Crisis of the Humanities," *October* 53 (Summer 1990), p. 11–23.

43. See Manfredo Tafuri, *Progetto e Utopia* (Bari, 1973); English ed., *Architecture and Utopia: Design and Capitalist Development* (Cambridge, Mass., 1976). See also "Per una critica dell'ideologia architettonica," *Contropiano* 1 (1969), pp. 31–79.

44. Asor Rosa, *Scrittori e popolo,* p. xiii.

45. Ibid., pp. ix–x.

46. Tafuri, "Austro-marxismo e città: *das Rote Wien,"* p. 259.

47. Manfredo Tafuri, *Teorie e storia dell'architettura* (Theories and histories of architecture) (Bari, 1973), p. 5.

48. What else is the history of a discipline—as Barthes noted in 1960—if not a simple accumulation of data following a fixed, congealed, and therefore nonhistorical organizing principle, that is, the artist's life and work or an artistic movement or style? See Roland Barthes, "History of Literature?" in *On Racine* (New York, 1964), pp. 154–155. Barthes suggests here studying literature as an institution in order to write a history of literature that would be real history, focusing on the literary function in given societies and periods. Interestingly enough this article was published by the *Annales* in 1960.

49. Jameson, "Architecture and the Critique of Ideology," p. 38.

50. Ibid. Jameson considers Tafuri's blend of Marxism has an ambiguous position and "betrays" that Adornian negativity in its "refusal to entertain the possibility of some properly Marxian 'ideology'" capable of offering alternatives.

51. Walter Benjamin, "Thesis on the Philosophy of History," *Illuminations* (1989), p. 256.

Notes to pages xxxiii–xxxviii

52. Ibid., p. 262.

53. Ibid., p. 262–263.

54. Thus I am not interested in writing the linear history since 1968 of the intellectual relationships among the people I have mentioned; I do not think it is important to follow chronologically a personal history nor the history of an institution like a school, or not what breaking offs occurred, what labels do or do not apply to individuals now.

55. This essay was published in Massimo Cacciari and F. Amendolaggine, *Oikos,* 1975. Officina published, among others, Giangiorgio Pasqualotto, Giorgio Ciucci, Georges Teyssot, Paolo Morachiello, and Donatella Calabi.

56. Giorgio Ciucci, Francesco Dal Co, Mario Manieri-Elia, and Manfredo Tafuri, *The American City: From the Civil War to the New Deal,* trans. Barbara Luigia La Penta (Cambridge, Mass., 1979) pp. x–xi.

57. Tafuri, *Teorie e storia dell'architettura,* p. 25. This argument I am summarizing is on pp. 24–28.

58. Carl Schorske, "The Ringstrasse and the Birth of Urban Modernism," *Fin-de-siècle Vienna* (New York, 1981), p. 84.

59. Ibid., p. 85.

60. Ibid., p. 100.

61. See, e.g., Renato De Fusco, *Storia dell'architettura contemporanea* (Bari, 1974, rpt. 1988), pp. 127–130. In "Loos and His Angel," Cacciari writes that it is "fundamentally impossible to assimilate him into the currents of progressive rationalism, in architecture and elsewhere."

62. Manfredo Tafuri, "The Disenchanted Mountain," in *The American City,* p. 403.

63. Cacciari mentions Aldo Rossi, "Adolf Loos," *Casabella* 233 (1959). See also Rossi's introduction to Adolf Loos, *Spoken into the Void: Collected Essays 1897–1900* (Cambridge, Mass., 1982), pp. viii–xiii; and Rossi's preface to Gravagnuolo, *Adolf Loos* pp. 11–15.

64. Aldo Rossi, *A Scientific Autobiography* (Cambridge, Mass.), p. 76. Rossi insists on the importance of the *Chicago Tribune* project in his preface to Loos's essays, and considers Loos's piece on that competition, together with "Ornament and Crime," essential to the understanding of architecture in general: "This latter piece is to my mind particularly pertinent today, at a time when 'post-modernism' is being praised with the same superficiality and the same arguments as modernism was: with everything packaged into a discussion of form—forms which 'change as quickly as a lady's hats.' For Loos the experience with the *Chicago Tribune* competition is a decisive one. In this experience he measures himself against the classical world, the great architectural works, and the American city, which made such a deep impression on him. . . While European modernists were getting excited about the constructions of Wright, dreaming about who knows what sort of exotic democracy, Loos was resolutely exploring the streets of downtown New York, amazed at the dark, immense buildings of Broadway and the perspective offered by the buildings of Wall Street. The beauty of this nucleus

of American business struck him in much the same way that the beauty of aristocratic and capitalist London had once struck Engels" (Introduction to Adolf Loos, *Spoken into the Void,* p. x). Rossi perceives no contradiction between the Loos of "Ornament and Crime" and the creator of the *Chicago Tribune* project and feels in it the presence of that Metropolis that Loos discovered in New York. Tafuri and Cacciari perceive, in the words of Tafuri quoted by Cacciari, "that in 1922 Loos seemed to have lost touch with the clarity of his prewar attitudes" (Tafuri, "The Disenchanted Mountain," in *The American City,* p. 432). If we reread today Tafuri's words in *Theories and History* we can say that, unlike Rossi, he hinted at a postmodern element of the *Chicago Tribune* project: "The Doric column planned by Loos for the *Chicago Tribune* competition, as a first and violent experiment in extracting a linguistic element from its context and transferring it to an abnormally sized second context, is the anticipation of a caustic and ambiguous Pop Architecture" (p. 84).

65. The horror of this figure—the architect-artist-dominator—appears in a satire by Loos that sounds almost like one of Baudelaire's prose poems, told as an old story. The poor little rich man thought that he needed art in order to be happy, and the architect tries to give him a beautiful home. But the despotic law of the architect who has designed and considered *everything* for him does not allow him to really live in his home and enjoy it. The rich man is not even allowed to buy a painting at the Secession! See Adolf Loos, "The Poor Little Rich Man," in *Spoken into the Void,* pp. 125–127.

66. The real loyalty to negative thought cannot be completed nihilismus, nor "weak thinking," as Gianni Vattimo calls our postmodern thought that abandons any systematic attempt to organize the world; see Gianni Vattimo and Pier Aldo Rovatti, *Il pensiero debole* (Milan, 1984). Franco Rella, who also teaches in Venice's Department of Critical and Historical Analysis, writes: "There is a turning point within the modern: a tradition that up to now has been concealed and almost undetected by the power of the great progressive and negative narratives. It is the emergence of a thought of metamorphosis that allows us to grasp and understand mutation beyond the mortal horizon of loss. . . . As Rilke wrote in the foreword of *Duino Elegies* to Hans Carossa: it is 'in the permanent realm of metamorphosis' that we can find 'the image that is saving us' " (Franco Rella, "Nihilisme et mutation: Les frontières du nouveau," *Critique* 452–453, [January–February 1985], pp. 142–143). Rella also discusses these themes in *Metamorfosi: Immagini del pensiero* (Milan, 1984).

67. "Desire is after all the desire to reconcile with the 'naturality' of Desire" (Cacciari, "Il problema del politico in Deleuze e Foucault," p. 66.)

68. Ibid., p. 68.

69. Cacciari, *Dallo Steinhof,* p. 31. At the end of a chapter on Trauerspiel, Cacciari quotes Roberto Bazlen: "True life means: to invent new places

where to be able to shipwreck . . . every new work is nothing but the invention of a new death" (p. 49).

70. See Charles Jencks, *The Language of Post-Modern Architecture* (New York, 1977). For a critique of this postmodernist immediacy, see Kenneth Frampton, *Modern Architecture: A Critical History* (New York, 1980), p. 292. See also Anthony Vidler, "Academicism: Modernism," *Oppositions* 8 (Spring 1977), pp. 1–5, where, almost in a *Contropiano* tone, he declared: "It is not the intention of *Oppositions* to found a new orthodoxy [such as postmodernism], nor to chronicle the events of the past as accomplished, knowable facts. Rather, we hope to encourage the investigation of the recent past as an instrument for the analysis and the criticism of the present, not once more as any fulfillment of the 'spirit of the age,' but now as an aid to understanding the impossible contradiction of our own practice" (p. 5).

71. Cacciari, "Eupalinos or Architecture," p. 115.

72. Ibid.

73. Manfredo Tafuri, *The Sphere and the Labyrinth* (Cambridge, Mass., 1987), p. 4. Cacciari expresses the same type of fear about the sense of multiplicity when he talks about the *revêtment* character of linguistic games expressing "a single thought" or "a single ideal dimension."

74. Ibid., pp. 4–5.

75. See Manfredo Tafuri, *Venice and the Renaissance* (Cambridge, Mass., 1988). First published as *Venezia e il Rinascimento* (Turin, 1985).

76. See Michel Vovelle, *Idéologie et Mentalités* (Paris, 1982), English trans., *Ideologies and Mentalities* (Chicago, 1990). See especially the introduction on Marxism and the Annales School, pp. 2–12.

77. Manfredo Tafuri, "Réalisme et architecture," *Critique* 476–477 (January–February 1987), p. 23. Tafuri posits the problem similarly to the historian Paul Veyne who suggested that in order to conceptualize history according to different main concepts, "represent to your mind the index of an ideal history of the human kind, and suppose that its chapters would not be titled: 'the East, Greece, Rome, the Middle Ages,' but, for example: 'from power as subjective right to power through mediation' " (Paul Veyne, *L'inventaire des différences* [Paris, 1976], pp. 48–49).

78. On the question of orthodoxy, the conflict over expressionism between Benjamin and Lukács is important. See Ernst Bloch et al., *Aesthetics and Politics* (London, 1977), including Frederic Jameson's "Reflections in Conclusion," pp. 196–209.

79. Lucien Febvre, "Avant-propos," in Charles Morazé, *Trois essais sur histoire et culture* (Paris, 1948), p. vii.

80. Benjamin, "Thesis on the Philosophy of History," pp. 257–258.

81. Friedrich Nietzsche, *The Birth of Tragedy and the Genealogy of Morals* (New York, 1956), p. 157.

82. Cacciari, *Dallo Steinhof*, p. 31.

83. As in Baudelaire's "Correspondances": (*Les Fleurs du Mal*, p. 11)
    La Nature est un temple où de vivants piliers,

Laissent parfois sortir des confuses paroles:

L'homme y passe à travers des forêts de symboles

Qui l'observent avec des regards familiers.

(Nature is a temple where living pilasters

Sometimes utter confused words;

Man passes here through a forest of symbols,

That watch him with familiar gaze.)

84. Cacciari, *Dallo Steinhof*, p. 13.

85. Ibid., p. 48.

86. Ibid., p. 29.

87. See Cacciari, *Dallo Steinhof*, pp. 76–80. Cacciari devoted an entire essay to the power of singing: see "Il fare del canto," *Le forme del fare* (Naples, 1987) pp. 47–74.

88. Ibid., p. 31. One can also think of Cacciari's early fascination with Chomsky. See "Vita Cartesii est simplicissima," *Contropiano* 2 (1970), pp. 375–399.

89. This is the title of a chapter of Claudio Magris's *Il mito asburgico nella letteratura moderna* (Turin, 1963, pp. 185–260), which contains essays on Trakl, Schnitzler, Hofmannsthal, and Kraus. See also Claudio Magris, *L'anello di Clarisse* (Turin, 1984), especially the essay often related to Cacciari's reading of Hugo von Hofmannsthal, "La ruggine e i segni: Hofmannsthal e *La lettera di Lord Chandos*," pp. 32–62.

90. Massimo Cacciari, "Intransitabili utopie," in Hugo von Hofmannsthal, *La Torre*, trans. Silvia Bortoli (Milan, 1978), p. 158.

91. Roland Barthes, "Longtemps, je me suis couché de bonne heure," in *The Rustling of Language* (New York, 1986), p. 286.

92. Aldo Rossi, for example, in his *Scientific Autobiography* (1981), perceives the passing of time with a poetic touch, in his more and more intimistic way of reading architecture, in that ever stronger identification, in the late seventies and early eighties, of his architecture and memory—personal and collective memory and a sort of melancholic nostalgia for youth and for the great hopes of the past, not unlike Loos's Veillich, in an intense *pietas* for things: "And this also meant knowing that the general condition must be experienced personally, often through small things, because the possibility of great ones has been historically precluded" (p. 83).

93. Asor Rosa, *Scrittori e popolo*, p. 10.

94. Cacciari, "Eupalinos or Architecture," p. 114.

95. See Carl Schmitt, *The Concept of the Political* (New Brunswick, N.J., 1976), and George Schwab's introduction, pp. 3–16.

96. Leo Strauss, "Comments on Carl Schmitt's *Der Begriffe des Politischen*," in Schmitt, *The Concept of the Political*, p. 81.

97. Massimo Cacciari, "Sinisteritas," in Massimo Cacciari et al., *Il concetto di sinistra* (Milan, 1982), p. 12.

98. Manfredo Tafuri, "The Historical Project," in *The Sphere and the Labyrinth*, p. 5.

99. See Cacciari, "Eupalinos or Architecture," pp. 113–114.

100. Georg Simmel, "Roma, Firenze, e Venezia," in Cacciari, *Metropolis,* p. 197.

Chapter 1. Metropolis

1. G. Simmel, "Metropolis and Mental Life," in *On Individuality and Social Forms,* ed. Donald E. Levine (Chicago, 1971). There are two Italian translations of this essay, in Autori Vari, *Immagini dell'uomo* (Milan, 1963) and in Autori Vari, *Città e analisi sociologica* (Padua, 1968).

2. W. Benjamin, "The Paris of the Second Empire and Baudelaire," *Angelus Novus* (Turin, 1962).

3. The crisis of the avant-garde constitutes the overall framework of the analyses of this book. I have written about this in *Krisis* (Milan, 1976) and elsewhere. Manfredo Tafuri devoted the central part of *Sphere and Labyrinth* It. ed. (Turin, 1980) to this subject.

4. Simmel, pp. 227–228.

5. A. de Tocqueville, *Souvenirs* (Paris, 1850).

6. Simmel, p. 229.

7. Simmel, p. 232.

8. Ibid., p. 233.

9. Regarding the term *negative thought,* I refer the reader to my *Krisis.* The discussion in Italy that ensued after the publication of this book brought forth some important *mises au point* regarding this concept, but unfortunately I do not have the space to present them here.

10. Simmel, p. 237.

11. Ibid., p. 242.

12. G. Lukacs, *Georg Simmel* (1918), in Autori Vari, *Buch des Dankes an Georg Simmel* (Berlin, 1958). Similar to Lukacs's definition of Simmel's thought is that given by Ernst Bloch—*Vielleichtsdenker,* the philosopher of maybe—in a 1958 essay, now in *Philosophische Aufsätze* (Frankfurt am Main, 1969). But for Bloch the term has an essentially negative value: it shows lack of content and decision. It is unnecessary to point out that Lukacs's position with regard to Simmel would change radically in *The Destruction of Reason* (1954).

13. On the concept of transcrescence, see J. A. Schumpeter, *Capitalism, Socialism, and Democracy,* part II Italian trans. (Milan, 1955).

14. Reactionary criticism of the metropolis has been for some time one of the favorite themes of critical theory. Cf. A. Mitscherlich, *Il feticcio urbano,* Italian trans. (Turin, 1968); and H. Berndt, A. Lorenzer, and K. Horn, *Ideologia dell'architettura,* Italian trans. (Bari, 1969).

15. Benjamin, pp. 91–97.

16. Here Benjamin cites Freud's 1921 opus, *Beyond the Pleasure Principle.* On this subject, see the essay by E. Benevelli, *Angelus Novus* 23 (1972).

17. Benjamin, pp. 97ff.

18. Ibid., p. 140.

Chapter 2. On the German Sociology of the City
at the Turn of the Century

1. F. Tönnies, *Comunità e società,* Italian trans. (Milan, 1963).

2. Ibid., p. 32.

3. Ibid., pp. 79–82.

4. Ibid., pp. 290–291.

5. F. Nietzsche, *Thus spoke Zarathustra,* tr. Walter Kaufmann, (New York, 1954), "The Wayfarer," pp. 152–155.

6. Ibid., p. 217. For a philologically precise explanation of these passages from Nietzsche, see E. Fink, *Nietzsches Philosophie* (Stuttgart, 1960).

7. This work was published in the Weberian "Archiv" in 1920–1921 and later included in *Wirtschaft und Gesellschaft.* Cf. R. Bendix, *Max Weber* (New York, 1962), p. 72.

8. M. Weber, *Wirtschaft und Gesellschaft,* Italian trans., Sec. 8, vol. 2 (Milan, 1961), p. 549.

9. By and large, the major studies on Weber have stopped at this most traditional aspect of his thought—an aspect which moreover may be easily related to the works of Glotz and Pirenne. Regarding the historiography of the city, see O. Handlin and J. Burchard, eds., *The Historian and the City* (Cambridge, Mass: MIT Press, 1963).

10. Weber, p. 619.

11. M. Weber, *Wirtschaftsgeschichte,* anastatic reprint of the 1923 edition (Berlin, 1958), p. 271.

12. W. Sombart, *Liebe, Luxus und Kapitalismus* (1912, Munich, 1967). Sombart discusses the modern industrial city in vol. 2 of *Der moderne Kapitalismus* (1927).

13. Sombart, *Liebe,* pp. 54–58. On the polemic regarding the luxury of the eighteenth century, cf. C. Borghero, ed., *La polemica sul lusso nel Settecento francese* (Turin, 1974).

14. W. Sombart, *Der moderne Kapitalismus,* Italian trans. (Turin, 1967), pp. 673–677.

15. Ibid., p. 684.

16. See my *Pensiero negativo e razionalizzazione* (Venice, 1977). The intersection between the analysis of *Rationalisierung* and the architectural-urbanistic debate was, in those years, a physical one. F. Naumann was one of the founders of the Werkbund; Th. Heuss would later become a member. Alfred Weber always divided his commitment between politico-sociological analysis and direct intervention in the problems of land organization: cf. his *Die Grossstadt und ihre sozialen Probleme* (Leipzig, 1908). H. Preuss, who played a decisive role in the definition of the Weimarian *Verfassung,* dealt with problems of urban development in *Die Entwicklung des deutschen Städtewesens* (Leipzig, 1906). M. Weber's essay on the city must be seen in this political and cultural context in order to be fully understood.

17. On the subject of the concentration of industry and financial capital, cf. J. Kuczynski, *Die Geschitchte der Lage der Arbeiter unter dem Kapi-*

talismus, vol. 14 (Berlin, 1962). Sombart was one of the first to analyze and understand the importance of these processes in *Die deutsche Volkswirtschaft im 19. Jahrhundert* (Berlin, 1903).

18. Regarding these themes, see chapter 3 below.

19. On the history of the Werkbund, cf. H. Eckstein, *Idee und Geschichte des deutschen Werkbundes* (Frankfurt am Main, 1958); also of importance as a testimony of the presence of the Naumann group in the Werkbund, Th. Heuss, "Notizen und Exkurse zur Geschichte des deutschen Werkbundes," in *50 Jahre deutschen Werkbundes,* (Berlin-Frankfurt am Main, 1958); J. Posener, *Anfänge des Funktionalismus* (Berlin-Frankfurt am Main-Wien, 1964); M. Franciscono, *Walter Gropius and the Creation of the Bauhaus in Weimar: The ideals and artistic theories of its founding years* (1971).

20. Posener, p. 22ff.

21. K. Scheffler, "Uber die Auseinandersetzung im deutschen Werkbund," in Posener, pp. 225–227.

22. K. Scheffler, *Henry Van de Velde* (Leipzig, 1913). This collection of four essays on Van de Velde, the first from 1900 and the last from 1913, was presented at the Nietzsche Archiv on the occasion of the architect's fiftieth birthday. In 1933, on the occasion of Van de Velde's seventieth birthday, Scheffler devoted a new essay to him in *Kunst und Kunstler* 32 (1933).

23. Scheffler, *Henry Van de Velde,* p. 84.

24. Regarding the various readings of Goethe during this period, see chapter 5 below. The first theoretician of Expressionism, H. Bahr, in the famous 1920 essay "Expressionism," connects this movement with the "Goethe-type." Simmel was the first, later followed in part by Lukacs, to attempt a "Goethian" interpretation of the avant-garde.

25. K. Scheffler, *Die Architektur der Grossstadt* (Berlin, 1913), the first chapter of which is summarized here.

26. Cf. the theses of Muthesius and the counter-theses of Van de Velde in Posener, pp. 205–207.

27. F. Naumann, "Werkbund und Weltwirtschaft," in Posener, p. 223. Naumann's position is not, however, so "linear"—see chapter 3 below.

28. A. Endell, *Die Schönheit der grossen Stadt* (Stuttgart, 1908).

29. On Dessoir and his school, see D. Formaggio, *Studi di estetica* (Milan, 1962), pp. 69–102.

30. Spengler, *The Decline of the West,* Italian trans. J. Evola (Milan, 1970), p. 1299.

Chapter 3. Merchants and Heroes

1. Harry Graf von Kessler spoke at great length of this experience in his "canonical" biography of Rathenau, *Walther Rathenau: Sein Leben und sein Werk* (Berlin, 1928), translated into French by the author in 1933, with an interesting introduction by Gabriel Marcel. All references here are from the French edition.

2. These concepts are taken from G. Simmel, *Soziologie: Untersuchungen über die Formen der Vergesellschaftung* (Leipzig, 1908).

3. This is also the thesis of Walther Rathenau's *Zur Mechanik des Geistes* (1913), which for this reason comes much closer to Spengler's notion of destiny than to Klages.

4. I. Révész, *Walther Rathenau und sein wirtschaftliches Werk* (Dresden, 1927), p. 26ff.

5. Kessler, *Tagebücher*, in which he recounts his first meeting with Rathenau after World War I, in February 1919. Kessler felt "annoyance" at his friend's attitude: Rathenau seemed to him one who was already "thinking about his own monument."

6. F. Meinecke, *Esperienze 1862–1919*, Italian trans. (Naples, 1971), p. 277.

7. E. Troeltsch, "Dem ermordeten Freunde," *Die neue Rundschau* 33 (1922), aside from the *Spektator-Briefe*, to which we shall return; M. Scheler, *Walther Rathenau: Eine Würdigung* (Koln, 1922).

8. R. Musil, "Anmerkung zu einer Metapsychik" (1914), in *Tagebücher. Aphorimen, Essays und Reden* (Hamburg, 1955) p. 637ff.

9. F. Naumann, *Die Kunst im Zeitalter der Maschine* (Berlin, 2nd ed., 1908), now in *Werke*, vol. 6, *Aesthetische Schriften*, which also contains all of his interventions in the Werkbund congresses. The title, as we shall see, should not lead one to assume affinities with the famous essay by Benjamin, even though in his final pages on photography, as a radical transformation of the way we see, and on its relation with the *Stadtkultur*, Naumann's discourse goes beyond an ingenuous apology for industrial art.

10. "The machine is not anti-Christian, since God wants it to exist. God speaks to us through the facts of history. . . . God wants technical progress, and hence he wants the machine." Naumann reached similar depths of *kitsch* in "Der Christ im Zertalter der Maschine" (1893), reprinted the following year in *Was heisst Christlich-sozial?*

11. Naumann, *Die Kunst*, p. 6.

12. A. Endell, *Die Schönheit der grossen Stadt* (Stuttgart, 1908). Naumann, in *Neue Schönheiten* (1902), in *Werke*, Vol 6, pp. 211ff., asserts that he would give all of the arcades of Germany and Italy for a brief stay in the Frankfurt railroad station or for a day in the shadow of the Eiffel Tower!

13. Naumann, *Die Kunst*, p. 23.

14. *Die Kunst* was followed by *Kunst und Industrie* (Berlin, 1906), and *Deutsche Gewerbekunst* (Berlin, 1908), both collected in *Anstellungsbriefe: Ein Buch der Arbeit* (Berlin, 1909); The second edition in 1913 had the title *Im Reiche der Arbeit*. Lastly *Der deutsche Stil* appeared (Leipzig, 1912). These essays, in addition to the interventions in the Werkbund congresses, bear witness to the exceptional importance that Naumann gave to his aesthetic activity.

15. The reference is to Van de Velde's *Werkbund und Weltwirtschaft*. For the Van de Velde side of the Werkbund, an instructive text is K. E.

Osthaus's apologetic volume, *Henry Van de Velde: Leben und Schaffen des Künstlers* (Hagen, 1920). An entire chapter could be devoted to the relations between the Van de Velde circle, of which Kessler was also part, and the Nietzsche-Archives of Weimar directed by Elisabeth Förster-Nietzsche. This side of the Werkbund actively collaborated in the ideologico-political construction of the myth of a reactionary Nietzsche and in those nationalization processes of the masses that G. L. Mosse examined from a perhaps too reductively popular perspective.

16. This was also T. Fischer's view in the early days of the Werkbund, cited in G. B. Hartmann and W. Fischer, "Zur Geschichte des deutschen Werkbundes," in *Zwischen Kunst und Industrie,* p. 16.

17. In his essay, "Englands Industrie," Rathenau writes: "The Englishman, well-off, healthy and strong, loves work, but has never devoted himself completely to it. He requires holiday periods, free hours, open-air recreation, sports. *Der Deutsche liebt seine Arbeit über alles*" (The German loves his work more than anything), In *Gesammeite Schriften,* vol. 4, p. 145.

18. W. Sombart, *Kunstgewerbe und Kultur* (Berlin, 1908). The essay was written, however, in 1906.

19. This notion of technique as all-encompassing "destiny" is of the greatest importance, even for the subsequent cultural debate in the Weimar Republik. Cf. in particular Ernst Jünger's *Der Arbeiter* (1932) and Spengler's *Der Mensch und die Technik*. We should not forget this climate (even though it is much more literary than philosophical), not even in Heidegger's discussion of technique.

20. For a critique of the Werkbund from the same period, cf. the interesting work by W. C. Behrendt, *Der Kampf um den Stil im Kunstgewerbe und in der Architektur* (Stuttgart-Berlin, 1920), pp. 97ff.

21. Aside from the "classical" J. J. Lador-Lederer, *Capitalismo mondiale e cartelli tedeschi tra le due guerre,* Italian trans. (Turin, 1959), pp. 100–101; cf. H. J. Henning, *Das westdeutsche Bürgertum in der Epoche der Hochindustrialisierung, 1860–1914* (Wiesbaden, 1972); W. G. Hoffmann, ed., *Das Wachstum der deutschen Wirtschaft seit der Mitte des 19. Jahrhunderts* (Berlin-Heidelberg-New York, 1965). An interesting book on this period is by G. Stolper (editor of the magazine *Der deutsche Volkswirt*), *German Economy, 1870–1940* (New York, 1940).

22. R. Musil, *Der Mann ohne Eigenschaften,* Italian trans. (Turin, 1957), vol. 1, pp. 635–636.

23. W. Gropius, "Die Entwicklung moderner Industriebaukunst," in *Werkbund-Jahrbuch 1913,* cited in *Zwischen Kunst und Industrie,* p. 73.

24. Cited in T. Buddendsieg and H. Rogge, "Peter Behrens e l'architettura dell' AEG," *Lotus 12* (September 1976). The writings of Behrens most relevant to understanding his participation in the AEG are "Was ist monumentale Kunst?" in *Kunstgewerbeblatt* (December 1908): "An art that one cannot love, in front of which we fall down, an art that dominates us spiritually . . . its secret is proportionality, a conformity to

rules expressed in architectural relationships"; "Kunst und Technik," in *Elektrotechnischen Zeitschrift* (June 1910: "The works of the engineer are still lacking in style, the result of an artistic will fully aware of its goals, that triumphs over the restraints of purpose, material and realization"; "Einfluss von Zeit und Raumausnützung auf moderne Formentwicklung," *Jahrbuch des deutschen Werkbundes 1914:* "Our age has not yet achieved unity in its formal vision, which is the premise as well as the testimony for a new style . . . Nothing is more common than haste . . . it is the fundamental basis of our production, but it cannot yet become a cultural form dominated by art. It still has something of a 'parvenu' character; we have not yet succeeded in getting at the heart of it"; and "Zur Aesthetik des Fabrikhaus," *Gewerbefleiss* (July-September 1929). Among the more important books on Behrens and his activity in this period are F. Hoeber, *Peter Behrens* (Munich, 1913); P. J. Cremers, *Peter Behrens: Sein Werk von 1909 zur Gegenwart* (Essen, 1928); and K. Scheffler, *Die fetten und die mageren Jahren* (Berlin, 1946). Of particular importance is the essay by Adolf Behne, "Peter Behrens und die toskanische Architekture des 12. Jahrhunderts," in *Kunstgewerbeblatt, 1912,* in which Behrens's work is seen as a perfection of the classical Tuscan architectural tradition. The attainment of such perfection represents a point of no return. The avant-garde was a consequence of the total exhaustion of the classical tradition and its language. On Behrens, see also the essay by S. Anderson, "Modern architecture and Industry: Peter Behrens, the AEG, and Industrial Design," *Oppositions* 21 (1980).

25. On the concept of *heterotopia* used here, cf. M. Foucault, "Des espaces autres," *Cercle d'Études architecturales,*" March 14, 1967.

26. Gropius, *Die Entwicklung.*

27. Regarding the "spirit of '14", cf. K. von Klemperer, pp. 47–55; K. Sontheimer, chapter 5; A. M. Kaktanek, pp. 182ff.; C. von Krochow, *Die Entscheidung: Eine Untersuchung über Ernst Jünger, Carl Schmitt, Martin Heidegger* (Stuttgart, 1958), pp. 39ff.; H. Lebovics; in addition to the works on the numerous authors who were more or less profoundly infected by this spirit, from Sombart to Scheler to Simmel and Troeltsch.

Chapter 4. Negative Thought and Artistic Representation

1. This interpretation is a critically revised version of the *cogito* of J. Lacan in "Science et Vérité," *Écrits* (Paris, 1966).

2. G. Lukacs, *History and Class Consciousness,* (*Geschichte und Klassenbewusstsein,* 1923), Italian trans. (Milan, 1967). Lukacs is still the only one to have comprehensively treated, from this perspective, the ethical-theoretical relationship in the foundation of bourgeois ideology. In this vein, partially, see Goldmann, *The Hidden God.*

3. It is, in fact, entirely consummated in *Der Konflikt der modernen Kultur* (Munich-Leipzig, 1918).

4. See my "Sulla genesi sel pensiero negativo," *Contropiano* 1 (1969).

5. M. Foucault, *La parole et la chose,* Italian trans. (Milan, 1967).

6. C. Baudelaire, "Notes nouvelles sur Edgar Poe," in *Curiosités esthétiques: L'art romantique* (Paris, 1962), p. 637.

7. Typical of this figure of the "traveler" are the opening pages of *Tristes Tropiques* by C. Lévi-Strauss.

8. Baudelaire, p. 616.

9. M. Bense relates this Melville story to the "epic form" of Kafka in an important essay, "Metaphysische Beobachtungen an Bartleby und K.," in *Aesthetica* (Baden-Baden, 1965). Regarding Bense, his relations with Benjamin, and many other issues discussed here, I refer the reader to G. Pasqualotto, *Avanguardia e tecnologia* (Rome, 1972).

10. On Mallarmé, cf. O. Mannoni, *Chiavi per l'immaginario*, Italian trans. (Bari, 1971).

11. W. Benjamin, *Briefe*, vol. 2 (Frankfurt, 1966), pp. 756–764.

12. Bense, pp. 80–95.

13. Franz Kafka, *The Castle*, trans. Willa and Edwin Muir, (Harmondsworth, England, 1957), pp. 25, 27.

14. W. Benjamin, *The Work of Art in the Age of Mechanical Reproduction*, Italian trans. (Turin, 1966). This important text is intrinsic to the process of the "positivization" of the negative and should be read "against" the technological aesthetics of Bense. This sort of critical approach would settle, once and for all, the quarrel between Adornians and engagés regarding Benjamin (cf. the debates/clashes in *Alternative*, Perlini's essays in Italy, etc.)

Chapter 5. Essay and Tragedy

1. Meinecke's volume came out in 1936. Simmel had published his monograph on Goethe in 1913; the German version of the Brandes volume, *Goethe*, is from 1922.

2. Even for Lukacs (*Goethe und sein Zeit*, 1947), Goethe provides all the answers, including a typical interpretation of classicism—order-equilibrium, and so on, for the historicist-reactionary interpretation—but, to an equal degree, a critical consciousness, a full awareness of the crisis. In sum: a full comprehension of reality for Lukacs. Baioni, in *Classicismo e Rivoluzione, Goethe e la Rivoluzione Francese* (Naples, 1969), definitively criticized both these tendencies. For a discussion of Baioni's book and of Mittner's important contributions on this subject, see my essay, "Entsagung," in *Contropiano* 2 (1971).

3. W. Dilthey, *Studien zur Geschichte des deutschen Geistes*, in *Gesammelte Schriften*, vol. 3 (Stuttgart-Göttingen, 1962); *Esperienza vissuta e poesia*, Italian trans. (Milan, 1947).

4. E. Cassirer, *Freiheit und Form* (1916, Darmstadt, 1961).

5. On January 31, 1912, Kafka wrote about a project for an essay entitled "The frightening nature of Goethe!" See *Diaries*, vol. 1, Italian trans. (Milan, 1959), p. 226.

6. G. Simmel, *Schopenhauer und Nietzsche* (Leipzig, 1907).

7. G. Lukacs, *Georg Simmel,* p. 172. The following quotations are taken from this short piece.

8. Whereas Lukacs speaks of Simmel as a Monet who does not *yet* have a Cézanne to follow him. Bear in mind Scheffler's essays on Van de Velde.

9. Antonin Artaud has been alone in grasping the true meaning of Nietzschean tragedy, even if only on the level of dramatic representation. J. Derrida devoted an important essay to the Nietzsche-Artaud connection, "Le théâtre de la cruauté et la clôture de la représentation," in *L'écriture et la différence* (Paris, 1966).

10. G. Lukacs, "The Metaphysics of Tragedy" (1910) in *Soul and Form,* Italian trans. (Milan, 1963).

11. On the *Trauerspiel,* particularly as regards the young Lukacs, cf. G. L. Boella, *Il giovane Lukacs* (Bari, 1976); E. Matassi, *Il giovane Lukacs* (Naples, 1979); M. Cacciari, *Intransitabili utopie,* in *H. von Hofmannsthal, La Torre* (Milan, 1978); Feher-Heller-Markos-Vajda, "Studies on the young Lukacs," *Aut-Aut* 157–158 (1977).

12. Lukacs, p. 311. On the Lukacs-Ernst-Simmel connection, cf. the works indicated in note 129.

13. A. Asor Rosa, "Il giovane Lukacs," *Contropiano* 1 (1968).

14. G. Simmel, "Aus dem nachgelassenen Tagebuch," *Fragmente und Aufsätze* (Hildesheim, 1967), p. 17.

15. Ibid.

16. G. Lukacs, "On the nature and form of the essay," in *Soul and Form.*

17. G. Simmel, "Bridge and Door," in *Brücke und Tür.*

18. Lukacs, "On the nature and form of the essay," p. 12.

19. Ibid., p. 16. Also evident here is the allusion to Nietzsche who, after the "aphorism," supposedly attempts to formulate a system, that is, *The Will to Power.* This absolutely erroneous interpretation can be traced directly back to P. Gast and to Elisabeth Förster-Nietzsche.

20. This theme of transitoriness treated together with that of the releasing of new energy—this theme of the consolation-overcoming of Vergänglichkeit—appears in one of Freud's most "hermetic" sketches, entitled "On Transience," from 1915, now in *Essays on Art, Literature, and Language,* vol. 1, Italian trans. (Turin, 1969).

21. On the difference between the aphorism and the essay see my "Aforisma, Lirica, Tragedia," in *Nuova Corrente* 68–69 (1975–76).

Chapter 6. The City as Essay

1. G. Simmel, *Rom* (1898), in *Zur Philosophie der Kunst* (Potsdam, 1922), pp. 17–28.

2. The entire debate over Kant in those years concerns the problematics of the thinking "I" and the transcendental schematism—a problematics resolved in the terms of a generalized reassumption of the teleological judgment. The teleological form also dominates the area of the analysis of historical processes: think of Husserl's position. It was Heidegger, in

his 1929 book on Kant, who made a clean sweep of this tradition (even while taking up several fundamental indications from *History and Class Consciousness*).

3. The Bergson-Simmel connection is an important one in the German culture of the first two decades of the twentieth century. Bergson's presence is constant in Simmel's images of the city. Moreover, *Matière et Mémoire* is from 1896, and the *Essai sur les données immédiates de la conscience* had come out in 1889. Bearing close affinities with this Simmelian perspective, and equally shaped by the influence of Bergson, was Husserl's position in these same years, especially in *Lessons on the intimate conscience of time* (1905). In 1914 Simmel devoted an essay to Bergson, now in *Zur Philosophie der Kunst*, pp. 126–145.

4. G. Simmel, "Florenz," (1906), in *Zur Philosophie der Kunst*, pp. 61–66.

5. E. Bloch recapitulated all of these positions of the radical, principally European architecture and urbanism of these years in a section of *The Principle of Hope*, vol. 2 (Frankfurt, 1959), p. 847ff., p. 863ff. After having exalted, in the same terms as Scheffler and Endell, the *ewiges Werden* of the Gothic spirit against the clerical-bureaucratic *Ordnung*, Bloch delineated the task of *Stadtplanung* as the formation of a *Heimat* for man—and Marxism as the means for the reconquest of this Homeland. The same search for a Homeland pervades Simmel's essays on the city.

6. W. Benjamin, *Images of the City*, Italian trans. (Turin, 1971).

7. On anti-bureaucratic Kultur see my "Sul problema della organizzazione: Germania, 1917–1921," in *Pensiero negativo e razionalizzazione* (Venice, 1977). For an analysis of the concrete ties between such a Kultur and the experiences of architecture-urbanism, cf. the important essay by M. Tafuri, "Austromarxismo e citta: 'Das rote Wien,'" *Contropiano* 2 (1971).

8. M. Proust, *Du côté de chez Swann*, in *A la recherche du temps perdu*, Italian trans. (Turin, 1961), vol. 1, p. 413.

9. G. Simmel, "Venedig," in *Zur Philosophie der Kunst*, pp. 67–73. Cf. S. Bettini, *Forma di Venezia* (Padua, 1960).

10. H. von Hofmannsthal, *Andreas oder die Vereinigten*, Italian trans. (Milan, 1971).

11. H. von Hofmannsthal, *Viaggi e saggi*, Italian trans. (Florence, 1958).

12. In an equally radical manner, Karl Kraus also shattered all nostalgia for the city Gemeinschaft, which he saw symbolized, at bottom, in Viennese decadence. Cf. K. Kraus, *Sprüche und Widersprüche*, 1909, Italian trans. (Milan, 1972), pp. 233–235; pp. 311–313. "In Vienna, safety is already a concession: the coachman never runs down the passers-by because he knows them personally."

Chapter 7. Loosian Dialectics

1. "Ornament and Crime," is from 1908, as are "The Superfluous Ones (Deutscher Werkbund)," "Culture," and "Cultural Degeneration,"

"Architecture" is from 1910 (Italian trans. in A. Loos, *Parole nel vuoto* (Milan, 1972). See *The Architecture of Adolf Loos* ed. Y. Safran and W. Wang (London, 1985). The Kärtner-Bar (Loos-Bar) is from 1907; the house on the Michaelerplatz is from 1910, as is the Steiner house. Schönberg's Opus 15 is from 1908. In 1907 and 1908 Mahler composed *Das Lied von der Erde*. The collection of Kraus aphorisms, *Sprüche und Widersprüche,* was published in 1909. In 1911, Schiele founded the Neukunstgruppe. Aside from the works to be cited, see *Wien um 1900,* catalog of the exhibition held in Vienna in 1964; *Arnold Schönberg Gedenkausstellung* (Vienna, 1974); L. Brion-Guerry, ed., *L'année 1913. Les formes esthétiques de l'oeuvre d'art à la veille de la première guerre mondiale,* 3 vols. (Paris, 1971–73); A. Janik and S. Toulmin, *Wittgenstein's Vienna* (New York, 1973); W. M. Johnston, *The Austrian Mind* (Berkeley: 1972); M. Cacciari, *Dallo Steinhof: Prospettive viennesi dell'inizio del secolo* (Milan, 1980).

2. Nietzsche is a constant presence in the above-mentioned authors. They even share Nietzsche's contempt for the "decadent," anti-Mozartean aspects of Vienna.

3. See part I above.

4. F. Naumann, "Werkbund und Handel," in *Die Kunst in Industrie und Handel,* "Jahrbuch des deutschen Werkbundes 1913" (Jena, 1913).

5. "A maxim of Brecht's: to ally oneself not with the good Old, but with the bad New." W. Benjamin, "Conversations with Brecht," Italian trans. in *Avanguardia e rivoluzione* (Turin, 1973).

6. In 1896 Hermann Muthesius was sent to England by the Prussian government to observe English architecture and industrial art. Upon his return, he made numerous lecture tours, during the course of which he came into contact with the Viennese circles. On Muthesius, see the three volumes of *Das englische Haus* (1904, 2nd ed. 1908–1911). Muthesius opposed the Jugendstil Nervenleben with the original English gentleman, in whose mode of dwelling "alles atmet Einfachheit, Bürgerlichkeit, Ländlichkeit," with the refuge of individuality in the circle of the family, and with a *natürliche Lebensauffassung.* The tone of the book deceived even Loos, who appreciated it even though his notion of gentleman was far removed from Muthesius' *Ländlichkeit.*

7. On Morris, cf. M. Manieri Elia, *William Morris e l'ideologia dell'architettura moderna* (Bari, 1975). Of great importance in the development of Morris' ideas and the movements influenced by them is the rarely analyzed essay by John Ruskin, *The Political Economy of Art,* which discusses the main themes of the two conferences held in Manchester in July 1857.

8. "Ockham's razor naturally is not an arbitrary rule or one justified only by its success in practice: it dictates that unnecessary signic unities don't mean anything." L. Wittgenstein, *Traetatus-logico-philosophicus,* "Schönberg said that the most important thing in composition is the eraser." A. Webern, *Toward a New Music,* (writings and letters), ed.

H. Jone and J. Humbern. This notion of composition is similar to that of Karl Kraus.

9. The expression is R. Calasso's, from his Introduction to Kraus, *Detti e contradetti* (Milan, 1972).

10. Cf. A. Schönberg and W. Kandinsky, *Briefe: Bilder und Dokumente einer aussergewöhnlichen Begegnung,* ed. J. Hahl-Koch (Salzburg, 1980). Regarding Schönberg's relations with Kandinsky and Der Blaue Reiter, cf. the important biography of Schönberg by H. H. Stuckenschmidt, *Schönberg: Leben, Umwelt, Werk* (Zurich, 1974), and also L. Rognoni, *Espressionismo e dodecafonia* (Turin, 1954).

11. Cf. Schönberg's 1909 interview with P. Wilhelm and his 1931 Berlin radio discussion with Preussner and Strobel. But all of Schönberg's work shows a critical-analytical approach to Wagner's music (*Harmony, Style, and Idea*). This was the kind of approach that Nietzsche himself anticipated. On Nietzsche's importance to the "new music," cf. U. Duse, *La musica nel pensiero di Nietzsche e Wagner,* in A. Caracciolo, ed., *Musica e Filosofia* (Bologna, 1973). Schönberg's attitude toward Wagner was, moreover, just like Mahler's: cf. U. Duse, *Gustav Mahler* (Turin, 1973).

12. Naumann, *Werkbund und Weltwirtschaft.*

13. The reference is to the "suspended tonality" that Schönberg and Webern discuss. This is a moment in the process of the disaggregation of basic tonality, a process that begins with R. Wagner and Brahms and reaches its point of crisis around 1908 (the *Drei Klavierstücke,* Opus 11 of Schönberg), when the suspension of tonality becomes total and the piece finishes in silence.

14. This concept of *composition* (multiplicity of languages, differences, the analysis of such differences, the attempt to put them in order as such and not through a priori, external interventions) is characteristic not only of the great works of "suspended tonality" (Mahler), but also of the later experiments of Schönberg. It is this fundamental aspect of the development of the "new music" which completely eludes the Adornian dialectic (T. W. Adorno, *The Philosophy of Modern Music.*)

15. Olbrich had designed his *Künstlerkolonie* on the Mathildenhöhe of Darmstadt. The roofs of the houses were covered with tiles of gaudy colors that recalled those of the flowers and plants in the flower beds designed by Olbrich himself. Even the restaurant waiters' uniforms were designed by Olbrich. The single buildings were supposed to appear, in this scene, as living organisms harmonized according to new tonal relations. They were the surfaces (and the surface!) of Klimt and the early Secession. For a rich source of information on the Künstlerkolonie, see A. Koch, ed., *Die Ausstellung der darmstädter Künstler-Kolonie* (Darmstadt, 1901). For the work of Joseph M. Olbrich, cf. *J. M. Olbrich: Das Werk des Architekten,* catalog of the exhibit for the Olbrich centenary (Darmstadt, 1967).

F. Naumann also visited the first *Ausstellung* of Darmstadt. His *Post-*

karten vom Künstlerpark in Darmstadt were printed in *Hilfe* in 1901 and reprinted in F. Naumann, *Form und Farbe* (Berlin, 1909). Naumann, too, was taken in by the organicity of the Olbrich project ("all of these elements belong to one single body"), but from the start he emphasized its dialectics: what relation is established between these forms and contemporary technique? What relation exists between this organism and the technique of these constructions, this kitchen, this lighting? What, in brief, is the meaning of this organism? Why this beauty? "I do not deny that these objects are beautiful, but they are beautiful only in the world for which they were necessary." In the final analysis, Naumann was a kind of tourist in Darmstadt—he had made an aesthetic pilgrimage. From that point on, he was a stranger to the value of Darmstadt and the Olbrich project; indeed, he finished his last card from the exhibition with an invocation of an Ausstellung of projects of working-class houses to be rented, beautiful and practical: *"doch das ist alles Zukunftsmusik."*

16. Schumpeter's work was published for the first time at the end of 1911. The preface to the first edition is dated Vienna, July 1911. When I say that Sombart, and Weber especially, brought the neo-classical philosophy to the point of crisis, I am referring to the political quality of their investigations, which is a far cry from the nineteenth century *Historismus* of the likes of Roscher and Knies. And this overall vision of the same economic facts (in which also originates Schumpeter's analysis of innovative processes) is opposed to the reductive logic and pretended universality of the marginalist position.

17. On this matter, as well as for some of the issues mentioned in the preceding note, see my *Pensiero negativo e razionalizzazione* (Venice, 1977).

18. A. Loos, "The Superfluous Ones," p. 208; "Hands Off" (1917), p. 287.

19. Loos, "The Superfluous Ones," p. 210.

20. A. Loos, "Cultural Degeneration," p. 212.

21. Ibid., p. 214.

22. Mahler's music "never mends the break between subject and object, and rather than feign an achieved reconciliation, it prefers to fall apart." (T. W. Adorno, *Mahler: A Musical Physiognomy*). The tendency, from Mahler to Schönberg, is to remove all natural innocence from the language of Western music. And this is an exact parallel to Loos's program for modern architecture.

23. Cf. G. Simmel, "On the problem of naturalism," Italian trans. in *Saggi di Estetica* (Padua, 1970).

24. The goal of the Blaue Reiter was to achieve such a synthesis. Cf. W. Kandinsky, *On the Spiritual in Art* (1912), Italian trans. (Bari, 1968) and now in vol. 2 of *Tutti gli scritti,* (Milan, 1974).

25. For this interpretation of the *Affinities,* see my "Entsagung," *Contropiano* 2 (1971).

26. Loos, "Architecture," p. 256.

27. The influences of his American sojourn (and of Louis Sullivan in par-

Notes to pages 109–112

ticular) are evident in this building. Its quality lies solely in the materials of the entrance and in the design of the interiors onto which it opens.

28. A. Loos, "Potemkin City," in Loos, *Spoken into the Void: Collected Essays 1897–1900* (Cambridge, Mass., 1982), p. 105.

29. Loos, "Architecture," p. 246. Olbrich's plan is indeed splendid. One can in this way assert that the real project lives in its being-as-plan: rhythmic values are exalted therein—they appear in a pure state, uncompromised by the material. This quest for absoluteness is in fact implicit in the concept of the plan. See J. M. Olbrich, *Die Zeichnungen in der Kunstbibliothek Berlin: Kritischer Katalog*, K. H. Schreyl, ed. (Berlin, 1972).

30. A. Loos, "The Principle of Cladding," (1898), in Loos, *Spoken into the Void*, p. 80.

31. A. Loos, "Building Materials," (1898), in Loos, *Spoken into the Void*, p. 75.

32. F. Busoni, *Aesthetik der Tonkunst*, (mit Anmerkungen von Arnold Schönberg) (Frankfurt am Main, 1974), p. 75.

33. A. Schönberg, *Letters*, Italian trans. (Florence, 1969), pp. 213–214.

34. L. Wittgenstein, *Lezioni e conversazioni sull'etica, l'estetica, la psicologia e la credenza religiosa*, Italian trans. (Milan, 1967). The lectures are in English, and not by accident. The remarks on aesthetics were presented at Cambridge University in the summer of 1938.

35. This too is Wittgenstein, and not just his taste. Note, in the letters to Paul Engelmann, Italian trans. (Florence, 1970), the recurrence of the names of Goethe, Brahms, and so on. Also see the beautiful *Letters to L. von Ficker*, Italian trans. (Rome, 1974), and the biographical sketches of Engelmann, Malcom, von Wright, Wittgenstein's sister Hermine, among others.

36. G. Simmel, "Stefan George" (1901), in *Zur Philosophie der Kunst* (Potsdam, 1922). Also bear in mind the young Lukacs's essay on the same poet in *Soul and Form*.

37. Loos, "Architecture," p. 254. Also see part III below.

38. Ibid., p. 253.

39. A. Loos, *The modern Siedlung* (1926), p. 346, p. 356.

40. Schönberg also contributed to the volume with the essay entitled "Music." It is significant that, in its reprinting, Schönberg prefaced it with these lines: "I wrote this brief essay immediately after the defeat . . . when everyone was seeking escape in suicide alone and a new, better reality in fantasy alone. . . . No reasonable visionary can hope for a fulfillment of his dreams that goes beyond the reprinting of one of his articles." The enchantment was hence very short-lived—for Loos, instead, as we have seen, it was to worsen.

41. See what Wittgenstein wrote to F. Waismann after the publication of the *Wissenschaftliche Weltauffassung* of 1929, the "manifesto" of the Wiener Kreis, in F. Waismann, *Wittgenstein und der Wiener Kreis* (Frankfurt am Main, 1967), p. 18.

42. Wittgenstein, *Letters*, p. 12.

43. His sister Margarethe was perhaps the most "profound" member of the family (in the sense in which Wittgenstein understood the term). A reader of Schopenhauer, Kierkegaard, Weininger, a friend of Klimt and of the entire Secession circle, she also financed, together with her sister Hermine, the construction of the Olbrich Palace. Wittgenstein's brothers—like Wittgenstein himself—were, instead, more interested in music than the figurative arts. Paul became a famous pianist; after he lost a hand in World War I, Maurice Ravel wrote the famous Concerto for Left Hand for him. Kurt was a cellist, and a virtuoso in several instruments. Hans, Kurt, and the remaining brother, Rudi, a theater buff, all died as suicides. Between the apparently assimilated environment of the Viennese *Kunstfreunde* and the tragedy that Wittgenstein does not deny nor overcome, but only sets in order, there are hence many more cryptic relationships than Broch, to use an example, suspects. Wittgenstein's *oikos* would also be the definitive Grabmal of the Viennese Kunstfreunde (and a very well-known Kunstfreund was Ludwig's father Karl. It should also be remembered that the project presented by Olbrich for the St. Louis Exposition of 1904 was entitled "Summer residence of a Kunstfreund.")

Chapter 8. The Contemporaries

1. Cited in H. Weiser, *Josef Hoffmann* (Geneva, 1930). None of the "great Viennese masters of language" has ever shared this intellectual Buddhism of a Spenglerian stamp, this struggle against mechanization in the name of the Geist, a struggle that ignores and obscures the fact that mechanization is the work of the Geist. Schönberg expressed himself in these same critical terms in a still-unpublished fragment from 1931. On Hoffmann, see G. Veronesi, *Josef Hoffmann* (Milan, 1956).

2. A. Loos, "Unseren jungen Architekten," *Ver Sacrum* 7 (1898). The most comprehensive document on the Secession is R. Waissenberger, *Die Wiener Secession* (Munich-Vienna, 1971); also see, on Klimt, F. Novotny and J. Dobay, *Gustav Klimt* (Salzburg, 1967), and W. Hoffmann, *Gustav Klimt und die Wiener Jahrhundertwende* (Salzburg, 1970). Hermann Bahr and Ludwig Hevesi were the two critics most representative of the movement.

3. A. Loos, "Cultural Degeneration," p. 214.

4. This coupling of Hoffmann and Loos is further borne out by the essays on Hoffmann collected on the occasion of his sixtieth birthday (Vienna, 1930), and how could it be otherwise if Mahler's gravestone is by Hoffmann? On the other hand, to get an idea of the normal Secession style that Loos, and Hoffmann, had to live every day in Vienna, see the volume edited in Vienna in 1902, *Wiener Neubauten in Style der Secession*.

5. Regarding these exceptional experiences, see the documentation collected for the Darmstadt Exhibition of 1976, *Darmstadt, Ein Dokument deutscher Kunst*, 5 vols.

6. J. M. Olbrich, *Ideen*, with an introduction by L. Hevesi, first edition

is from 1900 and the second from 1904. It is the manifesto of the new *Handwerk*: every object is redesigned—ennobled by the artist—and exhibited, so to speak, in the shadow of the leafy golden boughs covering the Palais-Secession of Vienna, begun in 1898.

7. This was the slogan of the second edition of *Ideen: Seine Welt zeige der Künstler die niemals war, noch jemals sein wird.*

8. L. Hevesi, introduction to *Ideen*.

9. Also on Olbrich, see G. Veronesi, *Joseph M. Olbrich* (Milan, 1948).

10. Compare, to measure the difference from Loos, an interior of the Friedman villa, or the *Schlafzimmer*, with the walls frescoed with delicate tree branches: "repose" as a clearing in the woods as well as a tangling-interlacement: a dream not yet analyzed—still a sensation, an impression. However—and this seems incredible in light of this interior—Freud's *Interpretation of Dreams* would appear two years later.

11. For documentation of the Frauenrosenhof, see the thirty tables collected in *Der Frauenrosenhof* (Berlin, 1930).

12. A. Behne, *Von Kunst zur Gestaltung* (Berlin, 1925).

13. Regarding this German Kultur, see W. Rothe, ed., *Der Aktivismus 1915– 1920* (Munich, 1969), and P. Raabe, ed., *Ich schneide die Zeit aus* (Munich, 1964), a wide-ranging and well-selected anthology of *Aktion*, the review of Franz Pfemfert.

14. P. Bommersheim, "Philosophy and Architecture," published in 1920 in *Frühlicht*, the review directed by Bruno Taut. Italian trans. *"Frühlicht" 1920–1922: Gli anni della avanguardia architettonica in Germania* (Milan, 1974).

15. Bruno Taut, *Der Weltbaumeister* (Berlin, 1920).

Similar ideas were translated into the expressionist conception-vision of the city typical of Scheerbart, Taut, and Behne. It should not be forgotten that the Gothic, while ultimately resolving itself in its purely utopian aspect, represents, like Glasarchitektur, an appeal for order, as well as a precise technical demand. One need only think of Bruno Taut's Pavilion for the 1913 Leipzig exposition. If the Gothic is a dissolution of the Eurocentric form—an invention of new languages—this in Taut's argument serves above all as a new perspective-measure for the organization of the city and city life. In *Die Stadtkrone* (1919), Taut is looking for a new center for the city. All of the contemporary reorganizations of the urban fabric appear sectorial, particular, disarticulated. The buildings are arranged like a series of headless busts. The city needs a "flag," a center, a "crown." And this is the reorganization of the city around its soul—around its cathedral: "In the idea of the new city the church is lacking." Thus, the element of reorganization is brought to light in more explicitly utopian-regressive terms, all of them worthy of the monkey's argument to Zarathustra in Nietzsche. But this reorganization (like the appeal for the Gothic cathedral emerging from the city surrounding it and protecting it) is eminently spiritual (hence its cosmic dissolution). It is eminently anti-political: indeed, it is an explicit struggle against all bureaucratic-institutional crystallization of city life. And it is socialist—an overcoming of the bourgeois-egotist particularities of the metropolis—but "not in a political sense, but seen as above politics, as remote from all forms of power." And here reappear the fundamental ideological assumptions of radical *Aktivismus*. It was the Jesuits who scattered the center of the Gothic city, who obscured it by confusing it in the urban fabric; in other words, it was the politicians par excellence of the Catholic tradition, the men of power. The alternative to them is the International Gothic of Behne: "Our Gothic is nothing but a sublime dream of the lands of the East . . . light in fact comes from the East." "Anyone who cannot confront in manly fashion the destiny of our age must be advised to return in silence . . . back into the mercifully open arms of the old churches." (Max Weber, *Science as Profession*). But the above-mentioned authors could not make even this gesture "without turning it into publicity," with frankness and simplicity. For a good documentation of Expressionist architecture, see W. Pehnt, *Die Architektur des Expressionismus* (Stuttgart, 1973); regarding Bruno Taut's circle in particular, see *Die gläserne Kette,* Catalogue of the Exhibit at the Leverkusen Museum of Berlin, with an introduction by Max Taut 1963.

16. The value of the Gothic, which we have discussed, would be theorized by Ernst Bloch in *The Principle of Hope*, vol. 2 (Frankfurt am Main, 1959), p. 847ff., p. 863ff., *Bauten, die eine bessere Welt abbilden, architektonische Utopien*. It should also be remembered that Bloch collaborated on several reviews of Aktivismus.

17. O. Wagner, *Moderne Architektur* (Vienna, 1895). The title was changed for the fourth edition (Vienna, 1914) to *Die Baukunst unserer Zeit*. Baukunst, not Stilarchitektur à la Muthesius! But Busoni as well had entitled his book *Aesthetik der Tonkunst*—not *expressive Musik!*

18. Starting with his early works, Wagner's pure-visibilistic formal inspiration constantly controls the stylistic tendencies that emerge in them, and establishes a process of the simplification and rationalization of style itself. All historicist influence is in this way tested and criticized, and never assumed in natural, traditional terms. Cf. A. Giusti Baculo, *Otto Wagner* (Naples, 1970).

19. O. Wagner, *Grossstadt* (Vienna, 1911).

20. For the history of these developments, see M. Tafuri, "Austromarxismo e citta: "Das rote Wien," *Contropiano* 2 (1971), and, by the same author, *Architecture and Utopia* (Cambridge, Mass., 1976).

21. Wagner, *Grossstadt*, pp. 22–23.

22. Compare H. Geretsegger and M. Peinter, *Otto Wagner* (Salzburg, 1964). Wagner's unresolved "dialectic" is philologically analyzed, in its origins, in the essay by O. A. Geof, "Wagner and the Vienna School," in J. M. Richards and N. Pevsner, eds., *The Anti-Rationalists* (London, 1973).

23. G. Simmel, "Der Konflikt der modern Kultur," Italian trans. (Turin, 1925). For Simmel, the contradiction between life and form becomes

Notes to pages 127–131

progressively more flagrant and irreconciliable as forms "present themselves as the true meaning and value of our existence—hence perhaps as civilization itself grows." (p. 73) "But it is also a prejudice of mummified pedants to maintain that all conflicts and problems exist purposely to be resolved." (p. 74) Modern metropolitan life is but the force that drives things forward toward those transformations due to which a problem can be resolved only "by means of a new problem, and a conflict by means of another conflict." (p. 75) This important text of Simmel—though it came out in 1918—recapitulates his categories for interpreting contemporary historical reality; but it does so by centering these categories around those of conflict and crisis. Hence it is not only a harbinger of the end of Wilhelmian Kultur, but also of the *Finis Austriae*.

24. The apocalypse was somber, not gay, as H. Broch counters in his essay, "Hofmannsthal e il suo tempo," Italian trans., in *Poesia e conoscenza* (Milan, 1965).

Chapter 9. The oikos of Wittgenstein

1. For an excellent documentation of the Wittgenstein house, which nevertheless does not even touch upon the problems dealt with here, see B. Leitner, *The Architecture of Ludwig Wittgenstein* (Halifax-London, 1973).

   I use the Greek term *oikos* to point out the values of the *place* (instead of the *space*) and the priority of the *living* in *this* place compared to the simple dwelling. (*Oikos* refers also to the *demos,* on the one hand, and to the Latin *vicus* [village], on the other). Similarly, Heidegger speaks of the priority of inhabiting compared to the building of a home.

2. A "classical" dimension that is not ideal, but comprehensible and perceptible, one that can be "logicized." An immanent "classical." But also lived in all its contradictions: hence both Greek and Goethian.

3. A. Webern, *Letter* to Willi Reich of February 23, 1944, in *Toward a new music,* pp. 121–122.

4. Loos, "Architecture," p. 256.

5. Ibid., p. 253. The most complete documentation of Loos can be found in L. Münz and G. Künstler, *Der Architekt Adolf Loos* (Vienna-Munich, 1964). This volume contains an invaluable memoir by Oskar Kokoschka about his friend: "He was a *civil* man," a stranger to all "esprit," to all external vivacity—he used to say, "the age of man has not yet begun."

6. M. Tafuri, "The Disenchanted Mountain," in Ciucci et al., *The American City: From the Civil War to the New Deal* (Cambridge, Mass.: Bari, 1979). But Tafuri, immediately afterward, correctly perceives that Loos's "phantom" could also have been interpreted as an attempt at "dimensional control" of the new object, the skyscraper, an attempt at a "total possession of the compositional elements." Loos's proposal can hence also be read as the proposal of a formal essence, an ordering essence, for the skyscraper-edifice.

Notes to pages 131–134

7. *Die Wiener Genesis* of Franz Wickhoff was published in Vienna in 1895; the *Spätrömische Kunstindustrie* of Alois Riegl was published in Vienna in 1901.

8. It is therefore erroneous to interpret *Kunstwollen* in neo-Kantian terms, as a kind of a priori of the artistic act, as Erwin Panofsky tried to do in his essay, "The concept of *Kunstwollen*," published in 1920.

9. In *Malerische Einflüsse*, a manuscript of 1938, Schönberg writes at length about his relations with Gerstl and Kokoschka (for those with Gerstl, cf. H. H. Stuckenschmidt, *Arnold Schönberg*, cited above). He insists on the uniqueness of his painting, especially with respect to Gerstl, whom he correctly sees as still influenced by the German school of Liebermann, but also with respect to Kokoschka. Schönberg insists on the so to speak spiritual-musical aspect of his work, as opposed to Expressionist representation. "I have never painted faces, but, since I have looked at men in the eyes, only their looks have I painted. The result is that I am able to paint the look in a man's eyes. With one look, a painter grasps the whole man—I grasp only his soul." (*Gedenkausstellung*, p. 202 and 207).

10. W. Benjamin, *The Origin of German Tragic Drama* (1928), Italian trans. (Turin, 1971).

11. On the close relationship that existed between Benjamin and Hofmannsthal for a period of time, see my *Intransitibili utopie*, cited above.

Chapter 10. Loos and His Angel

1. W. Benjamin, "Karl Kraus," (1931) in *Reflections*, English trans. (New York, 1979).

2. K. Kraus, "Die Schoenheit im Dienste des Kauffmanns," *Die Fackel* 413–417 (1915).

3. K. Kraus, in *Die Fackel* 89 (1901), p. 21.

4. K. Kraus, *Nachts* (1918), Italian trans. in K. Kraus, *Detti e contradetti* (Milan, 1972), pp. 293–294.

5. K. Kraus, "Untergangder der Welt durch schwarze Magie," *Die Fackel* 363–365 (1912).

6. K. Kraus, "Tagebuch," *Die Fackel* 279–280 (1909), p. 9.

7. Kraus, *Nachts*, p. 287: "the aesthete is the true champion of *Realpolitik* in the realm of beauty": the autonomy of the political as art for art's sake!

8. See part II, above.

9. Benjamin.

10. This is the dominant theme in the last of the *Duino Elegies*. But the *Lied* of Wolf and Mahler is also *Klagendelied*.

11. W. Benjamin, *Über den Begriff der Geschichte*.

12. See my essay and others in M. Cacciari, ed., *Crucialità del tempo* (Naples, 1980).

13. We also find this theme—the critique of constructive *Aufbauen*—in

Wittgenstein cf. *Vermischte Bemerkungen* (Frankfurt am Main, 1977), p. 22.

14. G. Scholem, *Walter Benjamin e il suo Angelo* (1972), Italian trans. (Milan, 1978), p. 61.

15. W. Benjamin, *Agesilaus Santander,* second definitive version, (1933), in Scholem, p. 23.

16. Ibid., p. 24.

17. Kraus, *Nachts,* p. 290.

18. Scholem, p. 109.

19. Benjamin, "Karl Kraus," p. 132.

Chapter 11. Being Loyal

1. A. Loos, "A Letter" (1910), Italian trans. in A. Loos, *Parole nel vuoto* (Speaking into the Void) (Milan, 1972), p. 239.

2. K. Kraus, *Nachts,* p. 280.

3. A. Loos, "Guidelines for Building in the Mountains" (1913), in Loos, *Speaking into the Void,* Italian trans., p. 272.

4. Strictly speaking, we should speak of the "second" Wittgenstein. But on this matter see in particular the more recent essays of A. Gargani, *Stili di analisi* (Milan, 1980), and *Wittgenstein tra Austria e Inghilterra* (Turin, 1979), in particular the section devoted to Loos, pp. 41ff.

5. For this chapter, see the important essay by K. O. Apel, "Lo sviluppo della 'filosofia analitica del linguaggio' e il problema delle 'scienze dello spirito'" (1964), Italian trans. in K. O. Apel, *Comunità e comunicazione* (Turin, 1977), p. 47ff.

6. A. Loos, "Architecture" (1910), *Speaking into the Void,* Italian trans., p. 246.

7. *Adolf Loos: Festschrift zum 60. Geburstag,* (Vienna, 1930).

8. L. Wittgenstein, *Philosophical Investigations,* Italian trans., M. Trinchero, ed. (Turin, 1967), p. 107.

9. Loos, "Architecture," p. 242. Also see p. 272; p. 278.

10. Apel, pp. 97ff. In this passage, Apel critically summarizes P. Winch, *The Idea of a Social Science and Its Relation to Philosophy* (1958).

11. E. Sibour makes some interesting observations in "Adolf Loos: un 'Sebastiano nel sogno'?" *Nuova Corrente* 79–80 (1979), p. 315ff.

12. A. Loos, "Josef Veillich" (1929), in *Speaking into the Void,* Italian trans., p. 373.

13. "We serve our tools. We are subordinate to our employees. . . . We consume so that those who produce may consume. We do not eat to live, but live to eat—no, we do not even live to eat, but so that others may eat."

14. R. M. Rilke, *Die erste Elegie,* vv. 13–17.

Chapter 12. The Other

1. On Altenberg, see my *Dallo Steinhof,* pp. 218–219.

2. P. Altenberg, "Was der Tag mir zuträgt," (Berlin, 1901), Italian trans. *Favole della vita* (Milan, 1981), p. 99.

3. A. Loos, "The poor little rich man," (1900), in *Spoken into the Void*, Italian trans., p. 149ff.

4. Cf. S. Dimitriou, "Adolf Loos: Gedanken zum Ursprung von Lehre und Werk," *Bauforum*, 21 (1970), an interesting issue dedicated to the anniversary of his birth, containing previously unpublished photographs of Loosian interiors.

5. A. Loos, "Interiors in the Rotunda," (1898), in *Spoken into the Void*, Italian trans., p. 32.

6. Hans Sedlmayr calls museums "pompous asylums without roofs." *Perdita del centro,* Italian trans. (Milan, 1974), p. 116.

7. Benjamin, "Karl Kraus."

8. A. Savinio, *Nuova Enciclopedia* (Milan, 1977), pp. 139–151.

Chapter 13. Tabula Rasa

1. On the Loos-Haus, cf. H. Czech and W. Mistelbauer, *Das Looshaus* (Vienna, 1976).

2. O. Stoessl, "Das Haus auf dem Michaelerplatz," *Die Fackel* 317-318 (1911). In the same issue of the review is a poem by Paul Engelmann, the architect friend of Wittgenstein, that praises Loos's house as "the first sign of a new epoch."

3. On these Heideggerian themes, see my essay "Eupalinos or architecture," *Oppositions* 21 (1980).

4. K. Kraus, "Adolf Loos: Rede am Grab," *Die Fackel*, 888 (1933). The same issue, the shortest of *Die Fackel* at only four pages, contains the splendid poem *Man frage nicht,* a kind of Lied of the friend left behind, concluding the farewell on the tomb (pp. 118–119).

5. Sedlmayr, pp. 124, 143.

6. A recurrent theme in L. Münz and G. Künstler, *Adolf Loos* (Vienna, 1964).

7. Regarding the following passage, see E. Severino, *Destino della necessità* (Milan, 1980), p. 283ff.

Chapter 14. The New Space

1. M. Heidegger, *Die Kunst und der Raum* (1969).

2. Severino, pp. 267–268, 274.

3. P. Assunto, "Le due città," *Rivista di estetica* 1 (1980).

4. M. Perniola, "Ars e Urbs," *Rivista di estetica* 1 (1980). But according to Severino (p. 349), this movement was already evident in the term *polis*.

5. C. Schmitt, *Der Nomos der Erde* (Cologne, 1950).

6. J. Derrida, *Truth in Painting* (1975), Italian trans. (Milan, 1978), p. 91.

7. Ibid., p. 93.

Chapter 15. The House

1. Severino, p. 349.

2. On this matter, see A. Seppilli, *Sacralità dell'acqua e sacrilegio dei ponti* (Palermo, 1977).

3. G. Simmel, *Bridge and Door* (1909), Italian trans. in *Saggi di estetica* (Padua, 1970). Simmel's reflection on these two symbols is of such importance that two of the most respected scholars on Simmel, M. Landemann and M. Susman, entitled a collection of their writings on Simmel *Brücke und Tür*.

4. E. Levinas, *Totalità e infinito. Saggio sull'esteriorita*, Italian trans. (Milan, 1980), pp. 155–177.

5. In Loos, this intimacy, as a premise of the home, is preserved by Woman more than any other dweller. These reflections on the relation between interior and the feminine in Loos are treated in my *Dallo Steinhof*, p. 119.

Chapter 16. Lou's Buttons

1. Lou Andreas-Salomé, "Zum Typus Weib," Italian trans. in *La materia erotica: Scritti di psicoanalisi* (Rome, 1977).

2. E. Lemoine-Luccioni, *Partage des femmes* (Paris, 1976); Italian trans. *Il taglio femminile* (Milan, 1977), p. 184.

3. R. M. Rilke, *Puppen*, in *Gesammelte Werke*, vol. 4 (Leipzig, 1927).

4. M. Eliade, *Mefistofele e l'Androgino* (Rome, 1971), pp. 154ff.

5. W. Benjamin, *Erfahrung und Armut*, in *Gesammelte Schriften*, B.-II-vol. 1, (Frankfurt, 1980), p. 216.

Chapter 17. The Chain of Glass

1. G. Agamben, *Infanzia e storia* (Turin, 1978).

2. W. Benjamin, "Erfahrung und Armut," in *Gesammelte Schriften*, B.-II-vol. 1, p. 218.

Chapter 18. Of Progress and Pioneers

1. *Adolf Loos: Festschrift zum 60. Geburstag* (Vienna, 1930).

2. H. Kulka, *Adolf Loos* (Vienna, 1931).

3. "Wer seiner Zeit nur voraus ist, den holt sie einmal ein" (He who limits himself to anticipating his times shall be caught up by them)—Wittgenstein, *Vermischte Bemerkungen*, p. 25.

Chapter 19. On Loos's Tomb

1. It was Boris Pasternak who spoke of the "extraterritoriality" of the lyric in his correspondence with Svetaeva and Rilke. In another letter, Svetaeva asserts that the past has no mother tongue.

2. Loos, "Architecture," p. 254.

3. Tafuri, *The Sphere and the Labyrinth*, pp. 333–334. On these problems of Loos, see also the essay by Aldo Rossi, "Adolf Loos," *Cacbella* 233 (1959), which is still quite interesting, in spite of its age.

4. Various Krausian themes, contained for the most part in *Nachts* (pp. 280–290), are summarized here. We should remember that for Kraus, the artist "is a *servant* to the word" (emphasis added), unlike the clerk who may presume to "dominate the language" (*Detti e contradetti*,

p. 136). In comparing the two assertions one discovers that flinging oneself against the wall of language is a way of serving the word, that trying one's hardest to achieve excess expresses the maximum tension and crisis of this language. Whoever truly serves the word tries again and again to transform the rules of the language; between the two moments there is a paradoxical mutual belonging and no contradiction of principle.

Epilogue

1. E. Canetti, "Karl Kraus, scuola di resistenza," in *Potere e sopravvivenza,* Italian trans. (Milan, 1974).

2. In his most recent works, Gianni Vattimo has forcefully brought attention to this concept, although from a perspective totally different from ours here. For a debate on this matter, see *Problemi del nichilismo* (Milan, 1981); also very useful is the entry by V. Verra, "Nichilismo," in *Enciclopedia del Novecento,* vol. 4 (Rome, 1979). An essential reference of my own work is E. Severino, *Essenza del nichilismo,* rev. ed. (Milan, 1982).

3. On the dialectic of *rythmos* and *a-rythmos,* from Greek science to Renaissance enharmonics up to contemporary musicology and philosophy, the work of Hans Kayser, in the wake of Albert von Thismus, is of a brilliance that needs to be rediscovered: it constitutes an extraordinary and practically forgotten chapter of modern culture. As an introduction to his more systematic works, see *Akroasis: Die Lehre von der Harmonik der Welt* (Basel, 1946, 2d ed. 1964).

4. This holds true for the entire constructive tradition of modern architecture, from the Werkbund and the Bauhaus to all of their architectural-urbanistic descendants. It is interesting to note, however, how the pairing of nihilism and culture is immediately negated at the beginning of the century by the most revolutionary philosophical figures of central Europe: Lukacs, Wittgenstein, Michaelstaedter, Weininger—suicides or . . . survivors of suicide.

5. On the traditional elements in Taut and Scheerbart—even though it is not always precise in its individuation of the limits of their reception—cf. I. Desideri, *L'altra trasparenza di Paul Scheerbart,* in P. Scheerbart, *Lesabendio,* Italian trans. (Rome, 1982).

6. On the aporiae of the project, see my essay "Progetto," in *Laboratorio politico* 2 (1981).

7. There is a close relation between Loos and the so-called "second" Wittgenstein, a relation discussed by Aldo Gargani in some central passages of his book *Wittgenstein tra Austria e Inghilterra* (Turin, 1979).

8. *Gli Schiavi di Efesto* (The slaves of Hephaestus) is the title of a rich collection of essays by F. Masini devoted largely to the German literature of the period that we are chiefly concerned with in this book.

9. This is the same "displacement" around which revolves the truly epoch-making book by Jacques Derrida, *De la grammatologie* (Paris, 1967).

10. Regarding the concept of *dwelling,* see my "Eupalinos or Architecture," *Oppositions* 21, 1980. This essay supports many of the arguments contained in this book.

11. Even such figures of contemporary culture as Simone Weil who are so apparently opposed to the "slaves of Hephaestus" of Nietzschean descent, seem to tie into the famous passage in *The Gay Science* where modern man is said to be defenseless in the face of the monstruous multiplication of interpretations, which destroys all possibility of divinizing the world (should not *Glasarchitektur* itself also be read as a countertendency of this destiny?)

12. The only work of historical breadth that seems to move in this direction is, to my mind, *The Sphere and the Labyrinth: Avant-gardes and architecture from Piranesi to the 1970s,* by Manfredo Tafuri (Cambridge, Mass.: MIT Press, 1987).

13. R. Klein, "Urbanisitica utopistica dal Filarete a Valentin Andreae," in *La forma e l'intelligibile: Scritti sul Rinascimento e l'arte moderna,* Italian trans. (Turin, 1975).

14. Useful treatments of the architecture-tuopia connection, other than those in Tafuri, may be found in G. Lapouge, *Utopie et civilisations* (Paris, 1978); J. Sevrier, *Histoire de l'utopie* (Paris, 1967); E. M. Cioran, *Histoire et utopie* (Paris, 1960). This type of literature seems to me more significant than the more specialized approach in which utopia is almost always understood naively in its obvious meaning as a prefiguration of liberation.

15. On these themes, cf. the excellent chapter "Symboles architecturaux" in H. de Lubac, *Exégèse médiévale,* Seconde Partie, vol. 2, pp. 41–60.

16. R. Guénon, "La città divina," in *Simboli della scienza sacra,* Italian trans. (Milan, 1975); but regarding the arguments mentioned here, cf. the entire part of the book "Simbolismo costruttivo" and compare them to the complementary research of A. K. Coomaraswamy collected in vol. I of selected papers, *Traditional Art and Symbolism* (Princeton, 1977).

17. Cf. R. Wittkower, *Architectural Principles in the Age of Humanism* (New York, 1962). Italian trans. (Turin, 1964), especially pp. 24–33.

18. On the notion of temple, cf. the excellent essay by H. Corbin, "L'Imago Templi face aux normes profanes," in *Temple et contemplation* (Paris, 1980). The material collected in this book—even more so than in those cited above—could provide a starting point for numerous studies in the traditional aspects of modern-contemporary culture.

Credits for Illustrations

page 3: Georg Simmel, "The Metropolis and Modern Life," in *On Individuality and Social Forms* (Chicago: University of Chicago Press) 1971, p. 324

page 23: Friedrich Nietzsche, *Thus Spoke Zarathustra* (New York: Viking Press), 1966, p. 176

pages lx and 42: Peter Behrens, Assembly Hall of AEG Turbine Factory, Berlin-Moabit (1909); photo courtesy of AEG Firmenarchiv

page 56: Edgar Allan Poe, "The Murders in the Rue Morgue," in *The Complete Tales and Poems* (New York: Random House), 1975, p. 141

page 67: Georg Lukacs, "On the Nature and Form of the Essay," in *Soul and Form* (Cambridge: MIT Press), 1978, p. 1

page 87: Walter Benjamin, "Paris, Capital of the Nineteenth Century," in *Illuminations* (New York: Schocken Books), 1969, p. 146

pages 98 and 120: Joseph Olbrich, Ernst Ludwig House, Künstler-kolonie, Darmstadt (1901); photo from *Joseph M. Olbrich, 1867–1908* (Darmstadt: Mathildenhole), 1983

page 101: Adolf Loos, Café Museum, Vienna (1899); photo © 1992 ARS, New York / VBK, Vienna, courtesy of Graphische Sammlung Albertina, Vienna

page 131: Ludwig Wittgenstein, Wittgenstein House, Vienna (1928); photo by Moritz Nachs

page 143: *Das Andere*, no. 1 (1903)

page 150: Josef Veillich, chair (undated); photo courtesy of Graphische Sammlung Albertina, Vienna

page 156: *Das Andere*, no. 1 (1903)

page 161: Adolf Loos, Michaelerhaus, Vienna (1909); photo © 1992 ARS, New York / VBK, Vienna, courtesy of Graphische Sammlung Albertina, Vienna

page 166: Adolf Loos, Rufer House, Vienna (1922); photo © 1992 ARS, New York / VBK, Vienna, courtesy of Graphische Sammlung Albertina, Vienna

page 175: Adolf Loos, "Ladies' Room," Müller House, Prague (1929–1930); photo © 1992 ARS, New York / VBK, Vienna, courtesy of Graphische Sammlung Albertina, Vienna

pages 140 and 179: Adolf Loos, Helene Horner House, Vienna (1912); photo © 1992 ARS, New York / VBK, Vienna, courtesy of Graphische Sammlung Albertina, Vienna

page 187: Adolf Loos, Kärntner Bar, Vienna (1908); photo © 1992 ARS, New York / VBK, Vienna, courtesy of Graphische Sammlung Albertina, Vienna

page 191: *Adolf Loos zum 60. Geburstag*; reproduced courtesy of the Avery Architecture and Fine Arts Library, Columbia University

page 195: Adolf Loos, sketch for Loos's tomb (1931); photo © 1992 ARS, New York / VBK, Vienna, courtesy of Graphische Sammlung Albertina, Vienna

Credits for Illustrations